Intra-Industry Trade

Intra-Industry Trade

Cooperation and Conflict
in the Global Political Economy

Cameron G. Thies and Timothy M. Peterson

Stanford University Press
Stanford, California

Stanford University Press
Stanford, California

Printed in the United States of America on acid-free, archival-quality paper

Library of Congress Cataloging-in-Publication Data

Thies, Cameron G., author.
   Intra-industry trade : cooperation and conflict in the global political economy / Cameron G. Thies and Timothy M. Peterson.
        pages cm. – (Emerging frontiers in the global economy)
    Includes bibliographical references and index.
    ISBN 978-0-8047-9133-5 (cloth : alk. paper)
    1. Intra-industry trade. 2. International trade. 3. International economic relations. 4. International relations—Economic aspects. I. Peterson, Timothy M., 1981– author. II. Title. III. Series: Emerging frontiers in the global economy.
HF1414.35.T44 2015
382—dc23

                                                                              2015014935

ISBN 978-0-8047-9720-7 (electronic)

For my family, who still often wonder what I do for a living—C.G.T.

For Susan, who inspires me—T.M.P.

Contents

Preface

THE ideas contained in this book go back some years for both of us. Cameron began puzzling about intra-industry trade as an undergraduate economics major at the University of Nebraska. Why did scholars continue to base our understanding of international trade on Ricardian models, when even in the late 1980s it was already apparent that intra-industry trade between developed economies was outpacing inter-industry trade? Similarly, Tim entered the University of Missouri with a strong desire to explore how the influence of trade on a variety of international political outcomes could be conditional on factors beyond the mere extent of trade ties. The convergence of these interests was made clear when Tim took Cameron's course in international political economy. Tim expressed interest in exploring the consequences of intra-industry trade—a first for Cameron, who had included material on the topic since his earliest graduate courses taught as an assistant professor.

The collaboration on this project began in earnest with our first conference paper in 2010. That first paper ultimately led to the initial publication of our ideas about the pacific nature of intra-industry trade, in the British Journal of Political Science in 2012. Han Dorussen provided thoughtful editorial guidance on this paper, and the reviewers urged us to perfect our argument and evidence. A more general paper outlining our thoughts on the understudied implications of intra-industry trade on political outcomes in security and economy was published as a chapter in the Oxford Handbook of the Political Economy of International Trade in 2015. We thank Lisa Martin for including us in the handbook and for her very useful feedback on that chapter.

Along the way, we have presented portions of the book manuscript at seminars, workshops, and conferences around the world. We would like to extend special thanks to Christophe Crombez for organizing a seminar in the Department of Economics at KU Leuven, Belgium, in 2013 and for the feedback provided by the many participants in attendance. We wanted this book to speak as much to economists as to political scientists, so this was an excellent trial run with a group outside of our discipline. We also benefited greatly from participation in the workshop "Transformation in International Trade Governance," convened by Manfred Elsig and Leonardo Baccini in the 2012 ECPR Joint Sessions of Workshops. In addition to our two conveners, we received excellent comments from Andreas Dür, Simone Guenther, Tobias Hofmann, Soo Yeon Kim, Jeffrey Kucik, Krzysztof Pelc, and Peter Rosendorff.

We have also presented early versions of these chapters as conference chapters at the American Political Science Association, Midwest Political Science Association, International Studies Association, International Political Economy Society, and the International Studies Association-Midwest annual conferences. We thank our many discussants and fellow panelists for their suggestions. In particular, Charles Boehmer, Brian Greenhill, Zeev Yoram Haftel, Daniel Kono, Mark Nieman, and Michael Rudy provided excellent advice as we reworked our conference papers.

Han Dorussen became an important guide in the work again as he served as one of the reviewers for the book project along with Anna Lanozska. We thank both reviewers for their detailed feedback as well as their support for the book. J. P. Singh and Margo Beth Fleming helped shepherd the book through the review process, providing both intellectual guidance and moral support. Finally, Tim would like to thank Oklahoma State University for funding a grant that enabled the purchase of commodity-level data and the University of South Carolina for additional support. Cameron would like to thank the University of Iowa for financial support from the McGregor Fellow position he held there, as well as additional support from Arizona State University.

Intra-Industry Trade

Part I

Introduction

Chapter 1

Trade Composition and the Global Political Economy

THERE are few who would dispute the claim that international trade and world politics are closely linked, and yet our understanding of this connection has evolved considerably over time. Before the twentieth century, political leaders and philosophers alike viewed trade largely as a lever of power and a complement of armed conflict. History is replete with clashes over valuable markets for trade, as well as with militarized aggression financed by revenues from international commerce. Indeed, the first major conflict subject to academic study—the Peloponnesian War—stemmed from the growing, trade-facilitated strength of Athens, whose powerful navy controlled trade throughout the Aegean Sea, creating an ever-growing threat for adversaries such as Sparta. Later, European commercial empires fought almost continuous wars from the fifteenth through the nineteenth centuries in an attempt to control valuable—and tradable—resources from around the globe. The relationship between trade and politics—and the role of the state in leveraging trade toward its political ends—from antiquity through the era of mercantilism can perhaps best be summarized by a quotation from Catherine the Great of Russia: "Wherever there is trade there are customhouses also. The object of trade is the exportation and importation of goods for the advantage of the state" (Ekaterina II 1971, 265).

Over the past two centuries, however, scholars have focused increasingly on the cooperative rather than competitive aspects of trade. Emphasizing that the mutual economic benefit of commerce ties together the interests of trade partners (a notion dating back at least as far as Montesquieu),[1] many argue that trade fosters cooperation and discourages political, as well as militarized, conflict. Sir Normal Angell (1913) advocated this view, making the memorable statement—unfortunately timed shortly before World War I—that the high degree of interconnectedness between economies rendered any possible profit from war a "great illusion."[2] However, political leaders appeared slow to adopt this scholarly logic, as the two global wars that followed this statement belied the optimistic implications of Angell's assessment. Although the next several decades saw a resurgence of scholars examining how trade promotes power and influence, potentially leading to coercion and conflict, the end of the Cold War and concurrent expansion of global trade has coincided with a return to a predominant view that trade promotes peace and cooperation.

The resurgence of the *peace through trade hypothesis* serves as a primary motivation for this book, given that it raises the question, why is trade such a powerful force for peace and cooperation today if it was not so historically? Importantly, there are a number of meaningful differences in the nature of trade that occurs in the contemporary global political economy. First, states are (relatively) more constrained in their influence over trade, given the proliferation of bilateral, plurilateral, and multilateral agreements to liberalize commerce through reductions in barriers to trade. The globalization of production also has changed the nature of trade, a smaller proportion of which today consists of goods produced wholly within a single country. These two major changes have occurred simultaneously with a third trend that is far less studied by political scientists: we now see more variation in the kind of commodities being traded and, specifically, in the *similarity* of commodities exchanged between trade partners. Whereas, historically, two states would trade commodities that were quite distinct (for example, wheat in exchange for textiles), today we witness trade of similar, often branded commodities (for example, exports of domestically produced passenger cars and imports of foreign brands). This two-way exchange of similar commodities is known as *intra-industry trade*, qualitatively dissimilar from *inter-industry trade* of distinct commodities. Although economists have developed theories explaining variation in the commodity composition of trade, there has been little or no examination of how this kind of variation could affect international political relationships. Accordingly, the research question that we address in this book is, how does the similarity of commodities traded between two countries affect the ability of these countries to cooperate, as well as their tendency toward conflict? Our primary argument, developed and tested empirically in the pages that follow, is that a larger proportion of bilateral trade of similar commodities—that is, a larger proportion of bilateral *intra-industry trade*—is associated with higher levels of cooperation and lower levels of conflict between states.

Inter-Industry Versus Intra-Industry Trade

Our goal in this book is to overturn the predominant views held by scholars of global political economy about the role that trade plays in shaping global institutions and the balance of peace and conflict between states. The importance of trade and war, as well as the relationship between these two processes, is well-known to scholars of systemic leadership (see, for example, Kindleberger 1973; Krasner, 1976; Gilpin 1981; Doran 1991; Findlay and O'Rourke 2007; Lake 2009), those in the interdependence and conflict literature (for example, Barbieri, 1996; Copeland 1996; Keshk, Pollins, and Reuveny 2004; Gartzke 2007), and those studying the formation of institutional arrangements (such as Gowa 1994; Mansfield 1994; Mansfield and Pevehouse 2000). Yet we believe these scholars and most others are laboring under outdated theoretical arguments about trade, as well as limited measures with regard to the kind of trade that matters. We think the time has come to completely rethink the relationship between trade and politics in our global political economy because, while the composition of trade has changed dramatically as we move into the twenty-first century, our thinking remains rooted in nineteenth-century understandings of trade and its political effects.[3]

Theoretically, most scholars in these varied literatures still rely on extensions of David Ricardo's classical logic that we now know as comparative advantage (1817), which suggests that there are gains from trade if states specialize in the production of goods they are most efficient at, then exchange them for different goods similarly produced by maximizing efficiency elsewhere. Ricardo provides a simple illustration of his theory using two countries (England and Portugal) and two commodities (textiles and wine). England can produce textiles more efficiently, while Portugal can produce wine more efficiently.[4] Accordingly, Ricardo argues that English production of wine and Portuguese production of textiles would be (relatively) wasteful. England and Portugal could increase their welfare if England exports textiles to Portugal while Portugal exports wine to England, each state foregoing production of the other good. In other words, Ricardo's model specifically predicts the emergence of inter-industry trade. The Heckscher-Ohlin (HO) model (for example, Ohlin 1933), which has become the dominant model of inter-industry trade, extends Ricardo's basic argument to incorporate three factors of production. Findlay and O'Rourke (2007) refer to the period between 1780 and 1914 as the "Great Specialization," a time during which the industrial revolution in combination with rapid and sharp decreases in transportation costs spurred trade of manufactured goods from Europe and North America in exchange for agricultural commodities and raw resources from the undeveloped global periphery. Indeed, until the twentieth century, essentially all international trade was inter-industry trade, explainable in terms of trading states' relative endowments of land, labor, and capital.

Although the theory of comparative advantage and the HO model remain relevant and useful today, scholars have noted that an increasing proportion of international trade no longer fits the expectations of these models. Since the end of World War II, there has been an increasing proportion of trade within, rather than between, industries—often among states with very similar factor endowments. Intra-industry trade has expanded considerably in the post–World War II period and now accounts for the majority of total international trade—between 55 and 75 percent, according to Milner (1999, citing Greenaway and Milner 1986, Table 5–3; see also Alt and others 1996). A large body of research in economics has followed from this observation that the composition of trade did not mirror extant theoretical expectations. To explain the two-way exchange of similar commodities, scholars have noted that states might seek to capture gains from scale rather than gains from specialization, as well as gains from the satisfaction of varied consumer tastes. Krugman (1979; 1981) contends that consumer demand for variety in conjunction with the existence of internally increasing returns to scale, both of which are ignored in classical economic models, facilitates intra-industry trade. Accordingly, whereas inter-industry trade consists of relatively homogenous commodities, intra-industry trade is characterized by the exchange of varied products suited to heterogeneous tastes (see, for example, Grubel and Lloyd 1975).

Early economists did not ignore the potential political consequences of trade; however, research in this vein focused on its consequences for lobbying and trade policy. Following from classical models of inter-industry trade, Stolper and Samuelson (1941) extended the Heckscher-Ohlin model to predict how returns to holders of scarce and abundant factors would respond to liberalization of trade. Expanding upon this research, others (such as Rogowski 1987) demonstrate that support or opposition to trade openness can be explained by the factor of production that a given group utilizes. Using similar logic, Viner (1950) predicted that increasing economic integration in Europe following

World War II could lead to heightened political resistance by groups harmed by foreign competition.

Yet protectionist backlash to European integration was minimal. Scholars noted that resistance to liberalization in Europe might be lessened because of the intra-industry nature of European trade in the post–World War II period (for example, Balassa 1961). Observing the two-way trade of similar commodities, scholars reasoned that adjustment costs could be lower when trade did not reflect comparative advantage stemming from distinct factor endowments. This follows because intra-industry trade does not lead to the elimination of relatively unproductive industries; although a given industry in a given state could be less productive, the unique variety of commodities produced therein remain marketable for export. Accordingly, given the presence of internal economies of scale, the industry is less likely to mobilize for protectionism when it is exposed to imports of other varieties of the same commodity. As a result, resistance to liberalization should also be lower in the presence of two-way trade.

However, a study by Gilligan (1997) suggests that intra-industry trade could increase lobbying by firms; it is associated with greater ease of overcoming collective action problems because differentiation in commodities suggests that the benefits of lobbying will not be distributed across the entire industry. Kono (2009) extends this work, noting that the nature of domestic political institutions will condition the influence of intra-industry trade on lobbying—whether for or against protectionism. Specifically, when institutions reward narrow interests, lobbying will increase when firms engage in intra-industry trade. Conversely, in the presence of intra-industry trade, lobbying will decrease when political institutions foster wider competition, such as along geographic or party lines. Recent work by Madeira (2013) suggests that intra-industry trade will cause shifts in the nature of political coalitions, reducing incentives to form industry-level associations and increasing firm-level lobbying. While an unproductive industry engaging in intra-industry trade is not likely to exit due to foreign competition, less productive firms *within* an industry will face pressure to exit. Taken together, these studies suggest that we could see a qualitative shift in the makeup of lobbying entities rather than a mere decrease in overall lobbying.

While political scientists have begun to explore the relationship between intra-industry trade and political competition, work has emphasized preferences toward liberalization, ability to organize for collective action, and trade policy outcomes. Wider, international political determinants and consequences of intra-industry trade have received considerably less consideration. Yet the studies conducted thus far suggest that there could be important links between the structure of trade and international politics. For example, Gowa and Mansfield (2004) argue that alliances should have a greater trade-facilitating impact in the presence of scale economies and similar factor endowments, such that increasing trade is more likely to flow within industries. Our previous work has examined the connection between intra-industry trade and conflict propensity among trade partners, noting that intra-industry trade should be robustly pacifying, while inter-industry trade has more ambiguous effects (Peterson and Thies 2012a). This follows because, at the state level, inter-industry trade can provoke asymmetric dependence more easily than can intra-industry trade. Specifically, inter-industry trade could lead one state to rely on its trade partner for its supply of vital commodities such as fuel, metals, or food. While the trade partner also benefits from such exchange, it could perceive potential to make a demand of the dependent state, using its advantageous position as leverage (see, for example, Hirschman 1945). Conversely, with intra-industry trade, neither state imports commodities that they do not also produce domestically. Furthermore, at the subnational level, a higher proportion of intra-industry trade suggests the presence of fewer interests opposed to trade exposure, who might otherwise lobby for protectionism and who could prefer militarized conflict to protect their bottom line. Finally, there could be consequences for the Kantian mechanism of increased cultural understanding for trade in branded commodities, which could lead to greater consumer awareness and deeper understanding of trade partners.

The Domestic and Interstate Politics of Trade Composition: Moving from the Monadic to the Dyadic Level of Analysis

Many analyses of trade politics build from one of two theoretical approaches to understanding how domestic coalitions form in the abstract as a response to a country opening up to trade.[5] Alt and others (1996) and Nelson (1988) frame these two approaches on the basis of the importance of factor specificity: the ease with which factors of production (land, labor, and capital) can move from one sector to another in an economy. The two approaches to explaining the demand side of trade policy have used diametrically opposed assumptions about factor specificity. The aforementioned Heckscher-Ohlin model, used by Rogowski (1989), assumes very low factor specificity. For example, workers— that is, owners of labor—could easily move from an industry with lower wages to an industry with higher wages. As a result, because market pressures lead to equalization of wages across industries, this model assumes that returns to each factor are equalized throughout a region's economy. Producers therefore should export goods that intensively use their abundant factors and import goods that intensively use their scarce factors. This results in owners of abundant factors favoring free trade and owners of scarce factors seeking protectionism. Trade policy coalitions will therefore be organized along factor or class lines. On the other hand, the Ricardo-Viner model assumes that factor specificity is very high (see, for example, Frieden 1991). It assumes that some factors are stuck in their present uses. For example, labor in each industry requires specific skills that do not transfer across industry lines, or factories that are specialized to produce one type of commodity could not easily be altered to produce another. Consequently, this model assumes that factor returns are not equalized throughout a region's economy, but are industry specific. Trade policy coalitions, therefore, should form along the lines of exporting versus import-competing industries. Later work by Hiscox (2001) suggests that factor specificity is itself a variable that can be used to predict the nature of political cleavages that form over trade policy. As factors of production become fixed, more class conflict is likely to arise; conversely, as factors of production become more mobile, more industry conflict is likely to arise.

Unfortunately, none of these models explains how preferences over trade policies are actually translated into political action (Alt and others 1996, 695). Nelson (1988, 806) notes that the mobility costs of the specific-factors model may be a result of productivity differentials; labor union activity; or individual preferences for membership in a given geographic area, industry, or firm (in other words, some form of solidarity). Alt and colleagues (1996) suggest that we can begin to understand this process by assuming that rational individuals make cost-benefit calculations. The Heckscher-Ohlin and Ricardo-Viner models tell us the benefits that individuals hope to receive, but the costs of collective action also intervene as they organize to achieve those benefits in the political system. Olson (1965) argued that small groups with specialized interests are easier to organize and more effective in securing economic rents than large groups with diffuse interests. Geographic and firm concentration may be useful proxies for collective action costs (Alt and others 1996, 697; McGillivray 1997; Busch and Reinhardt 1999; 2000), as spatial proximity should increase the ability of individuals to organize and monitor or sanction free-riding behavior.

Alt and colleagues (1996), building on Alt and Gilligan (1994), similarly argue that domestic political institutions affect this process. If the political system rewards small sectoral groups, then individuals will not pay the costs of organizing large intersectoral coalitions. If the political system rewards large mass movements (that is, majoritarianism), then individuals will have to pay the costs of organizing large intersectoral coalitions in order to achieve any benefits. Alt and Gilligan (1994) argue that collective action costs and political institutions are interactive with factor specificity. They suggest that Rogowski's HO framework (1989) requires low factor specificity, low collective action costs, and domestic political institutions that favor mass movements. Changes in one of these factors will change the type of coalitions that will form, or perhaps prevent coalitions from forming altogether. The Ricardo-Viner framework used by the endogenous tariff literature requires that factors are specific, collection action costs are high, and institutions are less majoritarian, with changes in any of these three variables also affecting the type of coalitions that form.

The supply side of trade politics is similarly underspecified (Alt and others 1996, 709). Nelson (1988, 818) suggests that analyses of the supply side of trade policy typically view the state as a rational dictator or as a passive register of demands. In the state-as-a-rational-dictator model, the state may be seen as either pursuing "good government" goals along a social welfare function or intervening in the economy for its own self-interested ends. The good-government approach views state actors as perceiving that their legitimacy is tied to some economic welfare goal. The self-interested model of the state views politicians as offering preferential trade policy to economic actors in exchange for political support (for example, Magee, Brock, and Young 1989; Grossman and Helpman 2002). On the other hand, pluralist theory typically views the state as a neutral aggregator of demands from groups in society. The supply of trade policy is then determined by the balance of power on any given issue. A variety of different characteristics of the political system are posited to affect the supply of trade protectionism, such as politicians' incentives to cultivate personal votes, the size of electoral districts, party fragmentation, federalism, presidential versus parliamentary systems, majoritarian versus proportional representation systems, and so on (see, for example, Rogowski 1987; Rodrik 1995; Nielson 2003). The empirical results concerning institutional channels for the supply side of trade politics are mixed (Thies 2015, 344–46).

We contend that the existing literature on trade policy that focuses on the coalitional politics of protectionism is not overly helpful for our purposes. The primary reason is that these models tend to be grounded in the conventional understanding that the composition of trade does not matter, or, perhaps more accurately, that inter-industry trade according to specialization is the norm. We suggest that intra-industry trade is qualitatively different from inter-industry trade, including in the way in which it affects domestic producers. Classical economic studies argue that when intra-industry trade is high, lessened distributional consequences associated with reducing trade barriers render liberalization—whether multilateral or preferential—politically more feasible (for example, Balassa 1966; Aquino 1978). However, more recent research challenges the conventional wisdom, demonstrating that firms engaging in intra-industry trade can more easily overcome barriers to collective action, taking measures to prevent liberalization that harms them (Gilligan 1997). Therefore, intra-industry trade may even lead to higher multilateral protectionism when a state's electoral institutions reward narrow interests (Kono 2009). While we tend to lean toward the expectations of the classical economic studies, the newer literature highlights a second reason we seek to move beyond most contemporary studies of trade policy.

Furthermore, contrary to the vast majority of studies discussed in the preceding, we are not interested in examining monadic decision making on trade policy, nor its consequences. The arguments we present are *dyadic* in nature, reflecting our belief that the link between trade and international politics is best understood when the attributes of the other state with which one state is interacting are considered. Thus, while work by Gilligan (1997) and Kono (2009) point to monadic responses to multilateral liberalization under conditions of prevalent intra-industry trade, we are more interested in interactions between *pairs* of states. For example, as we discuss later in Chapter 3, contrary to multilateral liberalization, the formation of preferential trade agreements (PTAs) is a highly competitive process. Firms face incentives to pressure states to pursue PTA membership in order to gain a global productivity advantage, or simply to avoid falling behind other states that are forming trade agreements. PTAs result in expanded markets, which allow firms engaging in intra-industry trade to benefit further from economies of scale. At the firm level, the existence of economies of scale alone is sufficient to encourage lobbying in favor of a PTA. Yet if firms in one state enjoy productivity advantages over their counterparts in a potential PTA partner, resistance to the agreement by their potential competitors could thwart their own support for PTA formation, regardless of how many resources they invest to lobby in favor of the agreement. Yet when intra-industry trade already exists, it suggests the presence of economies of scale and a mutual benefit thereof for firms in both states. Third-party effects also become important to the process of developing a commonality of interests among firms and governments within the two states. The dyadic unit of analysis is particularly useful because it allows us to account for factors within each dyadic state in a relativistic manner (for example, relative gross domestic product [GDP]), as well as factors external to the dyad, from the dyadic perspective (for example, the number of preferential trade agreements existing outside the dyad, which might create pressure for the dyad to form a countervailing agreement).

While dyadic analyses are quite common in the conflict literature, especially since the advent of the democratic peace literature, they are less common in the trade politics literature. Our work extends dyadic analyses of the type found in the trade interdependence and conflict literature both to institutional outcomes such as PTA formation and World Trade Organization (WTO) dispute initiation and to substantive areas more closely related to the conflict literature, such as the onset of a militarized interstate dispute as well as analyses of political affinity and alliance formation. We suggest that there are always possible combinations of political economy features in dyads that structure the degree of cooperation and conflict between them. Higher proportions of dyadic intra-industry trade reveal to us that complementary features exist across states, suggesting that existing cooperation should be maintainable—and that incentives exist for further cooperative agreements to form. For example, firms in both trade partners will recognize that, with a higher proportion of intra-industry trade, there is incentive to maintain and increase gains from scale. Import-competing firms do not act in the way predicted by the endogenous tariff literature, since they have carved out specific niches for their products both at home and abroad. While their branded goods do compete with other potential substitutes, consumers may prefer one brand to another, which allows them to profit through the expansion of foreign markets even as they compete for market share at home. Thus, as intra-industry trade increases as a proportion of total trade in the dyad, the prevalence and political strength of actors seeking openness should increase, leading to diminished strength of interests factoring in protectionism.

Among consumers in both trade partners, intra-industry trade suggests demand for continuing interaction because individuals prefer choices of goods and often attach loyalty to specific brands. Indeed, what separates our view of intra-industry trade from that typically held by economists is that we are primarily interested in brand-name trade in similar commodities, as opposed to value-added trade that occurs in production chains (which we suggest has political effects more similar to inter-industry trade). Proponents of the Kantian peace claim that trade reduces conflict by rendering nations members of global communities, facilitating information exchange and communication (see Dorussen and Ward 2010 for a review of this line of research). Yet the flow of a homogenous, non-branded commodity such as oil into the United States probably does little to improve citizen views of Saudi Arabians or Venezuelans. This would also be true in instances in which non-branded, undifferentiated commodities are exchanged between states, such as trade in similar grains or types of steel between the United States and European Union member states. Conversely, the flow of BMWs may indeed improve U.S. citizens' views of Germans, facilitating an interest in intercultural exchange. Importantly, the bilateral exchange of brands is possible only within intra-industry trade at the dyad level. U.S. goods flowing into raw resource exporting states may result in resentment as well as unilateral brand recognition, potentially fostering backlashes against globalization, and, ultimately, contributing to an ambiguous impact of inter-industry trade on conflict and institution building. Again, this fact suggests that a dyadic analysis is appropriate to understand fully how trade composition affects international political outcomes.

For policymakers in each trade partner, security concerns are lowest for intra-industry trade given the lack of strategic dependence or vulnerability associated with the importation of goods that one's country also produces. Conversely, inter-industry trade is a double-edged sword because it may be leveraged as political power by trade partners, if, for example, one trade partner faces lower costs associated with terminating trade—a phenomenon illustrated by Keohane and Nye (1977), who explore the case of the United States and Japan prior to World War II (see also Crescenzi 2003; Peterson 2014). Inter-industry trade may also be less stable due to the typically smaller trade gains and higher asset specificity associated with export of primary commodities relative to manufactured commodities (Galtung 1971), which may contribute to dependence of primary products-exporting states on their manufactures-exporting trade partners. This requirement to examine the *relative* costs for terminating trade—and the associated consequences for vulnerability and dependence—again compels the use of the dyadic level of analysis.

The Causal Link Between Trade Composition and International Cooperation

The focus of this book is on how the composition of existing bilateral trade affects the preferences of interest groups in each trading state—specifically influencing the *similarity* and *complementarity* of those preferences in ways that affect the trading states' political dealings with each other. Our central argument is that a higher proportion of dyadic intra-industry trade suggests the presence of complementary interests that translate into a higher likeli-hood of cooperative interaction as well as a reduced likelihood of conflictual interaction. However, the question arises as to whether the causal mecha-nisms connecting intra-industry trade to increased cooperation follow from some other factor that encourages both a higher proportion of intra-industry trade and more cooperative international relationships. In other words, is the relationship between intra-industry trade and international cooperation spu-rious? While it is true that we can identify factors promoting the emergence of intra-industry trade, we contend that each of these factors is, in isolation, insufficient to promote cooperation between two trade partners. We intro-duce this argument further on and expand on each component in subsequent chapters.

First, (mutual) development is one factor that arguably is necessary for the emergence of intra-industry trade. Although two less-developed states could trade distinct agricultural products, we find relatively small volumes of such trade in our data. Conversely, mutually developed states—primarily in Europe and North America—tend to have higher proportions of intra-industry trade, as well as higher overall trade levels. Accordingly, one might suspect that the link between intra-industry trade and cooperation is spurious given the find-ings of previous research that development can encourage states to pursue more cooperative means to prosperity (for example, Rosecrance 1986). Specifically, in the choice between the two "worlds" of aggression or commerce, more developed states should favor peace and commerce because this condition is associated with relatively higher trade gains, higher economic and political war costs, and lower benefit from occupation. However, later research has disputed the latter point, showing that sometimes conquest and occupation of territory can "pay," leading to a net benefit of aggressive behavior (Liberman 1993). Liberman points to Hitler's successful capture and subsequent use of European industry as the fundamental example of how development alone does not preclude benefits of conquest. We contend that mutual development, while perhaps correlating with cooperation on average, is not sufficient to promote cooperation.

Related, the presence of similar factor endowments is associated with trade following from (horizontal) intra-industry specialization (for example, Krugman 1979; 1981). Indeed, similarity of factor endowments could follow from joint development, as already discussed. However, we contend that similar factor endowments alone do not necessarily promote cooperation. Conversely, throughout most of history, states with similar export profiles (suggesting similar factor endowments and thus similar underlying comparative advantages) tended to compete for international markets. This pattern is perhaps best illustrated by the mercantilist era, during which European states (including Portugal, the Netherlands, the United Kingdom, France, and Spain) fought numerous wars for access to strategic markets and territory in Asia and the Pacific region, as well as in North America, Latin America, and Africa. While competition today tends not to escalate to the level experienced during imperial wars, states do compete with trade policy to maximize their economic performance (see, for example, Gilpin 1981). For example, states have begun forming preferential trade agreements that benefit insiders at the expense of outsiders (for example, Bhagwati 1991). Such behavior could facilitate a competitive PTA formation process (Baldwin 1995), and in some cases could foster increased hostilities between members and nonmembers of trade agreements, given outsiders' perception of economic threat from exclusive arrangements (Peterson 2014). In short, this potential for economic competition implies that similarity of factor endowments alone does not promote cooperation; rather, we must understand how states are interacting at the bilateral and multilateral levels in order to connect trade composition to political outcomes.

The presence of internal economies of scale is another factor implying that firms face incentive to engage in intra-industry trade. Yet, once again, we contend that the mutual presence of economies of scale among two (or more) states is insufficient to promote cooperation between them because this condition does not suggest that actors within each state have a stake in continuing amicable relations. Granted, firms could perceive the potential for lucrative exchange in the future—although this perception might follow only if each state faced internal economies of scale in the same industries. However, even if this more specific condition exists, the mere presence of scale economies does not imply the existence of opportunity costs following from commerce. Yet it is opportunity costs that are linked to incentives to cooperate—and specifically to avoid conflict.[6] While some recent studies have emphasized the potentially information-facilitating impact of commerce as more important than opportunity costs (for example, Morrow 1997; Reed 2003), this cooperation-enhancing impact too is absent when commerce remains only a possibility. Along these same lines, an increase in the variation of consumer tastes might suggest potential for intra-industry trade to emerge, yet provides no established commerce to provide opportunity costs or improve information flows.

The causal link between trade barriers and intra-industry trade is more tenuous. Yet this connection is important because a growing literature examines the contention that absence of trade barriers is necessary for trade to promote cooperation (see, for example, McDonald 2004; McDonald and Sweeney 2007). This effect follows from the fact that low trade barriers suggest the weakness of domestic protectionist interests who might otherwise lobby for conflictual foreign policy as well as for restrictions on trade. Two points contribute to the strength of this purported link. First, the absence of trade barriers suggests a weakness of domestic interests willing to pursue conflict as a means to protect their industry. Second, free trade is always more efficient in the aggregate, leading to welfare gains for each trade partner, promoting growing prosperity and satisfaction of citizens, on average.

If intra-industry trade followed from liberalization, then the argument we make in this book could follow from spurious correlation. Indeed, there is some evidence that low trade barriers (either multilateral or preferential) correlate with higher proportions of intra-industry trade. However, classical studies explain this correlation as a consequence of the fact that intra-industry specialization implies that industries will not be forced to exit following from economic openness (Balassa 1966; 1986). Thus, given the greater willingness of industries engaging in inter-industry specialization to lobby for protectionism, the highest trade barriers are likely to exist for commodities associated with inter-industry trade. It is reasonable to assume that the reduction in political strength of these protectionist interests could promote inter-industry trade more than intra-industry trade. Accordingly, while more intra-industry trade might lead to lower trade barriers, we are confident that the link between intra-industry trade and cooperation is unlikely to be spurious due to the effect of liberalization.

Indeed the uneven distributional consequences of liberalization further suggest that it could provoke discord. While the absence of trade barriers is efficient in the aggregate, the elimination of trade barriers does not necessarily improve welfare for all. While winners from liberalization will benefit relatively more than the losers suffer, the distributional impact of liberalization could nonetheless cause great dissatisfaction among a large proportion of a population following from the elimination of employment. This upheaval is likely to lead to demands of political leaders to take decisive action, the result of which could sew discord between trade partners. Yet in the presence of intra-industry trade, increasing exposure to trade does not lead to the elimination of industries, and thus does not reduce employment. Accordingly, we could make a counterargument that the apparent association between liberalization and peace is in fact spurious, due in reality to the pacifying impact of intra-industry trade, which, when composing a higher proportion of bilateral trade, suggests less incentive for protectionist trade policy to emerge.

As we discuss in later chapters (particularly in Chapter 3), intra-industry trade might promote the emergence of common interests among trade partners to benefit relative to third parties. Growth of intra-industry trade bestows productivity advantages among trade partners, which could translate to a competitive edge relative to the rest of the world. However, this point might lead one to wonder if causation is reversed: does improved cooperation (perhaps due to a common external adversary) facilitate more intra-industry trade rather than vice versa? Indeed, Gowa and Mansfield (2004) argue that the presence of alliance reduces the risk associated with trade because firms have less fear that contracts will have to be renegotiated. The authors find that alliance promotes intra-industry trade, but not inter-industry trade. Yet the authors examine only trade among major powers, which are relatively developed states. It's possible that these states are more likely to engage in intra-industry trade irrespective of alliance prevalence. A better test of whether alliance affects the composition of trade is to examine a wider variety of states. Presumably, asymmetric development among allies could promote inter-industry trade relatively more than intra-industry trade given the distinct comparative advantages that asymmetric states possess. Accordingly, we contend that intra-industry trade itself, rather than some other factor suggesting complementary interests among states, promotes political cooperation and discourages conflict.

Ultimately, some of the factors that promote intra-industry trade might lead to the perception that cooperation is feasible, and could prevent certain conflicts of interest from emerging and escalating. Yet only in the presence of intra-industry trade are there convergent interests and a mutual stake in continuing amicable relations. Perhaps more important, the presence of intra-industry trade potentially fosters common interests against economic competitors in third-party states. Although we are careful to avoid over-selling causation in our various empirical analyses given the shortcomings inherent in the use of observational data, our theory suggests a clear causal path from intra-industry trade to improved cooperation. Accordingly, the analyses presented in this book follow from a simple argument: irrespective of overall trade levels, trade barriers, and levels of development, a higher proportion of bilateral intra-industry trade suggests the presence of complementary domestic interests within each state as well as a mutual stake in cooperation. As we show in subsequent chapters, this complementarity of interests and symmetry of dependence promotes a greater frequency of cooperative interaction and fewer instances of conflictual interactions between trade partners.

Empirical Analysis of Intra-Industry Trade and Its Effects

Empirically, we are able to observe intra-industry trade using commodity-level dyadic trade data from the United Nations COMTRADE database. These data capture commodity flows from exporter to importer at a reasonably disaggregated level, spanning 1962 to 2010. We construct a bilateral measure of intra-industry trade using a procedure developed by Grubel and Lloyd (1975). In constructing the index, we are also mindful that many economists, such as Grimwade (1989, 101–106), show that measures of intra-industry trade can vary dramatically when different levels of aggregation are used. Therefore, it is vital to capture intra-industry trade consistent with theoretical expectations. Krugman's new trade theory suggests that (horizontal) intra-industry trade follows from consumer tastes for variety. In other words, an "industry" can be defined as a group of trade goods that can generally be considered substitutes by consumers (a group in which we include firms as well as individuals). However, this theoretical concern must be balanced against a more practical concern, given the scarcity of data available at various commodity levels. As we discuss in detail in Chapter 2, we argue that aggregating at the Standard International Trade Classification (SITC) 4-digit level satisfies both the theoretical and practical concerns associated with constructing a valid measure of intra-industry trade (see also Kono 2009).

As the empirical chapters of this book demonstrate, we wish to pursue how a reconceptualization of the underlying trade model used in studies of the global political economy is essential to future work. Most studies assume theoretically that "trade" is inter-industry trade operating according to the logic of comparative advantage. Inter-industry trade is clearly favored by neoclassical economists and liberal international relations theory. Operationally, this means that one simply looks at some measure related to the volume of trade, such as openness (total trade divided by GDP) or interdependence (bilateral trade divided by total trade or GDP). The results of these rough measures of trade lead to a great deal of inconsistency in the findings regarding militarized conflict (see, for example, Gartzke and Li, 2003). We contend that the most salient feature of trading relations today is the proportion of intra-industry trade to total trade in a dyadic relationship. In the substantive chapters we delve into greater detail about the theoretical reasons for this expectation, but suffice it to say that we believe that most of the inherent "good" properties ascribed to trade in terms of institutional outcomes and peace and conflict are a result of increased proportions of intra-industry trade. Or, perhaps more specifically, only in the presence of intra-industry trade do the "good" consequences of trade exist without corresponding "bad" consequences. Such trade should produce a higher likelihood of PTA formation, a lesser likelihood of WTO dispute initiation, a lesser likelihood of militarized conflict (even controlling for liberalization and levels of development), and a higher likelihood of preference similarity (in UN voting and alliance portfolios) and alliance formation.

The Plan of the Book

The other chapter in Part I tackles the important issue of how to conceptualize and measure intra-industry trade. We review several potential controversies in this regard, including the level of product-level aggregation, the separation of horizontal and vertical intra-industry trade, and whether state- or dyad-level intra-industry analysis is more appropriate. We make the case for our particular choices regarding these three issues for the analysis in the rest of the book. In particular, we advocate for product-level aggregation at the SITC 4-digit level, for a unique view on the distinction between horizontal and vertical intra-industry trade, and for the utility of the dyadic level of analysis. While researchers engaged in other areas of study may make different choices in these three areas, we think that these make the most sense for the majority of research on the global political economy. The bulk of the rest of the book is divided into two parts focused on substantive outcomes in international institutions and security.

In "Part II: Intra-Industry Trade and the Global Political Economy of International Institutions," we include a substantive chapter on preferential trade agreement formation and one on World Trade Organization dispute initiation. In Chapter 3, "Cooperating to Compete: Intra-Industry Trade and the Formation of Preferential Trade Agreements," we examine the connection between intra-industry trade and entrance into preferential trade agreements between 1962 and 2000. Given that PTA insiders typically benefit relative to outsiders, states face a strategic incentive to sign these agreements or else fall behind in global competitiveness. We argue that a higher proportion of bilateral intra-industry trade will increase the likelihood that states will form preferential trade agreements because (1) firms benefit from larger markets and increased efficiency, potentially gaining relative to firms in states left out of the agreement; (2) intra-industry trade suggests similar productivity, such that firms in member states are less likely to be harmed by preferentially reduced trade barriers; and (3) strategic considerations are lessened in the absence of inter-industry specialization. Empirically, we find support in our statistical analyses that a higher proportion of bilateral intra-industry trade is associated with a higher likelihood of PTA formation. We then discuss several implications of our results for the global political economy. First, while previous research has shown that intra-industry trade may hinder multilateral liberalization (for example, Kono 2009), PTAs may be attractive options to firms engaging in intra-industry trade when they are ineffi-cient relative to third parties because PTAs would enable these firms to benefit further from economies of scale while maintaining or even increasing trade bar-riers against firms in nonmember states. This could mean that even less-devel-oped countries can utilize them to protect infant industries, thus constituting short- to medium-term protectionism, but potentially "building blocks" to later multilateral liberalization. Second, our results also carry implications for the study of international cooperation and conflict resulting from trade patterns. For example, third parties may raise trade barriers in response to PTAs to which they are not a part in order to protect their firms from the productivity gains of firms within PTA members. Terms-of-trade competition could even drive the formation of rival PTAs in a pattern resembling an arms race, potentially foster-ing political—and ultimately militarized—conflict between PTA members and nonmembers. In fact, the link between intra-industry trade, PTA formation, and terms-of-trade competition could be behind the results found by Mansfield and Pevehouse (2000) that "peace through trade" follows only within PTAs.

Chapter 4, "Trade Composition and the World Trade Organization: The Effect of Intra-Industry Trade on the Dispute Settlement Procedure," explores the role that trade composition plays in dispute initiations with the WTO. While the existing literature has identified a number of factors relevant to dis-pute initiation and participation, such as legal capacity, the expected costs and benefits, relative size and power, and learning through previous participation in disputes, we examine the importance of trade composition. We develop a theoretical argument that suggests that a higher proportion of intra-industry trade is likely to reduce dispute initiation when trade flows are high in a dyad. Unlike the other cases presented in the book, we posit a conditional relation-ship between trade flows and intra-industry trade because trade itself is the source of potential conflict. If trade flows are low, then there is less potential for violations of WTO trade rules. It is only when trade flows are higher that the opportunity for conflicts arises. Once again, we expect that the higher the proportion of trade flows that are constituted by intra-industry trade, the less likely a dispute will be initiated, as the costs for engaging in a dispute far out-weigh any potential benefits in this situation.

In the next section, "Part III: Intra-Industry Trade and the Global Political Economy of Peace and Conflict," we examine how intra-industry trade affects a variety of outcomes in the international security realm. Recent studies of the link between trade and conflict suggest that the pacifying influence of trade could be conditional rather than absolute. In Chapter 5, "Beyond Liberalization and Development: Intra-Industry Trade and the Onset of Militarized Disputes," we examine three conditions identified in previous work that are thought to promote pacific interstate relations, including trade liberalization, which suggests weakness among interests potentially supporting conflict; levels of development, which may produce a "capitalist" peace; and a higher proportion of intra-industry trade, which uniquely promotes the emergence of similar interests and preferences, but not strategic vulnerability, among trade partners. We compare the influence of liberalization, trade composition, and development on the likelihood that states become involved in militarized disputes. We argue that liberalized trade policy and development can have countervailing effects on the stability of peace within dyads, while a higher proportion of intra-industry trade is robustly pacifying. We confirm these findings in a series of probit models.

Chapter 6, "The Political Economy of International Affinity: How the Composition of Trade Influences Preference Similarity and Alliance," explores the relationship between trade and political affinity between nations. Previous contributions to the literature disagree regarding whether trade flows foster amicable political relationships. In this chapter, we focus on how the *composition* of trade—specifically whether states engage more in intra- or inter-industry trade—influences political relationships. We contend that intra-industry trade provides mutual gains from scale and mitigates concerns with security externalities, since neither trade partner is dependent on the other for strategically important commodities. In addition, Kantian mechanisms linking trade to greater cultural understanding between nations may be greater for—or exclusive to—intra-industry trade. Accordingly, we argue that intra-industry trade promotes the emergence of similar foreign policy preferences among trade partners. However, we contend that the reverse case does not follow: more similar states do not necessarily engage in more intra-industry trade because restrictions on trade in strategic commodities are lower against friendly states. Simultaneous equations models and error correction models spanning 1962 to 2010 confirm that intra-industry trade promotes political similarity among trade partners, as well as the prevalence of alliances and the onset of alliance formation.

In the final section of the book, "Part IV: Conclusion," the concluding chapter reinforces the need to move away from nineteenth-century models of trade to models that more accurately reflect trade composition in the late twentieth and early twenty-first-centuries. We review the theoretical arguments and empirical findings associated with our two cases of institutional outcomes (PTA formation and WTO dispute initiation) as well as our two cases of peace and conflict (militarized conflict initiation and preference similarity and alliance or rivalry formation). We argue that each of these four studies demonstrates a major change in the way we think about trade's effect on institutions and peace in the global political economy. If our arguments and evidence are correct, then future work on intra-industry trade and political outcomes holds the possibility of overturning the predominant views held by scholars of international political economy about the role that trade plays in shaping global institutions and the balance of peace and conflict between states. Finally, we sketch out a research agenda that suggests ways to incorporate intra-industry trade into other areas of research in the global political economy.

A Note on Style

The results presented in this book rely on relatively sophisticated statistical analyses. However, in order to maximize readability to the widest possible audience, we emphasize the substantive conclusions of our analyses, presenting tables of regression coefficients and standard errors in supplemental appendices to Chapters 3 through 6. While very little experience with statistics or math is required to absorb our arguments and findings, readers knowledgeable in quantitative methods will be able to critique our analyses in accordance with standard social science practices.

Chapter 2

Conceptualizing and Operationalizing Intra-Industry Trade

W HILE theoretically there should be little controversy surrounding the notion that intra- and inter-industry trade may have different effects on policy outcomes, empirically demonstrating that this is the case poses some particular challenges. In this chapter, we review some of the basic controversies surrounding the measurement of intra-industry trade, making the case for what seems most appropriate for the kind of research typically carried out by political scientists—particularly the phenomena we examine in this book.[1] We argue that there are three critical questions to consider when designing studies linking intra-industry trade to international politics. First, what is the appropriate level of product-level aggregation? Second, is it appropriate to separate horizontal and vertical intra-industry trade? Third, is the state or dyad the appropriate level of analysis? We explore how the researcher's theoretical orientation typically suggests an answer to each of these three questions. As we show in the following, the answer to each of these questions carries important implications for empirical analyses.

Considerations

Product-Level Aggregation (What Is an Industry?)
Measures of intra-industry trade can vary when different levels of aggregation are used (Grimwade 1989, 101–106). Early research into intra-industry trade often disaggregated trade to the Standard International Trade Classification (SITC) 3-digit level. However, some argued that intra-industry trade was a statistical artifact of this aggregation; the resulting "industries" were arguably broad enough to obscure whether exchange consisted truly of similar commodities or whether internationalization of production led to the exchange of related, but distinct commodities (for example, Finger 1975). We argue that it is vital for the measure of intra-industry trade to be consistent with the theoreti-

cal expectations of the study. For example, in Peterson and Thies (2012a), we are most concerned with a measure that captures consumer substitutability of commodities. Given that our theory emphasizes that the benefits of intra-industry trade follow in part from the fact that a diverse selection of differentiated commodities satisfies consumer demand for variety, we define an "industry" as a group of trade goods that, while not identical (that is, homogenous), can generally be considered substitutes by consumers (a group in which we include firms as well as individuals). This distinction is useful because some trade that appears to flow within industries on the basis of identical commodity codes could in fact follow from the internationalization of production. Specifically, a case in which a commodity is imported, experiences further production, and then is re-exported while retaining the same commodity code, would likely be recorded as vertical intra-industry trade.[2] However, this scenario suggests that the value added to the traded commodity by each trade partner does not follow from intra-industry specialization, but rather from differing factor endowments. Indeed, this form of trade is most similar to classic Heckscher-Ohlin trade.[3] When two states trade in this manner, consumers will not benefit from a variety of similar goods. Accordingly, to operationalize intra-industry trade that reflects consumer tastes, disaggregated enough such that substitute commodities are coded the same while internationally produced commodities are distinct, we use data recording commodity flows from exporter to importer at the SITC 4-digit level (Peterson and Thies, 2012a).

Table 2.1, created using data available from the U.S. Census Bureau, presents a few examples of aggregation at the SITC 3-, 4-, and 5-digit levels. Table 2.1 demonstrates that the 3-digit level aggregates commodities that consumers would not view as substitutes. For example, all motorcars intended to carry individuals (other than public transportation), including passenger vehicles and racing vehicles, are aggregated into one commodity code. Similarly, all motorcycles and nonmotorized bicycles are aggregated to the same commodity code. Conversely, the SITC 5-digit level in many cases either offers no additional disaggregation from the 4-digit level or disaggregates commodities too much with respect to the goal of capturing consumer substitutes. For example, cars intended for passenger transportation are already disaggregated fully at the 4-digit level. On the other hand, motorcycles are grouped into a single 4-digit product code, whereas at the 5-digit level they are disaggregated into six different categories on the basis of relatively minor variations in engine

Table 2.1. Aggregation by SITC commodity codes.

SITC 3-, 4-, and 5-Digit	Description
781	**Motor cars and other motor vehicles principally designed for the transport of persons (not public transport), including station wagons and racing cars**
7811	*Vehicles specially designed for travel on snow; golf carts and similar vehicles*
78110	Vehicles specially designed for travel on snow; golf carts and similar vehicles
7812	*Motor vehicles for the transport of persons (other than public transport), (n.e.s.)*
78120	Motor vehicles for the transport of persons (other than public transport), n.e.s.
782	**Motor vehicles for the transport of goods and special purpose motor vehicles**
7821	*Motor vehicles for the transport of goods*
78211	Dumpers designed for off-highway use
78219	Motor vehicles for the transport of goods, n.e.s.
785	**Motorcycles (including mopeds) and cycles, motorized and not motorized; invalid carriages**
7851	*Motorcycles (including mopeds) and cycles fitted with an auxiliary motor, with or without side-cars; side-cars*
78511	Motorcycles with reciprocating internal combustion piston engine of a cylinder capacity not exceeding 50 cc
78513	Motorcycles with reciprocating internal combustion piston engine of a cylinder capacity exceeding 50 cc but not 250 cc
78515	Motorcycles with reciprocating internal combustion piston engine of a cylinder capacity exceeding 250 cc but not 500 cc
78516	Motorcycles with reciprocating internal combustion piston engine of a cylinder capacity exceeding 500 cc but not 800 cc
78517	Motorcycles with reciprocating internal combustion piston engine of a cylinder capacity exceeding 800 cc
78519	Motorcycles (including mopeds) and cycles fitted with an auxiliary motor, with or without side-cars, n.e.s.

Notes: Bolded text indicates 3-digit level; Italicized text indicates 4-digit level; plain text indicates 5-digit level.
n.e.s. equals "not elsewhere specified."

size. This latter disaggregation arguably fails to group together motorcycles of varying engine power that consumers might consider purchasing.

Practically, this level of product aggregation is useful because the United Nations Comtrade system records data at the SITC 4-digit level (revision 1) for the period spanning 1962 to the present. In addition, these Comtrade data include records for unit value, which allows for the disaggregation of vertical and horizontal intra-industry trade using price thresholds. However, the SITC 4-digit level is not used universally. For example, Kono (2009) advocates the

Harmonized System (HS) 6-digit level of aggregation. Notably, however, the SITC 4-digit level is quite similar to the HS 6-digit level, with close to a one-to-one concordance. Yet dyadic SITC 4-digit level data are more widely available on a yearly basis,[4] while dyad-year HS 6-digit level data are more difficult to obtain, particularly given that the UN limits the size of data downloads from the Comtrade database.

Horizontal and Vertical Intra-Industry Trade

The second important distinction in intra-industry trade that we examine involves whether heterogeneity of similar traded goods follows from variation in quality. Disaggregation of trade to the commodity rather than industry level, in conjunction with data on the quantity of trade as well as its value, has facilitated improvement in the measurement of intra-industry trade to account for price differentials. For example, a focus on commodities has led to the distinction between horizontal and vertical variants of trade within industries (for example, Falvey 1981). Horizontal intra-industry trade is the exchange of commodities that perform essentially the same function, but which are differentiated by variety. It occurs primarily among states with similar factor endowments and in the presence of monopolistic competition, and is determined primarily by consumer tastes for variety and the presence of increasing returns to scale for firms in each trade partner (Krugman 1979). Horizontal intra-industry trade as a share of total trade appears larger between states that have higher income per capita, and which have similar income levels (Fontagné, Freudenberg, and Péridy 1998). Conversely, vertical intra-industry trade is exchange of commodities that fulfill the same function, but which are distinguished by quality. For example, vertical intra-industry trade exists in a hypothetical case in which one state manufactures and exports cheap, low-quality engine components while importing expensive, high-quality variants of the same product. The United States and Mexico engage in a relatively high proportion of vertical intra-industry trade in which the United States provides luxury goods in exchange for more economical Mexican varieties, and, indeed, engine components are included in this form of U.S.-Mexico trade. In some ways, vertical intra-industry trade is more similar to inter-industry trade than to horizontal intra-industry trade (Blanes and Martín 2000). Specifically, vertical intra-industry trade can arise due to comparative advantage among states with differing factor endowments under the condition of perfect competition (Falvey 1981). According to the findings of Fontagné, Freudenberg, and Péridy, vertical intra-industry trade composes a larger share of dyadic trade when trade partners have differing incomes, as does inter-industry trade.

The distinction between horizontal and vertical intra-industry trade could have implications for international politics. Horizontal intra-industry trade suggests the presence of similar factor endowments (and, most likely, similar development levels as well). Accordingly, coalitions within each state are more likely to have complementary interests, as we discuss in Chapter 1. Critically, in the presence of horizontal intra-industry trade, participating firms in neither state have unilateral incentives to lobby for protectionism. With vertical intra-industry trade, distributional considerations could spark resistance in one or both participating states. Notably, however, this consequence is less certain than when trade follows primarily from inter-industry specialization.

Whereas horizontal and vertical intra-industry trade could vary somewhat in their influence on producers, we contend that the influences of both on consumer preferences, as well as on the structure of trade dependence, are similar. Accordingly, from our consumer-oriented, product substitutability perspective, horizontal and vertical intra-industry trade are nearly identical in their influence on a number of international political relationships.[5] Notably, if researchers wish to focus on the role of producers in lobbying for protection, then isolating vertical intra-industry trade could be important because exposure to it might involve relatively greater distributional consequences. However, we argue that quality distinctions are probably no more meaningful than horizontal variations, whether theorizing from a Kantian perspective that emphasizes intra-industry trade as a means by which consumers in each country become acquainted with and understanding toward the culture of a trade partner (see, for example, Oneal and Russett 1999; Russett and Oneal 2001) or from a perspective highlighting the influence of dependence and vulnerability stemming from trade ties (for example, Hirschman 1945, Barbieri 1996).

The (Sub)State and Dyad Levels of Analysis

An understanding of how intra-industry trade affects international politics depends in part on whether we examine the phenomenon at the state or the dyad level. At the state level, intra-industry trade exists when a given state imports and exports similar commodities in a given industry. As discussed in Chapter 1, such patterns of trade have implications for the productivity of firms, and therefore influence incentives to lobby for trade policy and ultimately influence observed levels of protectionism. However, there is no guarantee that country-level indicators of imports and exports within a given industry imply the existence of bilateral intra-industry trade with a given trade partner. For example, it is feasible that a state could export passenger cars to one trade partner while importing competing passenger cars from another. Indeed, although the United States exports passenger cars to numerous states, historically, it imported cars from Japan while exporting very few cars to Japan, which tended not to demand U.S. brands. In recent years, however, the flow of U.S. vehicles to Japan has increased somewhat, leading to a greater proportion of bilateral intra-industry trade in the U.S.-Japan dyad.

When two countries engage in bilateral intra-industry trade, there is potential for additional political consequences. All else equal, it is more likely that coalitions favoring the continuance of amicable bilateral trade relations will exist in both states. An examination of bilateral intra-industry trade is also important to consider given that economic and political agreements between states could be intended to create an advantage relative to third parties. We discuss this more fully further on, and in Chapter 3. For example, a firm might lobby for preferential trade agreements with trade partners with which it engages in intra-industry trade, while seeking protection against other states that could also export similar commodities, but with which existing intra-industry trade levels are low. Bilateral intra-industry trade suggests a *complementarity* of interests in the two participating states. As we noted in previous work (Peterson and Thies 2012a), bilateral intra-industry trade also suggests that gains from trade are extensive *and* symmetric. Dyads engaging in intra-industry trade should therefore be less likely to experience asymmetric vulnerability that could persist if one trade partner could more easily cut off trade ties than another (see, for example, Hirschman 1945; Crescenzi 2003; Peterson 2014), which could lead in turn to coercion attempts and conflict.

Operationalizing Intra-Industry Trade for Use in Models of International Politics

Taking the three considerations just discussed into mind, we suggest that a bilateral version of Grubel and Lloyd's intra-industry trade measure, using data disaggregated to the SITC 4-digit level, incorporating horizontal and vertical variants, is useful for many studies of international politics. Specifically, at the commodity level

$$G_{ij}^k = 1 - \left[\frac{\left| X_{ij}^k - X_{ji}^k \right|}{X_{ij}^k + X_{ji}^k} \right]$$

in which X_{ij}^k is the value of exports from country i to country j (or, conversely, imports of j from i) of commodity k, and X_{ji}^k is the value of exports from country j to country i (or imports of i from j) of commodity k. To create a single measure for a given dyad year, we take the weighted average of each commodity-level measure with respect to the proportion of dyadic trade composed by the given commodity, as follows:

$$G_{ij} = \sum_{k=1}^{n} G_{ij}^k * \frac{X_{ij}^k + X_{ji}^k}{X_{ij} + X_{ji}}$$

in which X_{ij} is the value of exports from i to j across all commodities and X_{ji} is the value of exports from j to i across all commodities. Our final measure varies from 0 to 1, where 0 represents no intra-industry trade and 1 signifies that *all* trade within the dyad, in a given year, flows within industries.

Notably, this measure might be less useful if one's theoretical aim is to explain firm lobbying for a state's multilateral trade policy. To explain firm- and industry-level preferences within a single state, researchers might prefer a measure of intra-industry trade that uses the combined total of imports from all other states to state i, rather than the dyadic measure we propose here. Looking within one state, researchers can use the industry or commodity as the unit of analysis. Doing so reduces possible aggregation bias inherent in the dyadic measure. Specifically, because the dyadic measure is a weighted average of intra-industry trade across all industries, an indicator of 0.5 obscures whether 50 percent of trade is two-way in every industry or whether some industries are characterized entirely by two-way trade while others are characterized entirely by one-way trade. Lobbying for protection at the industry level likely depends primarily on the proportion of two-way trade specifically in that industry.

Data and Measurement

To create the Grubel and Lloyd measure of intra-industry trade, we take data from the United Nations COMTRADE database. Specifically, we obtain data on direction of trade between pairs of states between 1962 and 2010, with trade flows disaggregated to the SITC 4-digit level.[6] Although the COMTRADE database records values for a state's imports to and exports from trade partners, we rely on import values for both directions of trade for two reasons: first, import data are recorded including the cost of insurance and freight, better reflecting the value of the goods for the importer;[7] second, import data tend to be more reliable because countries emphasize good record keeping on imports, for which they often receive tariff revenue. Accordingly, when calculating intra-industry trade for dyad$_{ij}$ on commodity k, we use state i's imports from j along with state j's imports from i. All values are reported in thousands of current U.S. dollars; however, because we calculate proportions by year, import values in constant dollars would return identical results.

Descriptive Statistics

We create 382,077 dyad-year observations for our measure of intra-industry trade. The number of yearly observations increases over time as more states enter the international system and record keeping improves. For example, there are 3,517 dyadic observations (including values for i's imports from j and j's imports from i) in 1962, and nearly four times as many observations—specifically, 12,681—in 2010. In total, we create intra-industry trade values for dyads composed of 190 states; however, this number increases over time as well (from 142 states in 1962 to 185 states in 2010).[8]

The final intra-industry trade value varies from 0 to 0.977, suggesting that some trade partners engage in no trade following from intra-industry specialization, whereas others (essentially) trade exclusively in similar commodities. The mean intra-industry trade value is small: 0.018, suggesting that 1.8 percent of the average dyad's trade follows from intra-industry specialization. Variation is modest, given a standard deviation equal to 0.062. However, these numbers have changed systematically over time. For example, in 1962, mean intra-industry trade is 0.005, with standard deviation equal to 0.028. Conversely, in 2010, mean intra-industry trade is 0.027, with standard deviation equal to 0.078. The left-hand graph in Figure 2.1 illustrates the increase in mean intra-industry trade over time. As this figure shows, there has been a steady increase over time in intra-industry trade as a proportion of total dyadic trade.

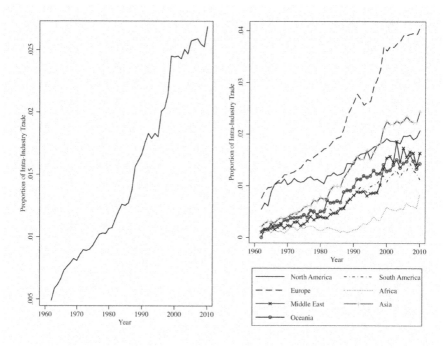

Figure 2.1   Intra-industry trade as a proportion of total dyadic trade, aggregated globally (left) and by region (right), 1962–2010.

However, the increase in intra-industry trade over time has not necessarily occurred evenly across space. The right-hand graph in Figure 2.1 breaks down mean intra-industry trade by region, specifically for North America, South America, Europe, Africa, the Middle East, Asia, and Oceania.[9] The figure shows that percentage increases in intra-industry trade have been similar across regions, but that the absolute magnitude differs by region. For example, Europe engaged in the highest proportion of intra-industry trade at all time periods, averaging just less than 1 percent of dyadic trade in 1962 and more than 4 percent in 2010. Africa engaged in the least intra-industry trade across all years in our data, with an average proportion of less than 1 percent even in 2010. At first glance, both the relative level of intra-industry trade and the rate of increase appear to correlate with development; Europe is a very developed region, while Africa has fallen behind the rest of the world (although very recent trends look more encouraging).

To examine variation on regional intra-industry trade proportions, Figure 2.2 shows boxplots of intra-industry trade proportions by region in the

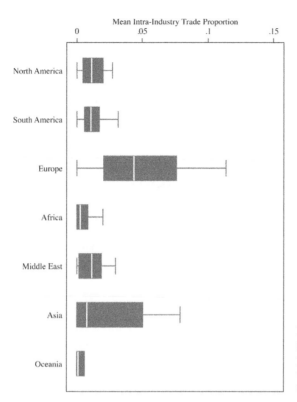

Figure 2.2   Boxplots of intra-industry trade as a proportion of total dyadic trade, by region, 2010.
NOTE: Values taken from 2010.

year 2010. For each region, the dark box outlines the inter-quartile range (IQR) of values (that is, the 25th percentile to the 75th percentile), with a solid line indicating the median level. The whiskers for each region highlight the most extreme value within 1.5 IQRs of the nearest quartile. The boxplots illustrate that Europe is the region with the highest average level of intra-industry trade as a proportion of dyadic trade. Europe also has higher variance in these values than any other region. Africa and Oceania have the lowest proportions of intra-industry trade on average. Interestingly, Asia has relatively low intra-industry trade proportions on average but also has a very large variance in these values.

Very high levels of intra-industry trade are rare: for example, the value for the 95th percentile of intra-industry trade proportion is only 0.10. There are only a few dozen dyadic values above 0.8, many of which include either Belgium or Armenia as one of the dyadic states. However, this fact that high levels of intra-industry trade appear to represent severe outliers could be misleading when considering *which* states and dyads tend to have high values. For example, the 95th percentile for intra-industry trade proportion in U.S. dyads is equal to 0.35. For U.K. dyads, the 95th percentile is 0.4. Belgium dyads, which are represented frequently among the largest intra-industry trade proportions, have a 95th percentile equal to 0.5. We contend that the extreme right-skewness of bilateral intra-industry trade proportions (with the vast majority of values close to 0) should not be taken as evidence that high values of intra-industry trade are unimportant aberrations. These bilateral values are considerably more common among larger, more developed states—exactly the states that tend to dominate international politics.[10] Accordingly, we turn to a discussion of the association between intra-industry trade and development.

Examining covariation in intra-industry trade and development (in terms of gross domestic product per capita [GDPPC]), we find a relatively modest correlation of 0.26. As we suspected, high values of intra-industry trade are most common—and, in fact, nearly exclusive to—dyads with a higher minimum GDPPC. However, there is wide variation in intra-industry trade even when lower dyadic development takes higher values. Figure 2.3 is a scatterplot that graphs the association between intra-industry trade and lower (logged) development—specifically, the lower of inflation-adjusted gross domestic product per capita taken from the Penn World Table 8.0 (Feenstra, Inklaar, and Timmer 2013).[11] Given the large number of dyadic observations, we examined separate graphs by year. The left-hand plot of Figure 2.3 presents the earliest year (1962), while the right-hand plot presents the latest year (2010). The plots demonstrate the increase in observations over time; however, both show the identical pattern: intra-industry trade is almost always low in the absence of mutual development, yet higher mutual development shows great variation in intra-industry trade levels. In other words, as we posit in Chapter 1, mutual development appears necessary but not sufficient for the emergence of intra-industry trade.

To illustrate Figure 2.3, we examined the mean and standard deviation of intra-industry trade conditional on lower development. From the left-hand plot, presenting values from 1962, we find that mean intra-industry trade is equal to 0.002 with a standard deviation of 0.011 when examining the least developed dyads—specifically, where (ln) lower development is less than 3, equivalent to 2,667 dollars in inflation-adjusted dollars.[12] However examining (ln) lower development between 3 and 6 (between 2,667 and 53,585 inflation-adjusted dollars of GDP per capita), we find that the mean intra-industry trade

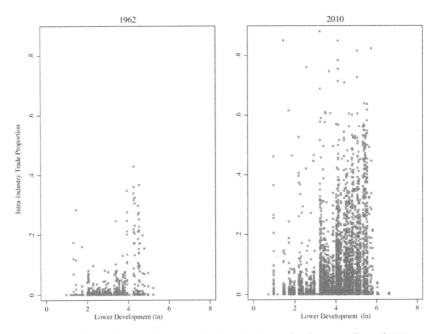

Figure 2.3   Bilateral intra-industry trade values by lower development (logged GDP per capita).

value is 0.009, with standard deviation of 0.040. This mean and variation is considerably higher than that for less developed dyads. In 2010, the equivalent less-developed dyads have a mean value of 0.005 with standard deviation 0.033. The equivalent more-developed dyads have a mean value of 0.041 with standard deviation of 0.094, again considerably higher on average, and with a much greater variation.

Intra-Industry Trade Value

Discussion of intra-industry trade proportions does not necessarily highlight the magnitude of bilateral trade composed of similar commodities. Indeed, dyad-year-level intra-industry trade proportions do not necessarily reflect the dollar value of similar and distinct commodities traded. For example, if very few dyads are responsible for most trade, and simultaneously engage in very high proportions of intra-industry trade, then it could be possible for the total dollar value of intra-industry trade to outweigh the total dollar value of inter-industry trade despite the fact that the average dyad's trade consisted of only 2 or 3 percent intra-industry trade. Previous studies (using extant measures of intra-industry trade) estimate that more than half of international trade by dollar value follows from intra-industry specialization (Milner 1999; Greenaway and Milner 1986). Accordingly, Figure 2.4 examines how the total (that is, system-level) dollar values of inter- and intra-industry trade have changed over the 1962–2010 period. The figure shows that, using our definitions of inter- and intra-industry trade, the total value of intra-industry trade has increased from about 10 billion U.S. dollars in 1962 to 3.37 trillion U.S. dollars in 2010 (an increase of over 330 times). Simultaneously, the total value of inter-industry trade has increased from 84 billion U.S. dollars in 1962 to 9.06 trillion U.S. dollars in 2010 (an increase of slightly over 100 times).[13]

Conclusion

As the preceding sections show, the composition of trade has changed markedly since 1962. The proportion of two-way trade in similar commodities has increased almost universally; although not all states and regions engage primarily in intra-industry trade, it has, on average, increased as a proportion of total trade in every region of the world. Notably, the increase, on average, in intra-industry trade has correlated with increasing global development. This trend is further supported by the fact that intra-industry trade levels appear higher, on average, in more developed states and regions. However, as we discuss in this and subsequent chapters, development could be necessary, but is not sufficient, for intra-industry trade to flourish. Accordingly, we expect to see considerable differences in the interactions of jointly developed states as a function of the degree to which these states trade similar or distinct commodities.

It is important to reiterate that our conceptualization and operationalization of intra-industry trade is somewhat distinct from that of economists, who typically are interested in vertical specialization, in part stemming from interest in the increasingly globalized production process. Conversely, we are interested in how the composition of trade influences the complementarity of domestic interest groups and the potential dependence (and therefore vulnerability) of trade partners on each other. We exclude vertically specialized trade except when the commodities in question would be considered substitutes by firms and consumers—sharing the same product code irrespective of price differential. Consequently, we develop a measure of intra-industry trade that captures the likelihood that domestic inter-

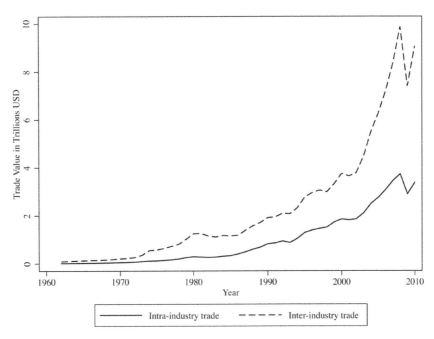

Figure 2.4   Intra- and inter-industry trade value in trillions of 2005 U.S. dollars, 1962–2010.

ests will favor cooperation over conflict, while ensuring that neither state depends on the other for strategically important commodities. Yet states engaging in two-way trade of similar commodities, as captured in our measure, will benefit considerably from increasing welfare. As we will show in subsequent chapters, our measure therefore captures an important economic determinant of political cooperation.

Part II

Intra-Industry Trade and the Global Political Economy of International Institutions

Chapter 3

Cooperating to Compete:
Intra-Industry Trade and the Formation
of Preferential Trade Agreements

A S of early 2015, 160 states belong to the World Trade Organization (WTO). As specified in the terms of WTO membership, these states must provide Most Favored Nation (MFN) status to all other members; that is, reduction in trade barriers to any state must be extended to all WTO members. However, even among WTO member states, preferential trade agreements (PTAs) remain as an authorized means of reducing tariffs for some states while excluding others. GATT Article XXIV, paragraph 8, authorizes that two or more states can enter into agreements to liberalize trade between them so long as the parties to such an agreement do *not* raise trade barriers against nonmembers. Over 270 such agreements have entered into force in accordance with Article XXIV, with nearly 40 more negotiations in progress.[1] As a result, the contemporary era is witness to an unprecedented degree of multilateral liberalization, as well as a resurgence of discriminatory, potentially competitive preferential liberalization (see, for example, Oye 1993). In this chapter, we investigate the role of intra-industry trade in explaining these trends, emphasizing its role in the formation of PTAs.

Conventional wisdom has long asserted a causal connection between the simultaneous increase in intra-industry trade and reduced protectionism in the post–World War II period. Classical studies argue that when intra-industry trade is high, lessened distributional consequences associated with reducing trade barriers render liberalization—whether multilateral or preferential—politically more feasible (for example, Balassa 1961; 1966; Aquino 1978). However, more recent research challenges the conventional wisdom, demonstrating that firms engaging in intra-industry trade can more easily overcome barriers to collective action, taking measures to prevent liberalization that harms them (Gilligan 1997). Therefore, intra-industry trade may even lead to higher multilateral protectionism when a state's electoral institutions reward narrow interests (Kono 2009).

This new body of work casts doubt on the conventional wisdom regarding intra-industry trade and *multilateral* liberalization, yet leaves open the question of how the composition of trade influences *preferential* liberalization. The proliferation of PTAs has been met with optimism regarding the impact of these agreements on peace between members (see, for example, Mansfield and Pevehouse 2000) as well as with warnings of their potentially detrimental influence on wider economic cooperation (for example, Bhagwati 1996; 2008). Contrary to multilateral liberalization, the formation of preferential trade agreements is a highly competitive process (Baldwin 1995). In this chapter, we model PTA formation as defection in a multiplayer prisoners' dilemma game. In this model, firms face incentives to pressure leaders to pursue PTA membership in order to gain a global productivity advantage, or simply to avoid falling behind other states that are forming trade agreements. The question becomes, with whom will states form these agreements? We connect a higher proportion of bilateral intra-industry trade to a higher likelihood that interests in favor of preferential liberalization can overcome institutional constraints to PTA formation; thus a higher proportion of bilateral intra-industry trade suggests a higher likelihood that a dyad enters into a PTA. Empirically, we find support for this argument in statistical models spanning 1962 to 2000.

This chapter has important implications for our understanding of the simultaneously cooperative and competitive nature of PTAs. Although at first glance our conclusion matches that offered by supporters of the conventional wisdom, we demonstrate that the causal mechanisms leading from high levels of bilateral intra-industry trade to increased propensity for PTA formation follow not simply because resistance to liberalization is lowered, but because domestic interests face a strategic imperative to increase global competitiveness through preferential liberalization. Even if they lobby against multilateral liberalization, industries will pursue PTAs with trade partners with whom intra-industry trade is high because rejecting PTAs in this case would lead to decreased competitiveness in the long run. Furthermore, our results may have implications for the capitalist peace that sees liberalization increasing the prospects for cooperation and reducing the likelihood of conflict (see, for example, McDonald 2004). Given that our argument portrays PTA formation as resulting from a highly competitive process, it might provide insight into the lines along which cooperative economic blocs will form and, potentially, where economic competition and political conflict may occur (for example, Peterson 2015).

More generally, this chapter is also important because it emphasizes the bilateral—as well as multilateral—nature of trade barriers. Rather than conceiving of liberalization as a phenomenon that states decide with respect to all parties, we emphasize that complementarity of domestic interests leads to reduction of trade barriers for specific, prioritized trade partners. While domestic politics is central to the process of liberalization, we must consider the domestic incentives of pairs (or groups) of states together in order to understand when cooperative agreements are likely to be made. As noted in Chapter 1, the primary argument of this book is that a higher proportion of bilateral intra-industry trade suggests complementarity of interests. This chapter highlights how those complementary interests lead to economic agreements that benefit trading states—perhaps at the expense of third parties with which agreement members do not see complementary incentives to lower trade barriers preferentially.

We proceed with a discussion of the current state of the political science literature examining PTA formation, noting its attention to institutional constraints, and particularly the role of veto players, on this process. We then present our theory, in which we focus on the willingness of domestic actors to enter PTAs, arguing that higher levels of intra-industry trade within dyads suggests a higher likelihood of PTA formation. Next, we present our research design and discuss the considerable challenges associated with operationalizing intra-industry trade. The following statistical analysis confirms that intra-industry trade facilitates PTA formation. We conclude with a discussion of the implications of our results to the literature on liberalization, suggesting extensions of our theory to the study of the capitalist peace.

Institutional Constraints to PTA Formation

One feature common to PTAs is the requirement that states adjust their trade policies toward each other in order to grant other members some type of preferential access to their markets. In democracies, this adjustment is usually accomplished through domestic legislation, while autocracies may rely on executive decrees. In either type of system, there are bound to be entrenched interests favoring the status quo and powerful political actors who may work to maintain existing trade policy on their behalf. This straightforward observation has led to the emergence of a body of work within the political science literature focused on the effect of veto players on PTA membership.[2] While there are many studies that look at other aspects of domestic institutional constraints, such as the role of regime type (for example, Mansfield, Milner, and Rosendorff, 2002; Baccini 2012), bureaucratic interests (Elsig and Dupont 2012), electoral concerns (Hollyer and Rosendorff 2011), the use of trade institutions as a means of locking in domestic commitment (Maggi and Rodriquez-Clare 2007), and interest groups (Grossman and Helpman, 2002), our brief literature review focuses on veto players as a shorthand way to think about domestic factors that could preclude PTA formation.

This work views veto players as impediments to opportunities for PTA formation. Mansfield, Milner, and Pevehouse (2007) propose, and demonstrate empirically, that an increased number of veto players reduces the likelihood of a state joining a PTA. We agree with their argument that a focus on veto players provides additional analytic leverage to understanding the influence domestic politics has on joining PTAs. First, veto players and regime type are conceptually distinct, as all types of regimes have veto players. Even a dictator is unlikely to exercise power without the support of key groups such as the military or a political party. While democracies are likely to have more veto players than autocracies, both types of regimes will have institutional or party actors who can block policy change.

Second, the veto player perspective also expects that interest groups operate to affect trade policy, since changes to the status quo will always have distributional consequences. Yet, as they note, it is very difficult to compare interest group activity across countries. Mansfield, Milner, and Pevehouse (2007) expect that interest group activity will, through lobbying activities, indirectly affect the preferences of the executive negotiating a PTA as well as the other veto players in a state. Veto players ultimately emerge as a useful surrogate for domestic political activity surrounding attempts to change the status quo trade policy in favor of joining a PTA. Mansfield, Milner, and Pevehouse's empirical analyses confirm that increasing numbers of veto players reduce the likelihood of PTA formation, regardless of model specification.

The importance of veto players has been demonstrated repeatedly in related studies. For example, Heinisz and Mansfield (2006) find that an increased number of veto players generally reduces the likelihood of changes in trade policy within democracies. Further, poor macroeconomic conditions are likely to lead to restrictions in trade as the number of veto players decreases in democracies, while good macroeconomic conditions and low numbers of veto players leads to increasing commercial openness. Thus, even within democracies, institutional variation measured by veto players produces a range of trade policy outcomes. Mansfield, Milner, and Pevehouse (2008) go on to show that democracies are more likely than autocracies to enter into a regional integration agreement, but as the number of veto players increases, that likelihood decreases. Veto players also affect the depth of integration, as higher numbers of veto players ensures that at least one actor will have incentives to block changes to the status quo.

This literature has demonstrated theoretical and empirical connections between veto players and PTA formation. We characterize this prior work positing a negative association between veto players and PTA formation as demonstrating an *opportunity effect* (Most and Starr 1989). This body of work assumes the existence of domestic producers who would be harmed by foreign competition following the entrance into force of a preferential trade agreement. Therefore, a higher number of veto players provides more outlets through which the demand for protectionism may be pursued, much the same as Ehrlich's concept of access points (2007). As veto players increase in number, interests opposed to PTAs have more opportunity to derail them; therefore, there is a lesser likelihood that trade agreements will ultimately be signed and entered into force.

Importantly, the determinants of domestic support for PTAs are largely left unexamined in this model—despite nods to interest group activity and distributional coalitions. While it is safe to assume that there will always be at least some resistance to these agreements, there may also be considerable variation in domestic support for PTAs.[3] All else equal, this variation should affect the likelihood that states enter into trade agreements. When there is considerable support for PTA formation (for example, when firms desire export markets or foreign products), we expect greater lobbying on behalf of the agreements. Conversely, we expect more lobbying against PTAs as detractors (primarily import competitors) proliferate. Government actors who translate interests into policy are likely to make decisions reflecting the preferences of powerful actors, even if our knowledge of exactly how these preferences are aggregated is incomplete (Milner 2002). We conceptualize this impact of domestic support for PTAs as a *willingness effect* (Most and Starr 1989). A more comprehensive understanding of PTAs requires analysis of both opportunity and willingness to form such agreements.

Intra-Industry Trade and Willingness to Form Preferential Trade Agreements

To understand why intra-industry trade is a key indicator of the willingness of domestic actors and their state representatives to prefer the adoption of a PTA, one must consider the third-party consequences of preferential liberalization. As Baldwin (1995) argues, the existence or even *potential* formation of PTAs among third parties forces states to consider pursuing these agreements. This incentive follows because states left out of a PTA lose productivity relative to members. The desire for such productivity advantages could compel domestic interests to seek out compatible interests in foreign states. Accordingly, the decision to engage in preferential liberalization constitutes a prisoners' dilemma (PD). To simplify the explanation of the PTA formation process as a PD, we can consider the behavior of two states that agree to liberalize multilaterally (cooperate) or form a preferential trade agreement with some third party (defect). One additional assumption is required: a preferential trade agreement between the two states is not feasible—or at least is not preferable to multilateral liberalization. Our argument suggests that the mutual gains from multilateral liberalization are likely greater in the aggregate than are the gains from mutual formation of PTAs with third parties. Yet for both states, given what the other state is doing, welfare is maximized by forming a PTA. For example, if one state liberalizes trade multilaterally, the other state can benefit from those low tariffs for its exports, while also forming a PTA with a third party, denying the other state similarly low tariffs.

While mutual, multilateral liberalization would provide the most welfare gains for all states, smaller groups of states face incentives to form PTAs to benefit from resulting productivity gains that advantage members relative to nonmembers. Once even a single PTA forms, the potential costs of not following suit become apparent, given that productivity gains for members translate to (relative) productivity losses for nonmembers. Indeed, Baldwin suggests that the disruption to the political equilibrium associated with the formation of one PTA should result in a domino effect in which states become increasingly likely to enter into such agreements. Regions may then experience a cascade of PTAs (a phenomenon consistent with tit-for-tat strategy in an iterated PD [for example, Axelrod 1984]). However, the general willingness to join a PTA due to the pressures of competition still does not answer the specific question of which states are likely to form an agreement. To answer this outstanding question, we must move the literature forward to consider an even more basic source of the willingness to form PTAs: the nature of dyadic trade and its effects on domestic firms' propensity to lobby.

We suggest that the composition of trade flowing within the dyad sheds the critical light on the propensity of domestic actors to lobby for or against dyadic PTAs, and therefore on the likelihood of entrance into trade agreements. Specifically, we focus on the role of intra-industry trade in this process. While classical models of trade protectionism rely on the neoclassical assumption of inter-industry trade and the resulting distributional coalitions formed to lobby for or against protectionism, we recognize the rapid decline of this form of trade, particularly among advanced economies. As noted in Chapters 1 and 2, previous research suggests that intra-industry trade now occupies a large share of global trade (Milner 1999; see also Alt and others 1996). Our own estimates from Chapter 2 suggest that the proportion of global intra-industry trade is closer to 30 percent, yet *bilateral* proportions of intra-industry trade vary from 0 to very close to 100 percent. Given this, the domestic response to trade exposure merits reexamination.

We contend that higher intra-industry trade within a dyad will encourage firms in each dyad member to lobby for preferential trade agreements in order to facilitate gains from increased trade without risking the potential loss that might accrue if trade barriers were reduced for all states. PTAs result in expanded markets, which allow firms engaging in intra-industry trade to benefit further from economies of scale (see, for example, Chase 2003; 2005).[4] However, whereas Chase examines industry-level determinants of lobbying in favor of a PTA, we consider the dyad-level likelihood of PTA formation. At the firm level, the existence of economies of scale alone is sufficient to encourage lobbying in favor of a PTA. Yet if firms in one state enjoy productivity advantages over their counterparts in a potential PTA partner, resistance to the agreement by their potential competitors could thwart their own support for PTA formation, regardless of how many resources they invest to lobby in favor of the agreement. When intra-industry trade already exists, it suggests the presence of economies of scale *and* a mutual benefit thereof for firms in each state. Accordingly, there is *mutual* willingness to form a PTA across state borders. One might argue that, logically, the increased competition from firms in partner states would cancel out the benefit associated with a larger market.

While ambiguous gain is perhaps true regarding multilateral liberalization, the net gain associated with PTA formation becomes evident once one considers the third-party effects of these trade agreements, as discussed by Baldwin (1995). In fact, we contend that it is in the strategic interest of firms engaging in intra-industry trade to pursue PTAs for one of two reasons.

First, PTA formation would result in productivity gains for member-state firms that engaged in intra-industry trade due to the enlargement of markets and reduced trade barriers (Baldwin 1995; Melitz 2003; Melitz and Ottaviano 2008); in such a case, competing firms in nonmember states are rendered relatively less efficient and therefore less competitive.[5] Second, and alternatively, if third-party firms are considerably more efficient than those in states contemplating a preferential trade agreement, PTA formation is attractive because it would lead to expansion of markets with similarly unproductive firms,[6] while trade barriers could be maintained or even raised against nonmembers (see Levy 1997).[7] This potential for PTAs to be "trade diverting" has been suggested repeatedly in extant literature (for example, Viner 1950; Bhagwati 1991). While trade diversion is typically viewed in negative terms, rational firms should pursue it when it protects them from more efficient competitors. Again, this compulsion likely follows a prisoners' dilemma structure, given that all states would be better off if no one practiced trade diversion, yet each actor has a unilateral incentive to behave in ways that result in trade diversion. Thus there should be considerable domestic lobbying for entrance into PTAs on behalf of sectors and industries engaged in intra-industry trade.

Furthermore, because intra-industry trade signifies that trade partners do not specialize (as they do under conditions of inter-industry trade), it is less likely that firms (or entire industries) will be driven out of business because a trade partner has the comparative advantage in producing a given traded good. This means that there will be fewer losers due to expanded trade, and consequently there will be fewer actors lobbying against entrance into PTAs, relative to cases in which there is a high degree of inter-industry trade. It is important to note that, counter to conventional wisdom, this aspect of intra-industry trade would not be sufficient for PTA formation if not for the third-party competitive element discussed earlier. Yet the combination of substantial gains for exporters in both potential PTA members (relative to third parties) and relatively little loss for importers meets Grossman and Helpman's necessary conditions for the formation of a PTA (1995).[8]

Finally, security considerations leading governments to be wary of pref- erential market access are lowered as intra-industry trade increases. Specifi- cally, because intra-industry trade does not lead to specialization, it is less likely to invoke concerns for vulnerability to trade partners (see, for exam- ple, Keohane and Nye 1977). In our previous work (Peterson and Thies 2012a; 2012b), and in Chapter 5 of this volume, we find that bilateral intra-industry trade is uniquely associated with reduced conflict propensity between states because it ties these states' interests together. Although security consider- ations due to trade are given less attention in recent studies, we contend that they remain important among governments considering trade agreements. Recent events such as China's decision to reduce exports of strategically valuable rare-earth metals highlight the fact that security concerns remain salient to policymakers (Hounshell 2010). Indeed, increased trade with China is blamed for the decline of rare-earth metal production in the United States, given China's comparative advantage in this industry (Homans 2010).[9] In this case, if importers of Chinese rare-earth metals had domestic substitutes eas- ily available (in other words, if the industry had been characterized by intra- industry trade), they would likely have been less alarmed. Again, the absence of negative repercussion that might otherwise lead to resistance to PTAs sug- gests a lesser likelihood of lobbying against an agreement, relative to cases in which there is a higher degree of inter-industry trade between dyad members.

We do not make the claim that intra-industry trade is associated with lib- eralization unconditionally, as prior research suggests conditions in which intra-industry trade could actually lead to higher levels of protectionism (for example, Kono 2009). Specifically, Kono suggests the possibility that, although intra-industry trade could reduce the incentive to lobby for protectionism, it also increases the ability of interests to organize for collective action (see also Gilligan 1997). Kono therefore demonstrates that, for electoral systems in which narrow interests for protectionism are rewarded, intra-industry trade will be associated with more protectionism.

However, this prior work, which looks at intra-industry trade by state and by industry, does not preclude the possibility that bilateral intra-industry trade is associated with a greater demand for preferential treatment of a given trade partner in accordance with the argument presented here. Given that sustained global competitiveness requires expanded markets but does not necessarily isolate specific trade partners with which to liberalize, preferential agreements may be managed such that trade barriers are reduced only for states with which liberalization will have a net positive impact on domestic firms. Dyads experiencing higher levels of intra-industry trade are more likely to meet this criterion, as demonstrated earlier. Whereas liberalization overall might harm import competitors more than it helps exporters, states could seek out PTA partners for which overall interests favor freer trade, while trade barriers could be maintained or increased against nonmembers (see, for example, Levy 1997). Indeed, the relative losses associated with avoiding PTAs, particularly if third parties are forming or considering the formation of trade agreements, will push states to join PTAs even as multilateral protectionism remains or increases.

As noted, the model of preferential liberalization as a prisoners' dilemma suggests that all states face unilateral incentives to pursue these agreements. As we illustrate, bilateral intra-industry trade is an excellent indicator that a given dyad's interests are aligned. However, given evidence that prior formation of third-party PTAs could be perceived as threats by policymakers, increasing the desire to form counteragreements (Baldwin 1995), there is reason to expect that the PTA-influencing impact of PTAs becomes stronger as the number of third-party PTAs increases. This expectation also mirrors the findings of Axelrod (1984) that tit-for-tat strategies suggest that a player will defect in a prisoners' dilemma after witnessing other players do the same. We therefore hypothesize the following:

Hypothesis 3.1: A higher proportion of intra-industry trade between states is associated with a higher likelihood of PTA formation.

Hypothesis 3.2: The magnitude of the association between intra-industry trade and PTA formation is weakest when there are no third-party PTAs in force, becoming larger as the number of third-party PTAs in force increases.

Research Design

We test our hypotheses using data consisting of dyad years between 1962 and 2000. Although we created intra-industry trade data from 1962 to 2010 in Chapter 2, the PTA formation data we use are available only until 2000. However, our start year allows us to examine the vast majority of PTAs formed during the twentieth century. Very few dyadic PTAs were formed prior to 1962, most of these emerging from the formation of the European Economic Community in 1957. Furthermore, although many PTAs involve more than two states, the dyad remains a useful unit of analysis because each pair of states must agree to bilateral liberalization; states will not join multilateral agreements unless they are satisfied with the expected consequences of liberalization with all members.[10] Of course, the dyadic level of analysis is also useful given our arguments in Chapters 1 and 2 regarding the importance of modeling dyadic intra-industry trade.

Our dependent variables, which capture the signing of PTAs in year $t+1$,[11] are taken from Mansfield, Milner, and Pevehouse (2007). We code four different versions of PTA formation in order to test for the robustness of our theoretical arguments on increasing degrees of economic integration. First, we code a binary variable equal to 1 for dyad years in which any PTA is formed, including reciprocal and non-reciprocal agreements.[12] The second variable captures reciprocal PTA formation. The third dependent variable excludes the least comprehensive PTAs, including only free trade areas (FTAs), customs unions (CUs), common markets (CMs), or economic unions (ECUs). This variable addresses the fact that low-level preferential agreements may not convey the same benefits as agreements requiring that "restrictive regulations of commerce . . . are eliminated on substantially all the trade" between members (GATT article XXIV, paragraph 8).[13] Further removing low-level agreements, our fourth dependent variable equals 1 only when CUs, CMs, and ECUs are signed (that is, it excludes FTAs as well as lesser agreements). This final dependent variable isolates agreements in which external trade barriers on specific industries can more easily be raised,[14] which may be more attractive to firms engaging in intra-industry trade, particularly if they are inefficient relative to firms in third-party states.[15] As an alternative to using separate dependent variables to capture multiple levels of PTA integration, we further specify models in which we simultaneously estimate the formation of a PTA and the depth of integration, which we capture using a five-point ordinal scale isolating the formation of (1) preferential trade agreements, (2) free trade agreements, (3) customs unions, (4) common markets, and (5) economic unions.[16] Of the 2,555 dyadic agreements in our dataset, 1,067 are non-reciprocal. Non-reciprocal agreements are likely to be simple PTAs (759 out of the 824 agreement dyads that are less than FTA dyads). Non-reciprocal agreements represent a smaller proportion of agreements that stipulate deeper integration: 262 of 860 free trade agreement dyads, 12 of 185 customs union dyads, 34 of 603 common market dyads, and 0 of 83 economic union dyads.

Each of these dependent variables is identical in cases of bilateral PTAs and multilateral PTAs because we expect that the process leading from intra-industry trade to increased willingness to sign PTAs does not depend on the size of the proposed agreement.[17] However, the size of PTAs varies dramatically, a pattern even more prominent at the dyadic level of analysis. For example, the Canada-United States Free Trade Agreement (CUSFTA) is coded as one dyadic observation, while the North American Free Trade Agreement (NAFTA)—its successor—is coded as three (U.S.-Canada, U.S.-Mexico, and Canada-Mexico). This variation is evident for example with the EU expansion to twenty-seven members, which is coded as 351 dyadic observations. Given this, we replicate all statistical tests separately on bilateral PTA formation and multilateral PTA formation, finding that all results are robust.[18]

To estimate the formation of PTAs using our four dichotomous dependent variables, we use probit models, including corrections for time dependence and non-independence of observations.[19] Specifically, to account for time dependence, we include a counter variable for the number of years since a PTA has been formed, as well as a square and cube term of this variable (Carter and Signorino 2010). We use a Heckman selection model to estimate formation and depth of integration simultaneously.[20]

Primary Explanatory Variables

Our key explanatory variable is the bilateral *intra-industry trade index* developed in Chapter 2. The variable ranges from 0, representing no intra-industry trade in the dyad, to 1, signifying that all dyadic trade flows within industries. Given that Hypothesis 3.2 suggests that the relationship between intra-industry trade and PTA formation is conditional on the number of *third-party PTAs* in existence, we also specify models in which we interact intra-industry trade with a count of all third-party PTA competition. Specifically, for a given dyad composed of states *A* and *B*, we create a variable that counts the number of third-party dyads (for example, dyad *C-D*) that are members of PTAs that *exclude* both state *A* and state *B*. This third-party PTA dyad variable is also useful to capture the overall increasing prevalence of PTAs over time.[21] In the interactive models, the coefficient for intra-industry trade represents its association with PTA formation under the condition that there are zero third-party PTA dyads. We must interpret the coefficients for intra-industry trade and third-party PTA dyads together in order to determine how our expected association varies depending on the extent of third-party PTA competition (see, for example, Braumoeller 2004).

Other Explanatory Variables

We include control variables to account for other factors that could correlate with intra-industry trade and also affect PTA formation. To capture the institutional opportunity to derail PTAs, we include a variable for veto players in each dyadic state. We follow Mansfield, Milner, and Pevehouse (2007), using Heinisz's measure of veto players (2000). This measure captures (1) the number of government branches that might check the power of policymakers and (2) the similarity of policy preferences across actors. For example, in the United States, the Senate is a check on the power of the president, and this check is weighted higher when the Senate and president are of opposing parties. As veto players may vary across dyad members, we take the higher of the two states' veto player scores. We contend that the *higher veto players score* within the dyad functions as a weak link in the PTA negotiation-ratification process.[22]

It is important to distinguish the nature of trade (that is, whether trade is inter- or intra-industry) from the extent of dyadic trade, given that prior levels of trade interaction are likely to affect the entrance into preferential agreements. Therefore, we code *lower trade dependence* as the lesser value within the dyad for dyadic trade flow divided by gross domestic product (GDP). We use trade flow data (state A's imports from state B and A's exports to state B) from the UN Comtrade database, and GDP data from the Penn World Table 8.0 (Feenstra, Inklaar, and Timmer 2013).[23] We also include variables capturing income, democracy, and affinity within the dyad.[24] Specifically, we include a variable for the *lower GDP per capita* within the dyad as well as the *difference* between the higher GDP per capita to the lower GDP per capita, taking both of these indicators from the Penn World Table. These variables control for the absolute and relative development of states, given that, for example, PTAs between a developed state and a less-developed state are more likely to follow from desire to reap gains from inter-industry specialization.[25] We also include a variable for the lower Polity IV 21-point democracy-autocracy score (Marshall and Jaggers 2010), as well as the difference between polity scores. To capture dyadic affinity, we include a dichotomous variable equal to one for mutual membership in the *General Agreement on Tariffs and Trade* (GATT) or World Trade Organization, as well as a dichotomous variable equal to one when the dyad has experienced a *militarized interstate dispute* (MID) in the previous year, using data from EUGene (Bennett and Stam 2000).

Given that PTAs are often formed in accordance with regional liberalization, we include a dichotomous variable equal to 1 for *contiguous states*.[26] Finally, we include a dichotomous variable equal to one for *European Union dyads*, given the potentially extraordinary experience of the European Union.

Potential for Endogeneity

There could be concern for endogeneity in the research design we propose if, for example, trade agreements boost intra-industry trade rather than vice versa (Egger, Egger, and Greenaway 2008). We highlight the cases of the United States vis-à-vis Canada and Mexico prior to the entrance into force of the CUSFTA and NAFTA as salient examples of the temporal relationship between intra-industry trade and trade agreement formation. While one might argue that intra-industry trade increased as a function of these agreements, our data suggest that intra-industry trade as a proportion of U.S.-Canada and U.S.-Mexico trade had already increased considerably in the 1980s prior to NAFTA negotiation.[27] We present Figure 3.1 to illustrate the change in U.S.-Canada and U.S.-Mexico intra-industry trade over time (specifically, the proportion of all dyadic trade that can be considered intra-industry), noting CUSFTA and NAFTA signing with vertical lines. As the figures show, the composition of U.S.-Canada and U.S.-Mexico trade became dramatically more intra-industry leading up to the formation of these agreements. Interestingly, the change in intra-industry trade as a proportion of dyadic trade is uneven after NAFTA enters into force. U.S.-Canada intra-industry trade appears to level off after approximately 1990, while U.S.-Mexico intra-industry trade appears to decline as a proportion of all trade after 1995. Although these figures provide anecdotal evidence against reverse causation, we test for the robustness of our primary results with simultaneous models for two endogenous variables, looking at reciprocal causation between PTA signing and intra-industry trade (see Keshk 2003 for a description of this method). Our primary results are unchanged in these simultaneous models (which are not presented due to space considerations, but are available on request).[28]

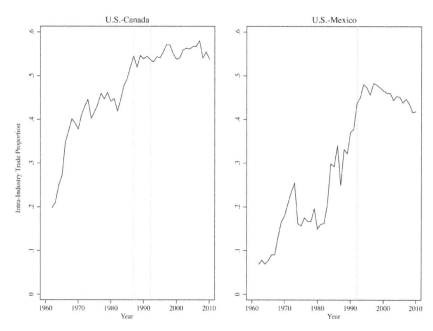

Figure 3.1   U.S.-Canada and U.S.-Mexico intra-industry trade proportion between 1962 and 2010. Vertical lines represent the signing of the U.S.-Canada FTA and NAFTA.

Analysis

As the preceding section makes clear, there are a number of important operationalization and modeling decisions that must be made in order to conduct a rigorous empirical test of our hypotheses. To ensure that our empirical results are robust to alternative measures of PTA formation as well as to modeling decisions regarding functional form, we specified several different models. The results of the ten most important models are presented in Tables 3.2 and 3.3, which we include in the appendix to this chapter. However, we present a summary of the conclusions from these tests in a series of figures that follow. As these figures show, our main hypothesis is strongly supported by the statistical analysis. Specifically, we find that intra-industry trade is associated with a higher likelihood of PTA formation. Furthermore, there is some evidence that this relationship becomes stronger as there are more third-party PTAs in existence.

Figure 3.2 presents the marginal effect of each explanatory variable from a basic probit model in which the dependent variable is a dichotomous indicator of PTA formation: equal to 1 when a dyad forms any preferential trade agreement in a given year (Model 3.1 presented in Table 3.1; this is a non-interactive

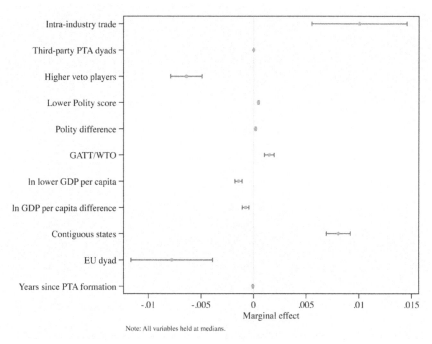

Figure 3.2 Marginal effects of explanatory variables on PTA formation with all variables held at their medians, including 95 percent confidence bounds. From Model 3.1.

specification).[29] In this figure, a vertical line at $x = 0$ represents a null association between an explanatory variable and PTA formation. Small circles represent the estimated marginal effect between each of our explanatory variables, while horizontal lines represent the 95 percent confidence interval for these estimates. The further an estimate is from the reference line, the larger is the magnitude of the marginal effect.[30] Indicators to the left of the reference line suggest a negative association with PTA formation, while indicators entirely to the right suggest a positive association with PTA formation. Any line that crosses the reference line represents a variable for which the association with PTA formation is not significant at the 95 percent level.

Figure 3.2 indicates that intra-industry trade has a positive and statistically significant association with PTA formation. All else equal, an increase in intra-industry trade from 0 to 100 percent of all trade is associated with approximately a one-percentage-point increase in the probability of PTA formation. Given that the baseline probability of PTA formation is quite small (0.5 percent), the impact of changing composition of trade from fully inter-industry to fully intra-indus-

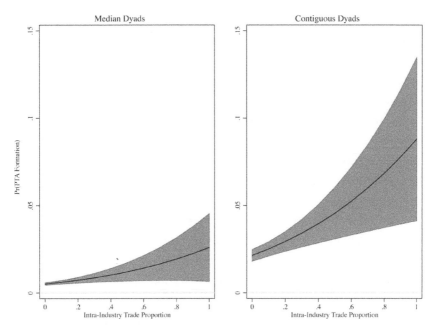

Figure 3.3   The probability of PTA formation over the range of intra-industry trade, including 95 percent confidence bounds, for median dyads and contiguous dyads. From Model 3.1.

try is large in relative terms: a 200 percent increase in the probability of PTA formation. Notably, the marginal effect of intra-industry trade is the largest in all our explanatory variables as presented in the figure. However, its substantive impact is not necessarily the largest given that its range is bound by 0 and 1, whereas some of our other explanatory variables have much larger ranges. For a more in-depth analysis of the impact of intra-industry trade, we present a visual representation of the change in probability of PTA formation as trade composition changes from entirely inter-industry trade (intra-industry trade = 0) to entirely intra-industry trade (intra-industry trade = 1).[31] Figure 3.3 (from Model 1) presents this change in probability for two cases: (1) holding all other explanatory variables at the median and (2) holding contiguity at 1, therefore examining how intra-industry trade is associated with PTA formation for proximate states that likely have more opportunity to form trade agreements.

The same pattern is evident in both graphs presented in Figure 3.3. Specifically, as intra-industry trade increases from its minimum to its maximum, the probability of PTA formation increases by a factor of approximately 4. Specifically, from the left-hand plot in Figure 3.3, we estimate that the probability that an otherwise median dyad forms at preferential trade agreement increases steadily from approximately 0.5 percent to approximately 2.5 percent. Similarly, in the right-hand plot of Figure 3.3, the probability of PTA formation increases from slightly over 2 percent to nearly 9 percent.[32] However, these changes in probability follow from Model 3.1, in which we examine the formation of any trade agreement. Figure 3.4 is a bar chart comparing the relative influence of intra-industry trade on differing levels of integration. The figure shows that increasing intra-industry trade has a stronger facilitating impact on agreements specifying deeper levels of integration. The results, from the left-hand graph in Figure 3.3, are reflected in the left-most bar. The increase from no intra-industry trade to complete trade within industries is associated with a 490 percent increase in the probability of PTA formation. However, if we examine only the impact of reciprocal PTAs (Model 3.2), free trade agreements (Model 3.3), and agreements that are at least customs unions (Model 3.4),[33] we see a stronger relationship. In the formation of reciprocal PTAs or FTAs (the middle two bars in Figure 3.4), a minimum-to-maximum change in intra-industry trade proportion is associated with more than a 1,000 percent increase in agreement formation. For customs unions (or greater level of integration), a minimum-to-maximum change in intra-industry trade proportion is associated with approximately a 9,000 percent increase in the formation of an agreement (shown in the right-most bar).

The impact of intra-industry trade on PTA formation can be illustrated using examples from our data. For example, the United States and the United Kingdom had intra-industry trade equal to approximately 20 percent of all trade in 1962, but it has increased to over 60 percent of all trade by 2000.[34] U.S. intra-industry trade with France and Germany has followed similar patterns of increase over time. This trend toward larger proportions of intra-industry trade over time could explain mounting pressure toward forming a PTA: specifically, the Transatlantic Trade and Investment Partnership, which is currently being negotiated between the United States and the European Union. Similarly, trade within European dyads tends to be considerably higher than average levels. These large proportions of intra-industry trade could be in part responsible for momentum toward increasing integration. Indeed, expansion of the EU typically has been preceded by periods of increasing intra-industry trade between existing and new members—particularly notable in patterns

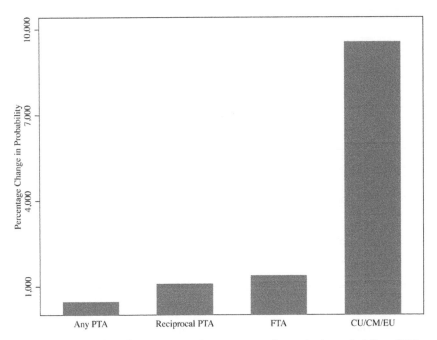

Figure 3.4   Bar chart demonstrating the percentage change in the probability of PTA formation. From Models 3.1 through 3.4.

of trade of the three largest powers (the United Kingdom, France, and Germany) with Romania and the Baltic States.

Interacting Intra-Industry Trade and Third-Party PTAs

Results of interactive models provide some evidence that the effect of intra-industry trade on PTA formation becomes stronger as the number of third-party PTAs in existence increases. As Table 3.2 (presented in the appendix) demonstrates, the interaction term for *intra-industry trade X third-party PTAs* is not significant in any of Models 3.6–3.10. However, interaction terms are of limited value in nonlinear models (Ai and Norton 2003). Accordingly, we graph the marginal effect of intra-industry trade on PTA formation over the range of third-party PTAs in our data. The resulting graph, presented in Figure 3.5, shows that the marginal effect of intra-industry trade appears to increase as the number of third-party PTA dyads increases. The effect is relatively modest as third-party PTA dyads increase from the minimum (approximately 100) to the maximum (approximately 5,000), an increase in the marginal effect

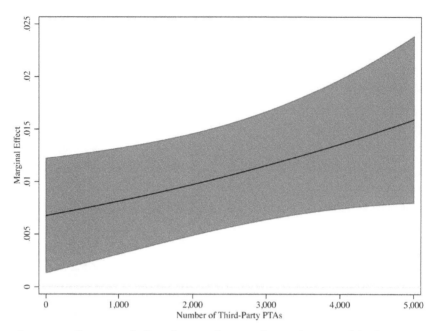

Figure 3.5   The marginal effect of intra-industry trade over the range of third-party PTA dyads, including 95 percent confidence bounds. From Model 3.6.

of intra-industry trade from approximately 0.5 percent to 1.5 percent.[35] This increase falls approximately within a standard deviation below to a standard deviation above the mean value within our data (mean = 2,371; standard deviation = 1,580). However, relatively wide confidence bounds suggest uncertainty in this increase; it is significant only at the 90 percent confidence level. Notably, our model predicts that intra-industry trade has a significant impact on PTA formation even when there are no third-party PTA dyads in existence. Ultimately, we expect that even the threat of third-party PTAs (or, conversely, the opportunity to be the first of such advantageous agreements) is enough to drive PTA formation. Therefore, the actual number of existing trade agreements has only a modest conditioning role.

Important Control Variables

To put the influence of intra-industry trade into perspective, we compare its association with PTA formation to that of other explanatory variables. Figure 3.2 illustrates these comparable effects, albeit with the caveat that all estimates represent the influence of increasing each explanatory variable by one unit. For example, we find, as expected, that PTA formation is more likely when there are more third-party PTAs in force. Thus we find support for Baldwin's argument that PTAs may form in a "domino effect" (1995). The magnitude of this effect appears very small (on the scale of 10^{-7}). However, there are as many as five thousand third-party PTAs in existence in a given dyad year. Accordingly, third-party PTAs can have a meaningful impact on the probability of PTA formation.

Notably, we find that preexisting dependence on trade (that is, trade divided by the less wealthy state's GDP) is not significantly associated with PTA formation. This result supports our expectation that the mere flow of trade could have crosscutting effects on willingness to engage in preferential liberalization. A higher flow of trade could suggest similar interests that favor PTA formation. Yet it could be that higher flows of trade occur because firms in one state hold a comparative advantage in the production of some commodity, which could spark resistance to liberalization from import competitors in the other trade partner.[36]

Finally, as expected, the coefficient for higher veto players is negative and significant in each of these six models, supporting findings by Mansfield, Milner, and Pevehouse (2007) that institutional opportunity to derail PTAs is associated with a reduced probability of PTA formation.[37] In further robustness tests not presented (but available from the authors), we specified models including an interaction of intra-industry trade and veto players, finding that the coefficients for intra-industry trade and veto players look as they do in models excluding the interaction, while the interaction term is not significant. An interpretation of interaction effects suggests that the effects of intra-industry trade and veto players are not conditional on the level at which we hold the other variable.[38]

Conclusion

Our results suggest that the nature of trade influences the likelihood of entrance into preferential trade agreements. More generally, we find evidence that domestic support operationalized by intra-industry trade, which we characterize as *willingness* to enter PTAs, operates along with the previously highlighted institutional constraints such as veto players, which we characterize as *opportunity* to impede PTAs. Furthermore, we find some evidence that this relationship becomes stronger as PTAs continue to proliferate throughout the international system. Our results have important implications for the study of economic agreements, as we find that the nature of preexisting trade is an important determinant of future preferential liberalization. Perhaps more important, an interpretation of our findings along with those of Gilligan (1997) and Kono (2009) may suggest that the conventional wisdom linking intra-industry trade to PTA formation may be too optimistic in assuming that intra-industry trade *always* lessens resistance to liberalization. Instead, scholars should account for the fact that PTAs could arise when intra-industry trade is high for more selfish reasons, as firms attempt to maintain or increase global competitiveness, while potentially also seeking to isolate themselves from more competitive third parties.

Accordingly, of particular interest for future research is the implication of our argument that PTA formation due to intra-industry trade might complement multilateral protectionism (see, for example, Levy 1997). Previous research has shown that intra-industry trade, in some circumstances, may hinder multilateral liberalization (for example, Kono 2009). PTAs may be attractive options to firms engaging in intra-industry trade when they are inefficient relative to third parties because preferential trade agreements would enable these firms to benefit further from economies of scale, while maintaining or even increasing trade barriers against firms in nonmember states. However, assuming that PTAs lead to productivity gains, perhaps less developed countries can utilize them in a manner similar to outward-looking import substitution industrialization to protect infant industries. PTAs in these cases might constitute short- to medium-term protectionism, yet they may also be "building blocks" to later multilateral liberalization.

Our results also carry implications for the study of international cooperation and conflict resulting from trade patterns. For example, third parties may raise trade barriers in response to PTAs to which they are not a part in order to protect their firms from the productivity gains of firms within PTA members. Terms-of-trade competition could even drive the formation of rival PTAs in a pattern resembling an arms race, potentially fostering political—and ultimately militarized—conflict between PTA members and nonmembers. In fact, the link between intra-industry trade, PTA formation, and terms-of-trade competition could be behind the results found by Mansfield and Pevehouse (2000) that "peace through trade" follows only within PTAs. Future studies should examine these and other related possibilities that emerge from our findings about the relationships between intra-industry trade and economic integration.

Appendix to Chapter 3

This appendix presents tables for Models 3.1 through 3.10, demonstrating the robust relationship between intra-industry trade proportion and the formation of a preferential trade agreement. Table 3.1 presents Models 3.1 through 3.5, non-interactive models in which *intra-industry trade proportion* and *third-party PTA count* are both included in an additive specification. The dependent variable in Model 3.1 is the formation of any PTA, while Model 3.2 restricts the dependent variable to the formation of reciprocal PTAs (excluding primarily agreements following from the generalized system of preferences, which typically occur among former colonies and their former masters). Model 3.3 restricts the dependent variable to the formation of free trade agreements, while model 3.4 is the most restrictive, examining only agreements that are at least customs unions, establishing a common external tariff as well as eliminating essentially all protectionist barriers within member states. The final two columns in Table 3.1 present Model 3.5, a Heckman probit model in which formation of any agreement is estimated simultaneously with the depth of integration.

As Table 3.1 shows, the coefficient for intra-industry trade is positive and highly significant ($p < 0.001$) in all four single-equation models, as well as in both equations in model 3.5. Notably, the results of Model 3.5 suggest that a higher proportion of intra-industry trade makes the formation of an agreement more likely, and also leads to deeper integration among agreements that are formed. This result complements that of Models 3.1 through 3.4, as demonstrated by Figure 3.5, which show that the impact of intra-industry trade becomes relatively larger for agreements specifying deeper integration.

The coefficient for third-party PTAs is positive and significant in all models as well ($p < 0.001$). Although the coefficient for third-party PTAs rounds to 0 because its magnitude is very small, the large number of possible third-party PTA dyads renders the effect of this variable potentially meaningful, as shown in our discussion of substantive effects presented in the chapter text. There are two remaining findings of note. First, the veto players measure is negative and significant at the 0.001 level in all models, suggesting that more access points through which opponents of preferential liberalization can influence policy results in a lesser likelihood of bilateral agreement formation. Second, the coefficient for trade level—specifically trade as a proportion of the poorer state's GDP—is not significant in any of our models, reaffirming our argument that trade (and specifically inter-industry trade) can have crosscutting effects on preferential liberalization.

Table 3.1 Probit and Heckman Probit coefficients and robust standard errors for non-interactive models examining the association between intra-industry trade, third-party PTA dyads, and PTA formation, 1962–2000.

	Model 3.1	Model 3.2	Model 3.3	Model 3.4	Model 3.5	
	Onset	Onset	Onset	Onset	Onset	Depth
Intra–industry trade	0.671***	0.903***	0.981***	1.739***	0.681***	3.603***
	(0.148)	(0.160)	(0.170)	(0.207)	(0.149)	(0.453)
Third–party PTA dyads	0.000***	0.000***	0.000***	0.000**	0.000***	0.000***
	(0.000)	(0.000)	(0.000)	(0.000)	(0.000)	(0.000)
Higher veto players	−0.428***	−1.035***	−1.036***	−1.304***	−0.419***	−1.440***
	(0.062)	(0.086)	(0.089)	(0.119)	(0.062)	(0.243)
Lower Polity score	0.030***	0.028***	0.029***	0.030***	0.031***	−0.002
	(0.002)	(0.003)	(0.003)	(0.004)	(0.002)	(0.008)
Polity difference	0.012***	−0.002	−0.002	0.007*	0.012***	−0.048***
	(0.002)	(0.003)	(0.003)	(0.004)	(0.002)	(0.007)
GATT or WTO	0.100***	0.088***	0.112***	0.145***	0.097***	0.113*
	(0.017)	(0.024)	(0.024)	(0.029)	(0.017)	(0.049)
Lower trade to GDP	−4.373	−1.768	−3.084	−2.233	−4.544	−1.468
	(3.037)	(2.779)	(3.589)	(4.058)	(3.075)	(4.316)
MID	−0.157	−0.067	−0.064	−0.133	−0.158	−0.028
	(0.087)	(0.092)	(0.093)	(0.127)	(0.087)	(0.166)
Lower ln GDPpc	−0.096***	−0.173***	−0.183***	−0.242***	−0.098***	−0.353***
	(0.012)	(0.016)	(0.015)	(0.023)	(0.012)	(0.040)
ln GDPpc difference	−0.051***	−0.165***	−0.167***	−0.165***	−0.052***	−0.468***
	(0.011)	(0.016)	(0.016)	(0.020)	(0.011)	(0.048)
Contiguous state	0.538***	0.604***	0.604***	0.554***	0.542***	−0.047
	(0.026)	(0.031)	(0.032)	(0.042)	(0.026)	(0.099)
EU dyad	−0.520***	−0.989***	−0.976***	−0.805***	−0.523***	0.992***
	(0.129)	(0.188)	(0.189)	(0.198)	(0.130)	(0.134)
Years since formation	−0.010	0.008	0.008	−0.042***	−0.004***	
	(0.005)	(0.007)	(0.007)	(0.009)	(0.001)	
Years since formation2	0.000	−0.001*	−0.001	0.002***		
	(0.000)	(0.000)	(0.000)	(0.001)		
Years since formation3	−0.000	0.000*	0.000*	−0.000***		
	(0.000)	(0.000)	(0.000)	(0.000)		
Constant	−1.858***	−1.713***	−1.745***	−1.395***	−1.902***	
	(0.056)	(0.074)	(0.076)	(0.098)	(0.048)	
Observations	194,688	193,620	193,551	192,979	194,688	2,489

continued

Table 3.1 Probit and Heckman Probit coefficients and robust standard errors for non-interactive models examining the association between intra-industry trade, third-party PTA dyads, and PTA formation, 1962–2000. (*continued*)

	Model 3.1	Model 3.2	Model 3.3	Model 3.4	Model 3.5	
	Onset	*Onset*	*Onset*	*Onset*	*Onset*	*Depth*
Cut 1						−3.444***
Cut 2						−2.291***
Cut 3						−2.040***
Cut 4						−0.638*
Rho						−0.360*
χ2	1348***	1689***	1699***	1379***	343.9***	
Log likelihood	−12790	−7568	−7237	−4416	−15603	

Notes: Robust standard errors adjusted for clustering on the dyad in parentheses.

*** p < 0.001, ** p < 0.01, * p < 0.05; two–tailed tests.

Table 3.2 presents coefficients for Models 3.6 through 3.10. These models are nearly identical to those in Table 3.1, except for the critical addition of a multiplicative interaction term for *intra-industry trade X third-party PTA dyads*. This interaction term allows us to address Hypothesis 3.2: that the impact of intra-industry trade becomes larger as the number of third-party PTAs increases. As noted in the chapter text, the interaction term is not significant in any of the models presented in Table 3.2. However, there is some evidence that the presence of more third-party PTAs is associated with a stronger impact of intra-industry trade on dyadic PTA formation.

Table 3.2 Probit and Heckman Probit coefficients and robust standard errors for interactive models examining the association between intra-industry trade, third-party PTA dyads, and PTA formation, 1962–2000.

	Model 3.6	Model 3.7	Model 3.8	Model 3.9	Model 3.10	
	Onset	Onset	Onset	Onset	Onset	Depth
Intra-industry trade	0.539*	0.690*	0.809**	1.078***	0.526*	2.437***
	(0.220)	(0.282)	(0.292)	(0.305)	(0.222)	(0.609)
Third-party PTA dyads	0.000***	0.000***	0.000***	0.000	0.000***	0.000***
	(0.000)	(0.000)	(0.000)	(0.000)	(0.000)	(0.000)
IIT X PTA dyads	0.000	0.000	0.000	0.000**	0.000	0.000*
	(0.000)	(0.000)	(0.000)	(0.000)	(0.000)	(0.000)
Higher veto players	−0.428***	−1.035***	−1.036***	−1.308***	−0.419***	−1.444***
	(0.062)	(0.086)	(0.089)	(0.119)	(0.062)	(0.250)
Lower Polity score	0.030***	0.028***	0.029***	0.030***	0.031***	−0.001
	(0.002)	(0.003)	(0.003)	(0.004)	(0.002)	(0.008)
Polity difference	0.012***	−0.002	−0.002	0.008*	0.012***	−0.048***
	(0.002)	(0.003)	(0.003)	(0.004)	(0.002)	(0.007)
GATT or WTO	0.100***	0.088***	0.112***	0.145***	0.097***	0.113*
	(0.017)	(0.024)	(0.024)	(0.029)	(0.017)	(0.049)
Lower trade to GDP	−4.233	−1.587	−2.933	−1.951	−4.383	−1.140
	(3.012)	(2.725)	(3.566)	(3.964)	(3.043)	(4.103)
MID	−0.158	−0.068	−0.064	−0.136	−0.159	−0.023
	(0.087)	(0.092)	(0.093)	(0.127)	(0.087)	(0.168)
Lower ln GDPpc	−0.096***	−0.173***	−0.183***	−0.244***	−0.098***	−0.352***
	(0.012)	(0.016)	(0.015)	(0.023)	(0.012)	(0.042)
ln GDPpc difference	−0.051***	−0.165***	−0.167***	−0.165***	−0.052***	−0.467***
	(0.011)	(0.016)	(0.016)	(0.020)	(0.011)	(0.050)
Contiguous state	0.539***	0.605***	0.604***	0.557***	0.543***	−0.044
	(0.026)	(0.031)	(0.032)	(0.042)	(0.026)	(0.104)
EU dyad	−0.525***	−1.007***	−0.990***	−0.874***	−0.529***	0.952***
	(0.129)	(0.184)	(0.185)	(0.198)	(0.131)	(0.118)
Years since formation	−0.010	0.008	0.008	−0.042***	−0.004***	
	(0.005)	(0.007)	(0.007)	(0.009)	(0.001)	
Years since formation2	0.000	−0.001*	−0.001	0.002***		
	(0.000)	(0.000)	(0.000)	(0.001)		
Years since formation3	−0.000	0.000*	0.000*	−0.000***		
	(0.000)	(0.000)	(0.000)	(0.000)		

continued

Table 3.2 Probit and Heckman Probit coefficients and robust standard errors for interactive models examining the association between intra-industry trade, third-party PTA dyads, and PTA formation, 1962–2000. (*continued*)

| | Model 3.6 | Model 3.7 | Model 3.8 | Model 3.9 | Model 3.10 | |
	Onset	Onset	Onset	Onset	Onset	Depth
Constant	−1.856***	−1.709***	−1.741***	−1.373***	−1.899***	
	(0.056)	(0.075)	(0.076)	(0.099)	(0.049)	
Observations	194,688	193,620	193,551	192,979	194,688	2,489
Cut 1						−3.481***
Cut 2						−2.330***
Cut 3						−2.079***
Cut 4						−0.668
Rho						−0.364*
χ2	1355	1703	1712	1404	362.8	
Log likelihood	−12790	−7567	−7237	−4413	−15600	

Notes: Robust standard errors adjusted for clustering on the dyad in parentheses.

*** $p < 0.001$, ** $p < 0.01$, * $p < 0.05$; two–tailed tests.

Chapter 4

Trade Composition and the World Trade Organization: The Effect of Intra-Industry Trade on the Dispute Settlement Procedure

THE creation of the World Trade Organization's (WTO's) dispute settlement mechanism in 1995 represented the culmination of efforts to bring trade disputes within a legalized, multilateral institutional format. The dispute settlement process under the General Agreement on Tariffs and Trade (GATT) regime was largely ineffective, as any contracting party could end the process at any point from the initiation of a dispute case, through the formation of a panel and the issuance and adoption of a panel report on the case. More troubling is that the faulty process provided few inducements for GATT contracting parties to bring their policies and practices into compliance with the specific rulings or general principles of the treaty framework. The WTO dispute agreement, formally known as the Understanding on Rules and Procedures Governing the Settlement of Disputes (a.k.a., Dispute Settlement Understanding, or DSU), created a binding dispute resolution mechanism that resolved many of the problems associated with the GATT dispute resolution process. Scholars have eagerly begun to analyze the effects that a more binding dispute resolution mechanism has had on the political economy of trade disputes.

This chapter adds a new dimension to our understanding of dispute initiation under the WTO regime. While the existing literature has identified a number of factors relevant to dispute initiation and participation, such as legal capacity, the expected costs and benefits, relative size and power, and learning through previous participation in disputes, we examine the importance of trade composition. We develop a theoretical argument that suggests that a higher proportion of intra-industry trade is likely to affect the degree to which dyadic trade flows lead to the initiation of a dispute. Unlike in previous chapters, we posit a conditional relationship between trade flows and intra-industry trade because trade itself is the source of potential conflict. If trade flows are low, then there is less potential for violations of WTO trade rules; perhaps more important, there is less opportunity for domestic producers to seek relief from foreign import competition. It is only when trade flows are higher that the opportunity for trade disputes arises. While higher trade flows increase the opportunity for disputes in most cases, we demonstrate that this relationship diminishes as the proportion of trade following from intra-industry specialization increases.

We begin with a brief overview of the dispute resolution process within the WTO regime, in order to demonstrate the costliness of this effort for firms and member governments. We continue by reviewing the existing literature on the origins of WTO trade disputes. While a variety of factors are identified that lead states to be more likely to initiate a dispute, none have addressed the composition of trade as an important conditioning variable. We then develop our theoretical perspective on the role of intra-industry trade in mitigating dispute initiation depending on the magnitude of trade flows in a dyad. Next we conduct an empirical analysis of WTO trade dispute onset from 1995 through 2009, and find that our theoretical expectations receive confirmation in the data. Finally, we conclude with some implications of the analysis for the WTO regime and extensions of the logic to other aspects of trade dispute analysis.

The Dispute Settlement Procedure in the WTO

As part of the agreements creating the WTO, the members agreed to use a multilateral system of settling disputes rather than take unilateral action if they believed other members were violating the rules.[1] The Dispute Settlement Body (DSB), composed from all members of the WTO, has the institutional authority to set up panels to consider dispute cases and to then accept or reject the findings established in panel reports. The DSB handles appeals, monitors compliance with rulings, and can authorize retaliation when a member does not comply. This legalization of the dispute settlement mechanism was a huge advance over the GATT system, in which a single contracting party could veto nearly every stage of the process, including the ruling. The DSB adopts rulings from panels automatically unless there is consensus among the member states to reject them. This obviously gives the WTO regime much more teeth in settling disputes than had the GATT.

Disputes arise when one member adopts a policy or practice that another member considers a violation of the WTO agreement. Such a policy or practice may cause harm to its domestic producers who export their products or compete with imported goods. As Davis and Shirato (2007, 278) suggest, firms in such a country have several options when confronted with such policies and practices. First, they could simply absorb the losses, or an exporter might try to get around trade barriers by shifting to foreign direct investment. Second, firms could lobby their government to negotiate with the offending country bilaterally, in WTO committees (for example, Technical Barriers to Trade, Sanitary and Phytosanitary Measures), or in regional or preferential trade agreement (PTA) fora. Third, firms could lobby their government to pursue WTO adjudication. Finally, in many cases, firms will work with governments to pursue several of the aforementioned options simultaneously, with WTO adjudication usually being the last option pursued. This is so because the WTO adjudication process is very costly.

Prior to filing an official complaint, discussions between firms and the government and intergovernmental negotiations take a great deal of time and money. Davis and Shirato (2007, 280) note that even cases settled during the consultation process can take up to a year, and those that proceeded to the formal panel process last on average three years. There are also the costs of legal teams and consulting firms that actually manage the process prior to and during the formal dispute resolution process.

The formal process begins with a member state requesting bilateral consultations with the offending member under Article 4 of the DSU. The consultation period lasts a minimum of sixty days before a member can request the formation of a panel from the DSB. The preferred solution to all disputes under the WTO regime is to have the two members resolve it between themselves, and even after a case may have proceeded formally to panel, consultation and negotiation are always available to the members to resolve the case. The consultation period should increase the amount and quality of information available to members, which in about half of the cases will lead to the end of a dispute. In other cases, disputants cannot agree on a resolution. If the preliminary consultations fail after sixty days, then a member can request the establishment of a formal dispute settlement panel under Article 6 of the DSU. The DSB selects panelists from a list of qualified governmental and nongovernmental individuals maintained by the WTO Secretariat. The members of the DSB negotiate the composition of the panel, and if there is no agreement, then the director-general of the WTO will make the selections.

Under Article 10 of the DSU, third parties may formally join in the dispute settlement after a panel has been formed. Third-party members can deliver testimony before panels in the attempt to shape the outcome. As Busch and Reinhardt (2006, 451) note, third parties acting in an informal capacity can actually join in at the consultation phase. In either case, third parties are expected to demonstrate a "substantial trade interest" in the particular dispute or a "systemic interest" in the way the dispute may affect interpretations and applications of WTO rules. The majority of disputes involve third parties entering at some phase in the formal process. Third parties are thought to participate for a number of reasons: to prevent a discriminatory settlement between the two members that would affect their own interests in their shared market (Bagwell and Staiger 2004), to increase the transparency of negotiated settlements (Busch and Reinhardt 2006, 454), and because they are strategic actors that represent the interests of all members in panel (Smith 2003). Busch and Reinhardt's argument (455–456) is that third parties increase disputants' bargaining costs because they serve as the main audience, thus increasing transparency, and as a participatory audience they engage directly in the dispute settlement. As a result, Busch and Reinhardt hypothesize and find evidence that third parties undermine early settlement in the consultation and panel phases, thus increasing the likelihood of an actual panel ruling.

The final panel report is provided to the disputing parties within six months of the formation of the panel. The panel process involves two hearings, expert testimony, a first draft and interim report, and a two-week review period, followed by a final report that is circulated to the DSB. After twenty days, but no longer than sixty days, the DSB must adopt the report unless consensus exists to reject it. The adopted report with the recommendation to bring the policy or practice into conformity becomes the ruling of the DSB. Either or both disputing parties may appeal a panel's ruling, but they must base the appeal on points of law rather than on reexamination of existing evidence or new evidence. Appeals of panel rulings are heard by three members of an appellate body of the DSB. The appellate body decisions are normally issued within sixty to ninety days, which must then be accepted or rejected with consensus by the DSB within thirty days. The member against whom a judgment is made is given thirty days or "a reasonable period of time" to bring its policies or practices into compliance with the ruling. Failing compliance, the member must enter into negotiations with the other disputant to determine compensation. Failing a negotiated compensation agreement, the harmed member may ask the DSB for permission to impose limited trade sanctions. The DSB continues to monitor the case until the underlying issue is resolved.

The process just described has been utilized relatively frequently since its inception in 1995. The left-hand graph of Figure 4.1 plots the number of dyadic disputes initiated each year between 1995 and 2010.[2] The figure also plots the average proportion of bilateral intra-industry trade over this same time period. Although these initial, system-level variables provide relatively little evidence, the frequency of dispute initiation appears to decrease over time as intra-industry trade increases. The right-hand graph of Figure 4.1 presents an alternative variant of this relationship: the mean number of dyadic WTO disputes initiated over time, along with the mean proportion of bilateral intra-industry trade. The pattern in this figure looks similar to that in the left-hand plot, although it suggests clearer—yet preliminary—evidence of an inverse correlation between intra-industry trade and WTO disputes over time.

As the overview of this process should make clear, the decision by a member country to launch a formal trade dispute under WTO auspices is a costly decision for that member and the firms it is representing, as well as for the member against whom the allegations are being made. As a result, a significant literature is developing to try to explain why members take such a costly decision to begin the formal dispute resolution procedure within the WTO.

The Origins of Trade Disputes Within the WTO

The transaction costs associated with filing formal disputes with the WTO are paramount in most of the literature. The central question becomes, under what conditions do firms and their governments deem the expected costs associated with the WTO dispute resolution procedure are worth the expected benefits? Davis and Shirato (2007) develop a firm-centered approach to understanding the likelihood of lobbying governments to pursue the most costly of negotiations over disputes, that of WTO adjudication. While recognizing that traditional sources of firm political action to mobilize for protection, such as size, concentration, and multinationality, are likely determinants of firm and industry lobbying, they wish to focus their explanation on the business environment. In their formulation, the business environment is

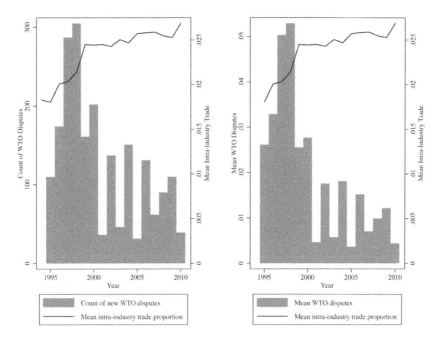

Figure 4.1   The frequency (left) and proportion by dyad (right) of WTO disputes, and mean bilateral intra-industry trade proportion over time, 1995–2010.

considered high velocity when there is "rapid and discontinuous change in demand, competitors, technology or regulation" as Eisenhardt and Bourgeois wrote (1988, 738). High-velocity environments provide incentives for firms to move product quickly and compete with many different product lines. Davis and Shirato (2007, 282) argue that, all things being equal, firms in high-velocity environments face greater opportunity costs for becoming involved in formal trade dispute processes than those in low-velocity environments. Firms in high-velocity markets have less need to defend a particular product against a particular trade barrier when they have multiple product lines and preexisting incentives to develop new products to compete. Time becomes an important transaction cost, and these firms prefer bilateral negotiations to quickly resolve disputes rather than the lengthy WTO adjudication process. Firms in low-velocity markets are much more willing to invest time and resources in a long-term adjudication process, since their product lines are narrower and their rates of product turnover are much slower. These firms have incentives to defend such products against trade barriers, since their losses are likely to be higher compared to firms in high-velocity environments facing the same type of trade barrier.

Davis and Shirato (2007) use the percentage of expenditures for research and development to total production to capture the velocity of the business environment. Their analysis demonstrates (in a study of Japan's experience) that high-velocity industries tend to have fewer WTO disputes than low-velocity industries. Electronics is the primary example of an industry in a high-velocity environment, while steel is an example of a low-velocity environment and automobiles lie somewhere in the middle. Our interest in the composition of trade probably cuts across the business environment, as some intra-industry trade is likely to be in high turnover, short-product-cycles areas, while others are likely to be in narrow product lines with more dedicated methods of production. Yet when comparing intra-industry trade to inter-industry trade as a whole, on balance the former probably has on average a higher-velocity business environment than the latter. This would be especially true for branded goods appealing to consumer tastes, since firms are constantly attempting to differentiate their consumer-oriented products by style and status recognition. This study also reinforces the importance of transaction costs in determining whether to launch a formal WTO trade dispute. Generally speaking, we might expect that the time and effort to launch a formal dispute process may not be as worthwhile for firms engaging in intra-industry trade, especially if the volume of trade is high, as opposed to those engaged in inter-industry trade.

Brown (2005) also develops an expected cost-benefit framework using an approach to both the benefits and costs different from that of the aforementioned Davis and Shirato (2007) approach. Brown actually theorizes the benefits and costs, rather than just the costs of WTO dispute participation. On the benefits side, he examines increased market access or trade liberalization in the disputed sector along with the probability of a successful dispute outcome with a state in which it is more bilaterally powerful. On the costs side, he examines the state's capacity to bear the legal costs of a dispute and the costs of potentially disrupting a relationship with an important trading partner. Brown also considers the possibility of free-riding, as a state observes the litigation of others either as a formal third party or just a spectator. Thus, all told, when the expected benefits outweigh the costs, we should expect states to initiate WTO trade disputes on behalf of firms in harmed industries. The empirical evidence presented suggests that states with a substantial economic stake are more likely to participate in a dispute, while those who are involved in a PTA, lack the institutional capacity, are poor or small, or are reliant on the other for bilateral assistance are less likely to participate.

There is a substantial debate in the literature about the ability of poor, small, or, more generally, developing states to initiate WTO disputes. The expected costs of the formal litigation process are often seen as just too great for such states to bear initially, even if the benefits might eventually outweigh those costs (see, for example, Smith 2004; Esserman and Howse 2003; Kim 2008). It is well-known that the major initiators of WTO disputes are the United States, the European Union, Canada, and Japan. But does this mean that the entry costs are too high for other states? According to Brown (2005), the answer is yes, which builds on previous findings by Blonigen and Brown (2003) and Brown (2004) that demonstrate that bilaterally powerless countries are more likely to be the targets of activities inconsistent with WTO rules. Horn, Mavroidis, and Nordström (2005) conversely find that structural features such as the value of trade and the diversity of a state's trading partners explain dispute initiation—these are features of the United States, the European Union, Canada, and Japan, and explain their behavior more than power or any institutional bias in the WTO. Busch and Reinhardt (2003) find that poor countries participate less in disputes than richer states (see also Shaffer 2003), though there is no evidence of bias in rulings against these countries (see also Moon 2006).

Davis and Bermeo (2009) suggest that there are institutional hurdles for developing countries to overcome in order to participate successfully in the WTO dispute settlement system. They suggest that there are economies of scale for dispute initiation that are the result of fixed costs for institutional capacity and knowledge. Both firms and governments must invest a considerable amount of time and effort in learning to use the dispute process the first time at the WTO, but that experience is then helpful in applications to future cases. Once the startup costs are paid, developing countries are likely to become repeat players at dispute adjudication through the WTO. Davis and Bermeo's empirical analysis demonstrates that prior involvement in trade dispute adjudication, as either a complainant or a defendant, increases the likelihood that developing countries will initiate disputes. Yet there are declining returns of experience after a state participates in five or six disputes.[3] Further, access to legal advice through the Advisory Centre on WTO Law increases participation, leading them to recommend assistance to developing countries to generate the institutional capacity and knowledge to participate fully in the WTO adjudication process.

Sattler and Bernauer (2011) add increased nuance to this debate by theoretically separating out three distinct arguments about potential discriminatory effects in WTO litigation present in the literature: legal capacity, standard power, and power preponderance. The legal capacity argument, just sketched out, is that poor countries lack the financial means and human resources to adequately navigate the WTO dispute settlement procedure. The standard power argument refers to the distribution of power within the dyad, such that the more powerful country is presumed to be able to impose its will on the weaker one (see, for example, Guzman and Simmons 2002). Sattler and Bernauer (147) also describe a variant of the standard power argument that they call power preponderance, which is the idea that powerful countries will attempt to compel weaker countries to lift trade barriers without WTO adjudication, or that powerful countries will resist the efforts of weaker countries to convince them to lift barriers, knowing that weaker countries will be unlikely to file a formal dispute with the WTO. Settlement prior to WTO procedures is thus more likely when power preponderance prevails.

Sattler and Bernauer's preferred argument (2011) is that all three of the empirical patterns may better be explained with a simple gravity model derived from the study of international trade. The gravity model, which explains trade in terms of economy size and distance, suggests that disputes are more likely as a result of larger economies, which facilitate greater trade volumes. States with more diversified economies and greater market sizes are much more likely to be targets of dispute litigation. This argument is similar to that of Horn, Mavroidis, and Nordström (2005), in that it suggests that structural features of the economy and the trading relationship are more important determinants of dispute initiation than the relative wealth and institutional capacity of states in the dyad. They test this gravitational argument against the other three arguments about discrimination and find that the absolute size of the complainant and defendant along with the trade volume of the dyad are strong predictors of disputes, both of which are consistent with the gravitational explanation. The predictors of the standard power argument (relative size and relative income levels) are insignificant. In terms of power preponderance, while income asymmetry is not significant, the economic size asymmetry is a significant factor in disputes. Finally, the measures of the legal capacity argument (GDP per capita, WTO delegation sizes of both countries) are not significant.

Our approach to understanding WTO dispute initiation similarly focuses on structural features of the economies and the trading relationship in question. Despite the increased nuance in theoretical specification and empirical testing introduced by studies such as Sattler and Bernauer's, the composition of trade (in any form) has not been considered by this literature. Some of the studies have looked at trade disputes in specific industries, but our approach takes a broader look at the composition of the trade in the dyadic relationship. In particular, we suspect that the intra-industry versus inter-industry composition of the trading relationship will have significant effects on WTO dispute initiation.

A variety of other factors are often introduced in explanations of WTO dispute initiation. Davis and Shirato (2007) mention the size of industry, since governments are more likely to advocate for firms in industries that employ large numbers of people (see, for example, Becker 1983). They also note that industries that give greater political contributions are also likely to have the government's ear on trade policy (see also Grossman and Helpman 2002; Hansen and Drope 2004). Some types of import relief measures, such as anti-dumping, countervailing, and safeguard duties, tend to be more highly contested by governments (see, for example, Tarullo 2004). Further, governments may be reticent to launch a formal dispute when they are concerned about spillover effects within a "sensitive diplomatic relationship" with the potential target country (for example, Alter 2003; Brown 2005). Finally, Davis and Shirato control for export dependence, foreign direct investment by industry, industry concentration, whether a trade barrier is product specific, the distortionary burden of a trade barrier, the GDP of the trade partner, the import penetration ratio, and employment share of the trade partner's industry (2007, 293–294). Other studies also mention the importance of democratic regime type, since democratic institutions create conduits for pressure groups to demand assistance (Busch 2000; Guzman and Simmons 2005; Davis and Bermeo 2009; Sattler and Bernauer 2011).

Overall, the literature thus provides a number of important ways to think about the likelihood of WTO dispute initiation. First, firms and states may engage in an expected costs–and-benefits analysis—exactly what those costs and benefits are depends upon the study, with some emphasizing aspects of the business environment (high or low velocity) and others focusing on more standard indicators of market access and trade liberalization as benefits versus legal and diplomatic costs. Second, some element of discrimination may exist in the dispute initiation process as legal costs, relative power, or power preponderance prevent weaker states from challenging stronger states, or what appears as discrimination may be better explained by gravity models focusing on economic size and trade volume. Third, a variety of structural features of economies and polities generate propensities toward dispute initiation, such as industry concentration or regime type, just as more agent-oriented activities, such as experience gained from participation in previous disputes or interest group lobbying, can convince governments to file formal trade disputes with the WTO. We draw on these lessons as we develop our own theoretical approach linking intra-industry trade to WTO dispute initiation.

Intra-Industry Trade and WTO Dispute Initiation

In this book, we spend considerable time demonstrating how the composition of trade matters to international conflict and associated political relationships, as well as to the political economy of international institutional outcomes. Higher proportions of intra-industry trade are expected to mitigate conflictual relationships between states; hence, trade is not the subject of conflict *per se* in this aspect of our inquiry. Yet in studying WTO trade dispute initiation, trade itself is the subject of conflict. This requires us to think somewhat differently about the effect of intra-industry trade on trade disputes.

We draw on the same logic underlying the gravitational model of trade disputes discussed earlier in thinking about the composition of trade (Sattler and Bernauer 2011). In particular, the effect of the composition of trade on dispute initiation will matter most when trade flows are high. When trade volume is low, we do not expect much in the way of dispute initiation between two states. Yet, as the empirical evidence suggests, once trade volume is high in a relationship, we suggest that the composition of trade may condition the likelihood of dispute initiation. It is important to note that this effect is separate from the economic size of either state in a dyad. The gravitational model argues that economic size exerts its own independent effects on dispute initiation. Sattler and Bernauer establish these logical and empirical findings about economic size and trade volume (155–156).

When trade flows are high between two states in a trading relationship, the potential for policies and practices to become sources of conflict is higher. Whether trade is primarily inter-industry or intra-industry, high volumes indicate that firms are profiting from access to each state's home market. Trade, of course, creates winners and losers domestically. Losers, particularly in democratic systems, will seek protection from governments for losses incurred to foreign competition. Many well-known factors intervene in the process of organizing to secure protection. Governments, especially of the democratic variety, tend to try to provide protection subject to many well-known constraints. One of the most pertinent constraints to our study of WTO dispute initiation is the set of rules contained within the WTO itself. Thus we return to the question posed earlier in the chapter: Under what conditions do firms and their governments decide that the expected costs associated with the WTO dispute resolution procedure are worth the expected benefits?

While the literature identifies many possibilities for factors that are incorporated into this decision-making process, we suggest that an underlying structural feature of the trading relationship will shape decision making. Trade composition, in the form of the proportion of trade volume that is intra-industry versus inter-industry, is the structural feature of interest here. Our analytic approach is thus in keeping with gravitational models' stress on structural features of economies and the trading relationship itself. We think this structural feature is consistent with underlying decision-making processes that likely flow from the kind of trade in the relationship.

Intra-industry trade, as trade in similar, often branded products, is quite different from inter-industry trade that occurs according to specialization. In keeping with the literature, intra-industry trade is probably on average occurring in more high-velocity business environments than inter-industry trade. This would be especially true for branded goods appealing to consumer tastes, since firms are constantly attempting to differentiate their consumer-oriented products by style and status recognition. The process of branding similar goods is itself a market-creating or market-segmentation exercise. Firms engaged in intra-industry trade are therefore more likely to pursue bilateral talks between governments or the use of WTO committees or PTA fora, rather than the more long-term, costly WTO dispute adjudication procedure.

We also know that joint membership in PTAs decreases the likelihood of WTO dispute initiation (Brown 2005). In Chapter 3, we theorized that higher proportions of intra-industry trade encourage the formation of PTAs. Higher intra-industry trade within a dyad will encourage firms to lobby for PTAs in order to facilitate gains from increased trade and expanded markets without risking the potential loss that might accrue if trade barriers were reduced for all states. Since intra-industry trade signifies that trade partners do not specialize, it is less likely that firms (or entire industries) will be driven out of business because a trade partner has the comparative advantage. There will be fewer losers due to expanded trade, and therefore there will be fewer actors lobbying against entrance into PTAs. Hence, the same underlying factors that lead firms to pursue PTAs also suggest that they are less likely to pursue WTO trade disputes within a dyad characterized by a high proportion of intra-industry trade. Firms in both states engaging in intra-industry trade gain from increased trade and expanded markets. Thus they are likely to pursue avenues such as PTA formation to institutionalize their mutual market access, and as trade volumes grow, they will be increasingly unlikely to formally initiate WTO dispute settlement procedures.

Conversely, when inter-industry trade prevails, we would expect to see WTO dispute initiation increase as trade volumes increase. Since inter-industry trade is on average characterized by a low-velocity business environment, such firms must defend against any potential barrier to their narrow product lines. Import competitors who lose out due to specialization are likely to pursue protection from foreign firms. To the extent that they are successful, we are more likely to see firms persuading their governments to pursue dispute settlement up to and including a higher likelihood of formal WTO adjudication.

Our theoretical expectations produce two hypotheses that we will test in this chapter:

Hypothesis 4.1: A higher proportion of intra-industry trade between states is associated with a lesser likelihood of WTO dispute onset. The magnitude of the association between intra-industry trade and WTO dispute onset is weakest when dyadic trade flows are small, becoming larger as dyadic trade flows increase.

Hypothesis 4.2: A higher level of dyadic trade is associated with a higher probability of WTO dispute onset in the absence of intra-industry trade. The magnitude of this relationship diminishes as intra-industry trade increases as a proportion of total trade.

Research Design

We test our hypotheses by combining our measure of intra-industry trade developed in Chapter 2 with data on WTO disputes from Horn and Mavroidis (2008). Our analysis covers nondirected dyad years spanning from 1995 to 2009. Our primary dependent variable is a count of the WTO disputes initiated by one dyad member against the other in a given year (that is, the sum of (original) disputes filed by state A against state B and those filed by state B against state A). Notably, we use a nondirected dyad-level measure of dispute initiation because we expect that higher trade flows, under the condition of a higher proportion of intra-industry trade—both of which are nondirected phenomena—lead to reduced incentive by both trade partners to initiate disputes; the identity of the claimant and respondent are irrelevant for our theory.[4]

Given that only WTO members may initiate WTO disputes, we design our analysis to overcome possible bias due to a selection effect. First, we specify models that exclude all non-WTO members from the analysis in order to isolate only those cases in which opportunity for dispute initiation exists. In a second set of specifications, we model WTO membership and dispute onset simultaneously to account for the fact that some unmodeled factors might influence both WTO membership and dispute initiation, leading to bias despite the exclusion of non-WTO members. First, we specify zero-inflated, negative binomial models for our subsample of WTO members. Given that our theory suggests that intra-industry trade conditions the willingness of states to file WTO disputes as a function of trade exposure, we attempt to account for zero inflation due to lack of *opportunity* for dispute initiation. We suspect that exposure to trade could affect each state's opportunity, as well as willingness, to initiate WTO disputes. Accordingly, we use the log of (1 plus) the distance between states, as well as the log of the higher of the GDP per capita, as inflation parameters. We chose these inflation parameters variables because they are causally prior to trade itself and yet strong determinants of opportunity for trade.[5] As a result, we have more confidence that the relationship between trade, its intra-industry composition, and the onset of WTO disputes is due to willingness of actors to initiate such disputes rather than the mere existence of opportunity for interaction.

In our second set of models, we estimate the number of WTO dispute onsets and WTO membership simultaneously using a Heckman probit selection model. Because we do not have the ability to specify such a model in which the outcome variable is a count, we recode our outcome equation dependent variable as a dichotomous indicator equal to 1 if there is at least one dyadic WTO dispute onset in a given year. This recoding allows for the use of a Heckman probit specification.[6] In our Heckman probit selection equations, we include two unique explanatory variables. First, we include a lagged measure of WTO membership, given strong duration dependence of membership in the organization. Second, we include a measure of UN voting similarity (Gartzke 1998), given that joint membership in the organization is likely a function of similar foreign policy preferences. Yet the link between similar foreign policy preferences and WTO dispute onset should be indirect.[7]

Accounting for the European Union

We design our models with one additional consideration in mind. Given that the European Union is a single customs territory with a single, common membership in the WTO, we must design our analysis to account for dependence among dyads that involve EU members. In all models, we exclude dyads in which both states are EU members. For dyads in which one state is an EU member, we use two alternative specifications. First, we specify models excluding these dyads. Accordingly, results from these models do not contain bias from the inclusion of dyads that are highly dependent, yet these results are limited because they exclude an actor that is involved in a large number of WTO disputes. In a second specification, we include dyads that involve one EU member but also include a dichotomous explanatory variable that identifies all such dyads. Although this variable might not capture the entirety of organization-based dependence, it acts similar to a weight for EU versus non-EU dyads, and allows us to determine whether the presence of the EU in the analysis leads to results different from those following from its exclusion.[8]

Primary Explanatory Variables

Our key explanatory variable is the *intra-industry trade* measure developed in Chapter 2. Again, this measure varies from 0, suggesting the absence of intra-industry trade in dyad, to 1, suggesting that all trade within the dyad follows from intra-industry specialization. However, given that our theory suggests that the proportion of intra-industry trade conditions the influence of trade exposure, we interact the intra-industry trade proportion with a measure of dyadic trade as a percentage of the less wealthy state's GDP (a.k.a., *trade dependence*). In alternate models, we also interact intra-industry trade with (1) the lower of the two states' *liberalization* scores (using the fixed-effects-based measures developed by Hiscox and Kastner [2002] and described further on) and (2) the lower level of *development*, coded as the lower of the states' logged GDP per capita, using data from the Penn World Table 8.0 (Feenstra, Inklaar, and Timmer 2013). These alternative specifications allow us to account for the possibility that liberalization, or development, rather than overall trade volume drives WTO disputes.

To measure the lower of the dyadic states' degree of liberalization, we use a measure of trade policy orientation developed by Hiscox and Kastner (2002). These authors estimate trade policy orientations for 82 states, spanning 1960 to 1992. To create trade policy orientation estimates that vary over time, the authors run separate models by year. The authors begin with a standard gravity model (for example, Anderson 1979; Bergstrand 1989), dividing both sides of the equation by the importer's GDP, such that the dependent variable is dyadic trade as a proportion of the importer's GDP. This transformed gravity equation has no importer-year-specific variables on the right-hand side; accordingly, the authors add an importer fixed-effect term, which is used as a state's trade policy orientation. We replicate Hiscox and Kastner's technique using updated data to derive measures of trade policy orientation for 162 states, spanning 1962 to 2010 (although the analysis in this chapter ends in 2009). A positive indicator suggests less restrictive trade than would be expected given each state's wealth, population, and the distance between the states, while a negative indicator suggests more restrictive trade than would be expected given these conditions. We take the lower of the two state's measures to capture *lower liberalization* within the dyad.

Other Explanatory Variables

We control for a number of factors that could confound our hypothesized relationships. First, we code the difference between the higher and lower development levels (that is, GDP per capita) within the dyad using the Penn World Table (Feenstra, Inklaar, and Timmer 2013). A higher disparity in development could suggest less similar factor endowments, and thus lower intra-industry trade. Simultaneously, a higher disparity could suggest dissimilar interests among domestic groups lobbying for free trade or protectionism. We also code the lower of the two states' combined 21-point Polity scores, using the Polity IV project data (Marshall and Jaggers 2010), to account for the fact that more democratic states might trade more and also could have more access points for protectionist interests to lobby. We include a measure of the lower of the states' GDP growth to account for domestic crises that could spur protectionist behavior as a signal to domestic populations that leaders are responding to foreign threat to domestic industry using Penn World Table data from Feenstra, Inklaar, and Timmer. Finally, we include a count of the years since the previous WTO dispute in order to capture possible duration dependence in protectionist behavior.[9]

Analysis

We find support for our hypotheses that a higher proportion of intra-industry trade in a dyad is associated with a reduced probability that a state in a dyad initiates a WTO trade dispute. As we hypothesize, intra-industry trade serves primarily to condition the role of trade levels on the probability that a trade dispute is originated. Complete tables of coefficients and standard errors for eight models are included in the appendix to this chapter. However, we illustrate the impact of intra-industry trade using a series of figures.

In general, we find that an increase in trade levels leads to an increase in the probability that a trade dispute is filed, as expected given that higher trade values correlate with higher opportunity for conflicts of interest to arise. However, we model the influence of trade level and intra-industry trade as an interaction, given our expectation that the influence of trade is conditional on the degree to which this trade follows from inter- or intra-industry specialization. The results of this interactive specification suggests that an increase in trade is associated with a large increase in the number of trade disputes filed when there is no intra-industry trade within the dyad. However, as the proportion of intra-industry trade increases, the magnitude of this relationship diminishes toward zero. In fact, when the proportion of intra-industry trade is very high (greater than 50 percent), an increase in trade levels is associated with a *decline* in the number of WTO trade disputes filed. Of course, there are relatively few dyads that have such a high proportion of intra-industry trade, given that the mean value is around 2.4 percent in the years included in this chapter. Notably, however, dyads that we might consider "important" due to wealth, military power, and so on have more interesting variation. For example, the U.S.-Russia dyad averages around 6 percent intra-industry trade between 1995 and 2009, while the U.S.-China dyad averages 16 percent, the U.S.-Japan dyad averages 36 percent, and the U.S.-U.K. dyad averages 57 percent. Accordingly, we contend that, despite

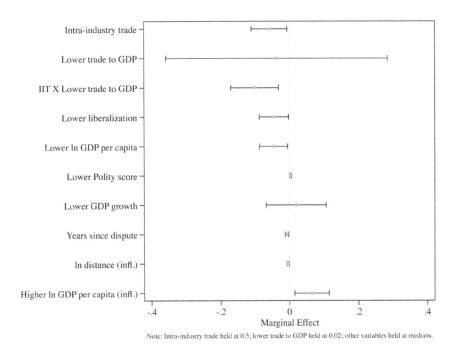

Note: Intra-industry trade held at 0.5; lower trade to GDP held at 0.02; other variables held at medians.

Figure 4.2   Marginal effects of explanatory variables on WTO dispute onset with control variables held at their medians, including 95 percent confidence bounds. From Model 4.1.

the very low mean value of intra-industry trade, we still find useful variation with which to explain the initiation of WTO disputes.

To illustrate these findings, first we present Figure 4.2, which plots the marginal effects of each explanatory variable (that is, the change in the count of disputes filed given a one-unit change in the variable) from a typical model in order to demonstrate the relative strength of each variable. The marginal effect of each variable depends on the value at which other variables are held. Accordingly, we hold all control variables at their medians. However, to produce marginal effects of substantive interest, we hold trade to GDP at 0.02 (that is, where trade value is equal to 2 percent of the less wealthy state's GDP), and intra-industry trade at 0.5 (meaning that half of dyadic trade follows from intra-industry specialization). The figure illustrates that the marginal effect of intra-industry trade is negative and statistically significant under these conditions. Conversely, the marginal effect of trade flows (as a proportion of GDP) is not statistically significant; although this variable has a negative marginal effect under these conditions, there is a very high

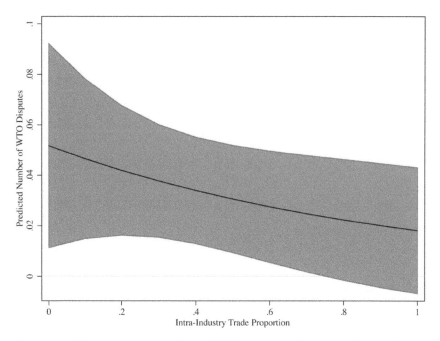

Figure 4.3   The expected count of new WTO disputes over the range of intra-industry trade, including 95 percent confidence bounds. From Model 4.1.

variation for this estimate. The final indicator of note is that the interaction term is negative and significant, suggesting that the effect of each constituent variable, intra-industry trade proportion and trade to GDP, becomes increasingly negative as the other variable is held at higher levels.

Figure 4.3 plots the number of predicted WTO dispute initiations as the proportion of intra-industry trade increases from 0 to 1, with other variables held at their medians. The figure shows that there is a positive and significant expected number of WTO disputes when there is no intra-industry trade within the dyad. However, the expected count declines as intra-industry trade increases as a proportion of dyadic trade. In fact, once intra-industry trade reaches approximately .75 (75 percent of dyadic trade), the expected count of dispute initiations loses statistical significance.[10] Notably, the predicted number of disputes is low, falling from approximately 0.052 to 0.018 as the proportion of intra-industry trade increases from 0 to 1. However, these low predicted event counts correspond to average (specifically, median) dyads. Absolute predictions are larger when we set variables to correspond to more proximate states, those with larger economies, or those with greater trade ties.

The effect of intra-industry trade on *relative* change in the predicted count of new WTO disputes becomes clearer if we examine the percentage change in expected counts as trade to GDP increases from 0 to 0.02 (that is, from 0 to 2 percent of the poorer state's GDP) at different levels of intra-industry trade. When there is no intra-industry trade, this increase in trade leads to more than a 7,000 percent increase in the expected count of such disputes. When intra-industry trade is equal to 25 percent of dyadic trade, this increase in trade leads to approximately a 700 percent increase in the expected count of new WTO disputes. When intra-industry trade composes half of the dyad's total trade, this increase in trade leads to a very slight decrease in the number of new disputes: approximately a 2.5 percent decrease (a change that is not statistically significant at the .05 level). When intra-industry trade composes 75 percent of dyadic trade, the expected count of new disputes decreases by over 88 percent. Finally, when all dyadic trade is intra-industry trade, the expected count of new disputes decreases by nearly 99 percent (keeping in mind that this last estimate is an extrapolation, which should be interpreted modestly). In short, when trade is primarily composed of a two-way exchange of similar commodities, an increase in total trade volume actually is associated with a reduction in both states' propensity to initiate trade disputes. This finding could follow because, in the presence of more intra-industry trade, there are fewer interest groups seeking protectionism, such that leaders are less likely to use WTO disputes as a tactic to gain political support. Figure 4.4 illustrates these changes (except for the case in which intra-industry trade equals 0, because the prediction in this case does not fit easily on the same scale).

On a more intuitive level, we can consider the trading relationships between the United States and India and the United States and China. In both cases, the trade-to-GDP ratio (based on the lower score for members of the dyad) has increased over time. WTO disputes follow increases in trade as we would expect. The United States and India have been involved in 14 disputes since the WTO was formed in 1995—an average of 0.7 disputes per year, with a decreasing rate of new dispute onset over time. The United States and China have been involved in 23 disputes since China joined the WTO in 2001—an average of 1.8 disputes per year; however, disputes have actually been filed at an increasing rate over time. Thus, consistent with Hypothesis 4.2, a higher level of dyadic trade is associated with a higher probability of WTO dispute onset. However, the U.S.-India ratio of trade to GDP is consistently higher and

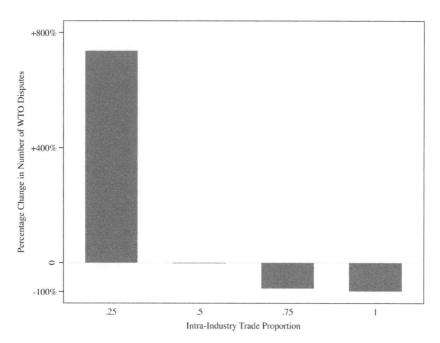

Figure 4.4   The percentage change in the expected count of new WTO disputes as trade increases from 0 to 2 percent of the poorer state's GDP, at increasing values of intra-industry trade. From Model 4.1.

has increased rather dramatically since 2000, so why has India been involved in relatively fewer disputes with the United States than has China? The U.S.-India trading relationship has consistently been composed of a higher proportion of intra-industry trade than the U.S.-China dyad. Consistent with our hypotheses, a higher proportion of intra-industry trade between states is associated with a lesser likelihood of dispute onset, while a higher extent of trade flow, under the condition of higher intra-industry trade, does not lead to a higher likelihood of dispute onset. Thus, despite relatively larger trade dependence between the United States and India versus between the United States and China, more of the former dyad's trade is intra-industry, leading to a diminished number and rate of WTO dispute filings. The United States and China, on the other hand, will likely continue to see more dispute filings as long as the composition of trade tends toward the inter-industry variety.

Conclusion

The WTO dispute resolution mechanism seeks to promote liberalized trade by legalizing the process through which states seek redress for perceived harm. The literature has generated a number of potential determinants of dispute initiation, such as the kind of business environment a firm inhabits, whether poorer and smaller states are discriminated against in the initiation process, the ability to learn from previous adjudication experience, and so on. Many of these approaches that focus more on decision making at the agent level are set in a cost-benefit analysis. On the other hand, gravitational models and other approaches that emphasize the structure of the economy and the nature of the trading relationship attempt to explain dispute initiation propensity from a more structural perspective.

Our approach identifies a structural feature of the trading relationship— the composition of trade, as a central explanatory factor in predicting the propensity to engage in formal WTO adjudication. The proportion of intra-industry trade within a trading relationship is a crucial factor affecting the likelihood of WTO dispute initiation. As trade volumes increase in a relationship, we would normally expect trade disputes to increase. Yet intra-industry trade conditions this relationship, making formal trade disputes less likely as trade volumes increase. This novel empirical finding is an important extension of our underlying argument that trade composition matters for the policy economy of international institutions.

The incentives faced by firms and governments in dyadic relationships characterized by high proportions of intra-industry trade are simply different from the incentives experienced by those in whose relationship inter-industry trade prevails. Firms engaged in intra-industry trade share a mutual interest in opening markets at home and abroad as they compete for brand loyalty. Higher volumes of trade with expanding markets is the perfect environment for intra-industry trade to flourish. Firms engaged in inter-industry trade will often find import competitors willing to bear the substantial costs of lobbying their government to pursue formal WTO dispute settlement procedures, as their very livelihood as a firm or industry may be threatened by competition. Higher volumes of trade and expanded market access exacerbate this dynamic under conditions in which inter-industry trade is prevalent.

There are numerous possible extensions of this work related to dispute initiation. We might consider the conditions under which the proportion of intra-industry trade affects the likelihood of being a complainant or a defendant—treating them separately as opposed to lumping them together within a dyad. We could examine the impact of third parties under conditions of higher intra-industry trade proportions, both prior to and during formal dispute settlement proceedings. We could examine stages of the negotiation process prior to the filing of formal WTO disputes to see if higher proportions of intra-industry trade lead to earlier settlement or not. We could also examine the phenomenon of forum shopping, since states engaged in intra-industry trade are also more likely to be members of PTAs. Do higher proportions of intra-industry trade mean that members may be more likely to use PTA settlement procedures, and therefore are just less likely to use the WTO dispute settlement procedure? These and many other questions are open for further discussion as we think about the role of trade composition on formal WTO dispute initiation.

Appendix to Chapter 4

This appendix presents the results of zero-inflated negative binomial models and Heckman probit models assessing the association between intra-industry trade and WTO dispute initiation. Table 4.1 presents the coefficients for six models examining the frequency of dyadic WTO dispute initiations. Models 4.1 and 4.2 include only an interaction term for intra-industry trade and lower trade to GDP; Models 4.3 and 4.4 add an interaction for intra-industry trade X lower liberalization; and Models 4.5 and 4.6 further add an interaction for intra-industry trade X lower GDP per capita. The odd models exclude any dyad that includes an EU member, while the even models include these dyads but add a dummy variable identifying the presence of an EU state.[11]

The coefficient for intra-industry trade is positive and significant (at the .001 level) in all six models presented in Table 4.1 At first glance, this evidence appears to disconfirm our main argument; however, the coefficient for intra-industry trade represents its association with the frequency of WTO dispute initiation when lower trade to GDP is equal to zero.[12] Accordingly, this coefficient is not particularly informative given that no intra-industry trade can exist if no trade exists at all. Similarly, the coefficient for lower trade to GDP is positive and significant in all six models. This coefficient, which represents the association between trade and WTO dispute initiation when intra-industry trade is held at 0, is more meaningful, given that it is possible for signifi-

Table 4.1 Zero-inflated negative binomial model coefficients and robust standard errors examining the association between intra-industry trade and WTO dispute onset, 1995–2010.

	Model 4.1	Model 4.2	Model 4.3	Model 4.4	Model 4.5	Model 4.6
	Excluding EU	Including EU	Excluding EU	Including EU	Excluding EU	Including EU
Intra-industry trade	6.687***	4.851***	7.124***	5.826***	12.729***	20.349***
	(0.689)	(0.489)	(0.801)	(0.654)	(3.724)	(2.701)
Lower trade to GDP	213.633***	181.912***	209.026***	168.192***	194.119***	140.943***
	(22.570)	(25.131)	(25.229)	(26.519)	(23.582)	(28.397)
IIT X low trade to GDP	−429.716***	−370.258***	−421.055***	−333.853***	−379.977***	−262.469***
	(49.291)	(61.208)	(53.857)	(63.142)	(47.681)	(74.629)
Lower liberalization	−329.858***	−353.239***	−363.983***	−454.872***	−349.969***	−428.422***
	(45.318)	(36.965)	(71.099)	(58.360)	(70.750)	(53.267)
IIT X low liberalization			173.620	576.779*	−3.981	294.849
			(203.803)	(254.514)	(229.794)	(222.425)
Lower ln GDP PC	−1.477***	−1.097***	−1.474***	−1.168***	−1.384***	−1.048***
	(0.333)	(0.226)	(0.340)	(0.227)	(0.305)	(0.212)
IIT X low ln GDPPC					−1.405	−3.158***
					(0.845)	(0.530)
ln GDP PC difference	−1.506***	−1.578***	−1.511***	−1.656***	−1.587***	−1.789***
	(0.313)	(0.225)	(0.320)	(0.227)	(0.290)	(0.214)
Lower Polity score	0.115***	0.043***	0.116***	0.043***	0.114***	0.047***
	(0.028)	(0.010)	(0.029)	(0.010)	(0.027)	(0.010)
Lower GDP growth	0.620	0.334	0.616	0.464	0.668	0.599
	(1.367)	(0.668)	(1.368)	(0.708)	(1.366)	(0.719)
Years since dispute	−0.253***	−0.309***	−0.257***	−0.314***	−0.258***	−0.320***
	(0.032)	(0.018)	(0.034)	(0.018)	(0.035)	(0.019)
Versus EU		1.837***		1.831***		1.949***
		(0.153)		(0.151)		(0.142)
Constant	3.161	2.246	3.125	2.628*	2.959	2.245
	(1.767)	(1.245)	(1.798)	(1.238)	(1.593)	(1.150)
Inflation parameters						
ln Distance	0.163**	−0.282*	0.158**	−0.317*	0.155**	−0.311*
	(0.050)	(0.139)	(0.051)	(0.160)	(0.051)	(0.158)
Higher ln GDP PC	−2.216***	−2.609***	−2.197***	−2.626***	−2.199***	−2.562***
	(0.313)	(0.310)	(0.310)	(0.311)	(0.285)	(0.304)

continued

Table 4.1   Zero-inflated negative binomial model coefficients and robust standard errors examining the association between intra-industry trade and WTO dispute onset, 1995–2010. (*continued*)

	Model 4.1	Model 4.2	Model 4.3	Model 4.4	Model 4.5	Model 4.6
	Excluding EU	Including EU	Excluding EU	Including EU	Excluding EU	Including EU
Constant	11.281***	16.209***	11.238***	16.752***	11.324***	16.517***
	(1.704)	(2.173)	(1.694)	(2.283)	(1.532)	(2.129)
Observations	62,447	93,358	62,447	93,358	62,447	93,358
χ2	549.7***	1751***	527.7***	2009***	512.4***	2089***
Log likelihood	−942.4	−4760	−942.1	−4751	−939.1	−4711

Notes: Robust standard errors adjusted for clustering on the dyad in parentheses.
*** $p < 0.001$, ** $p < 0.01$, * $p < 0.05$; two–tailed tests.

cant volumes of inter-industry trade to exist despite the complete absence of intra-industry trade. Accordingly, this positive and significant coefficient suggests that increasing trade is associated with a more frequent use of the WTO dispute process in the absence of intra-industry trade, as we hypothesize. The negative and significant (again at the .001 level) interaction term in all six models confirms our expectation that the proportion of intra-industry trade conditions the influence of trade levels on the incidence of WTO disputes. As our primary analysis in the chapter shows, high levels of trade promote more disputes when intra-industry trade is low, but this marginal effect decreases as intra-industry trade increases, eventually reversing. All six variants of our models confirm this hypothesized relationship.

Table 4.2 presents the results of two Heckman probit models designed to overcome a possible selection effect given non-observability of WTO disputes in cases in which states are not WTO members. Accordingly, we estimate the presence of a WTO dispute (a dichotomous indicator equal to 1 if there are any such disputes) simultaneously with joint WTO membership. Model 4.7 excludes EU states, while model 4.8 includes these states, as well as a dichotomous variable identifying their presence. The results for the WTO dispute initiation equation look essentially identical to those in Models 4.1 through 4.6. Interestingly, we find little evidence that intra-industry trade is associated with joint WTO membership. The only significant finding from the WTO membership equation is that higher trade flows (as a proportion of the poorer state's GDP) are associated with a lower probability of joint WTO membership

Table 4.2 Heckman probit model coefficients and robust standard errors examining the association between intra-industry trade and WTO dispute onset simultaneously with the association between intra-industry trade and WTO membership, 1995–2010.

	Model 4.7 Excluding EU		Model 4.8 Including EU	
	DV—WTO dispute	DV—WTO membership	DV—WTO dispute	DV—WTO membership
Intra-industry trade	3.504***	−0.119	4.149***	−0.221
	(0.855)	(0.638)	(0.732)	(0.664)
Lower trade to GDP	23.327***	−12.746*	28.728***	−15.148*
	(6.188)	(5.484)	(5.509)	(6.246)
IIT X low trade to GDP	−31.452*	25.930	−55.782***	26.934
	(14.472)	(26.562)	(16.821)	(28.204)
Lower liberalization	−118.997***	1.211	−134.208***	25.218***
	(28.978)	(5.256)	(23.279)	(4.694)
IIT X low liberalization	−48.294	268.680**	−187.560*	317.707**
	(107.888)	(98.536)	(84.646)	(99.338)
Lower ln GDP PC	0.191***	0.074***	0.298***	0.097***
	(0.047)	(0.010)	(0.040)	(0.009)
IIT X low ln GDPPC	−0.216	0.707***	−0.462**	0.847***
	(0.208)	(0.186)	(0.162)	(0.199)
ln GDP PC difference	0.054	0.123***	0.020	0.153***
	(0.050)	(0.009)	(0.042)	(0.008)
Lower Polity score	0.033***	0.043***	0.006	0.041***
	(0.009)	(0.001)	(0.004)	(0.001)
Lower GDP growth	0.182	1.004***	−0.088	1.205***
	(0.378)	(0.202)	(0.229)	(0.221)
Years since dispute	−0.090***		−0.134***	
	(0.013)		(0.007)	
Versus EU			0.715***	
			(0.056)	
WTO membership $_{t-1}$		4.709***		4.619***
		(0.032)		(0.026)
UN voting similarity		0.313***		0.354***
		(0.033)		(0.029)
Constant	−3.498***	−2.414***	−3.613***	−2.524***
	(0.186)	(0.052)	(0.192)	(0.048)

continued

Table 4.2   Heckman probit model coefficients and robust standard errors examining the association between intra-industry trade and WTO dispute onset simultaneously with the association between intra-industry trade and WTO membership, 1995–2010. (*continued*)

| | Model 4.7 | | Model 4.8 | |
| | Excluding EU | | Including EU | |
	DV—WTO dispute	DV—WTO membership	DV—WTO dispute	DV—WTO membership
Observations		138,413		186,017
rho	-0.271^{**}		-0.297^{***}	
χ^2	357.2		994.7	
Log likelihood	-10791		-16715	

Notes: Robust standard errors adjusted for clustering on the dyad in parentheses.
*** $p < 0.001$, ** $p < 0.01$, * $p < 0.05$; two–tailed tests.

under the specific condition that all trade is one-way trade in distinct commodities (that is, that intra-industry trade is equal to 0). The positive interaction term in the joint WTO membership equation suggests that trade becomes increasingly associated with WTO membership as its composition becomes increasingly intra-industry; however the interaction term is not statistically significant, and a subsequent analysis of marginal effects suggests that the marginal effect of lower trade to GDP merely loses statistical significance as intra-industry trade increases.

Part III

Intra-Industry Trade and the Global Political Economy of Peace and Conflict

Chapter 5

Beyond Liberalization and Development: Intra-Industry Trade and the Onset of Militarized Disputes

RAPIDLY expanding volumes of global trade, although reassuring to scholars supporting the peace through trade hypothesis, do not placate those who view the current trade environment as eerily similar to the period prior to World War I.[1] The unprecedented levels of trade and investment in the late nineteenth and early twentieth centuries did not prevent the two subsequent destructive world wars, casting doubt on the liberal view of trade as a universal pacifier of interstate relationships. However, recent research suggests that while trade may have had an uncertain relationship with conflict in the past (and perhaps even complemented aggression), contemporary trade occurs under conditions that are truly pacifying. For example, states today have more liberalized trade policy than their historical counterparts (see, for example, McDonald 2004). In addition, development may have facilitated the emergence of "trading states" that prefer commerce to war as a means to survive and thrive (Rosecrance 1986). Finally, and most interesting for this chapter, the composition of trade has changed markedly since the pre–World War I era. Although trade composition used to follow from inter-industry specialization in accordance with the Ricardian and Heckscher-Ohlin models, states today often exchange similar commodities following from intra-industry specialization (Krugman 1979; 1981). Intra-industry trade has been cited as particularly pacifying because it promotes similarity of interests and preferences among trade partners without evoking vulnerability, contrary to inter-industry trade (Peterson and Thies 2012a).

What makes the effects of these two conditions difficult to sort out theoretically and empirically is that the rapid growth of intra-industry trade has occurred simultaneously with considerable trade liberalization and development in the contemporary period. Accordingly, we compare intra-industry trade to liberalization and development with regard to their consequences for dyadic conflict. Focusing on the potential for trade to evoke vulnerability to trading partners, we argue that liberalization has a countervailing influence on the stability of dyadic peace because along with its beneficial aspects it could increase the degree to which states specialize, which in turn may lead one state to rely on another for strategically vital commodities. This specialization, although it generates trade gains and higher aggregate societal welfare, may also provide less dependent states with incentives to coerce their trade partners using their favorable position as bargaining leverage while evoking fear of this same coercion in more vulnerable states. Similarly, development does not necessarily confer a pacifying impact of trade, given the potential for vulnerable trade partners to seize other states' resources in order to eliminate vulnerability and to augment strength. Conversely, intra-industry trade (specifically as defined in Chapter 2) provides valuable trade gains resulting from mutual participation in global markets, often for branded commodities, and fosters complementary interests among domestic interest groups in each state, all without risking dependence and vulnerability. Accordingly, we contend that states engaging in more intra-industry trade are less likely to experience militarized conflict.

We proceed with a discussion of the literature linking trade to conflict, highlighting the dual nature of trade gains, reviewing arguments linking the absence of trade barriers to peace, and discussing the association between development and trade. We then present our arguments and discuss our research design. We test two hypotheses using data spanning 1962 to 2000, finding strong evidence to support the theory that more intra-industry trade within a dyad is associated with less militarized conflict, even when dyads are relatively protectionist overall. We also find support for a pacifying impact of multilateral liberalization, although its marginal effect appears to diminish when intra-industry trade composes a very large proportion of overall dyadic trade. Finally, we find, concurrent with Peterson and Thies (2012a), that joint development is insufficient to preclude conflict in the absence of intra-industry trade.

The Literature on Trade and Conflict

Scholars' assessments of the relationship between trade and conflict over time have tended to reflect the dominant theories of international relations. Prior to World War I, record levels of trade, spurred in large part by reductions in transportation costs, led Angell (1913) to conclude that interdependence between states would lead the victor in any war to suffer as much as the loser. Therefore, he argued that war (or, at very least, the profitability of war) was a "great illusion." The devastating scale of the world wars that followed resulted in realists' use of the term *idealism* to describe what they viewed as a body of optimistic, yet critically flawed work (see, for example, Carr 1964).

Realist scholars whose work reached its zenith during the Cold War tended to be skeptical of the pacifying effects of trade, some suggesting that high levels of trade might actually provide states with more reasons to fight (for example, Waltz, 1970). Concurrently, the interdependence literature challenged scholars to rethink the supposedly uniformly beneficial nature of gains from trade. Interdependence scholars recognized that reliance on trade also presents the potential for vulnerability and coercion (for example, Keohane and Nye 1977). Hirschman states concisely the dual nature of trade gains:

The influence which country *A* acquires in country *B* by foreign trade depends in the first place upon the total gain which *B* derives from that trade; the total gain from trade for any country is indeed nothing but another expression for the total impoverishment which would be inflicted upon it by a stoppage of trade. In this sense the classical concept, gain from trade, and the power concept, dependence on trade, now being studied are seen to be merely two aspects of the same phenomenon (Hirschman 1945, 73; quoted in Baldwin 1980, 478).

Although it still retains significant influence today, the interdependence literature has been overshadowed by a subsequent body of research once again advocating a pacifying impact of trade—a renewed view reflecting recent history and trends within broader international relations (IR) theory (Kegley 1993). The end of the Cold War was met with renewed optimism for the possibility of more peaceful global relations, which became evident in IR scholarship with the emergence of the democratic peace literature and, more broadly, neoliberal approaches. In these works, institutions—particularly democratic ones—constrain and inform states, reducing the likelihood of conflict. Indeed, subsequent literature suggests that trade may have similar effects. Trade may constrain states from engaging in aggressive behavior because valuable trade gains would be lost at the onset of conflict (see, for example, Polachek 1980; Oneal, Oneal, Maoz, and Russett 1996; Oneal and Russett 1997; 1999; Russett and Oneal 2001; Polachek and Xiang 2010). More recent research suggests that trade increases information flows, facilitating intercultural understanding (Dorussen and Ward 2010) and reducing information asymmetries that might lead to conflict (for example, Gartzke 2003; Reed 2003; Morrow 1999; see also Fearon 1995).[2]

Despite considerable gains in our understanding of how trade might affect conflict, there remains a divide in scholarly opinion as to whether and when the pacifying influence of trade gains is superseded by the potentially aggravating impact of dependence. Relatively few scholars advocate an aggravating impact of trade; those who do so tend to argue that asymmetric or particularly extensive trade ties are most likely to spark hostilities (for example, Barbieri 1996, Peterson 2014). However, some evidence suggests that the true causal relationship is reversed; conflict hinders trade while trade does not affect the likelihood of conflict (Keshk, Pollins, and Reuveny 2004; Keshk, Reuveny, and Pollins 2010). In an attempt to reconcile the markedly disparate views regarding the link between trade and conflict, other studies attempt to isolate boundary conditions that facilitate a pacifying impact of trade. Conditions posited to do so include joint development (Rosecrance 1986; Hegre 2000), symmetry of dependence (Oneal, Oneal, Maoz, and Russett 1996; Barbieri 1996, Peterson and Venteicher 2013, Peterson 2014), the type of issue under contention (Lu and Thies 2010), the settlement of prior contentious issues (Peterson and Quackenbush 2010), and the expectation that trade continues into the foreseeable future (Copeland 1996).

Other studies suggest that the militarized consequences of trade may depend on the nature of trade itself. For example, Dorussen (2006) contends that trade in manufactured goods has a stronger pacifying impact because the opportunity cost associated with this trade is higher than that for primary commodities (see also Crescenzi 2003). Most recently, Peterson and Thies (2012a) analyze the purported importance of development as well as the composition of trade to militarized conflict. They argue that development itself and overall trade have ambiguous effects on conflict, while intra-industry trade should be uniformly pacifying. Their statistical analyses demonstrate that higher proportions of dyadic intra-industry trade significantly reduces militarized conflict; overall trade interaction typically has no effect on the likelihood of dyadic conflict when controlling for intra-industry trade; and finally, development alone has no effect on the likelihood of dyadic conflict in the absence of intra-industry trade. We build on this work to continue the identification of important boundary conditions in the relationship between trade and conflict; in this case, liberalization and intra-industry trade as an important aspect of the composition of trade. We also revisit the relationship between development and peace in light of the possibly confounding factor of liberalization.

Liberalization and Specialization

Looking beyond the extent of international trade, recent studies contend that trade liberalization is associated with reduction in hostilities (McDonald 2004; 2009; McDonald and Sweeney 2007; Mansfield and Pevehouse 2000).[3] However, given the large body of recent work demonstrating that trade is not everywhere and at all times pacifying, we contend that the pacifying impact of liberalization may itself be a conditional phenomenon. A comparison of the first era of global trade (prior to World War I) with the current (post World War II) liberal regime highlights this possibility.

The nineteenth century saw some elements of liberalization, but trade was dominated by specialization in which European states exchanged finished goods for primary commodities produced by weaker states and colonies within their spheres of influence. Conversely, the contemporary trading environment contains states operating under varying degrees of liberalization, as well as variation in the degree to which bilateral trade reflects inter-industry specialization according to Ricardian comparative advantage (Ricardo 1820; Ohlin 1933), or intra-industry specialization, reflecting economies of scale and consumer demands for variety (Krugman 1979; 1981).

McDonald (2004; 2009) and McDonald and Sweeney (2007) suggest that protectionism enables states to pursue aggressive foreign policy objectives. The argument hinges on domestic political competition over the economic gains associated with whether commercial policy should be more or less restrictive. Free traders believe that interstate conflict damages their economic interests in expanded trade, while protectionists gain from trade barriers and may actually desire military conflict as a way of controlling foreign territory and capturing new markets. The winners of the argument over commercial policy also directly affect government revenues, since prior to World War II, most governments relied heavily on tariff revenues. If free traders win the argument over commercial policy, then governments must rely more heavily on taxation, which requires popular assent to government policy. If protectionists win the argument, then governments can rely on tariff revenues, which allow them the flexibility to pursue policies that domestic society may not fully support. Hence, societies whose commercial policies are characterized by more liberalized trade tend to be more peaceful in their interstate relations, while those who are more protectionist tend to pursue more aggressive foreign policies. The authors point to World War I as the quintessential example, given that rising protectionism in Germany and Russia led to increasingly aggressive diplomacy, and ultimately to war.

However, if our argument is correct, then the case for the unconditionally pacifying impact of free trade is questionable because there may be variation in the influence of liberalization on trade composition; it could lead to relatively more inter-industry trade or intra-industry trade. It is not difficult to think of cases in which protectionism, in the long run, facilitated intra-industry trade and consequently more peaceful dyadic relations. For example, South Korea employed protectionism in its manufacturing sector, developed globally competitive firms, and only later lowered some trade barriers to compete openly with foreign trade partners. Therefore, South Korea avoided a common fate of developing states: reliance on exports of primary commodities (following from inter-industry specialization), which typically involve low value-added relative to manufactured goods. Similarly, in the 1980s, the United States and Japan negotiated voluntary export restraints aimed at protecting the U.S. automotive industry. Arguably, this move saved U.S. auto firms from bankruptcy, an outcome that likely would have led to increasingly hostile views of Japan by U.S. citizens, as well as increased dependence of the United States on Japanese cars.

Development, Trade, and Conflict

The connection between development and conflict has drawn significant attention in the literature. This discussion is often depicted as a theoretical battle between realists and liberals, as has often been the case in the literature on interdependence and conflict (Mansfield and Pollins, 2001). Rather than revisit this debate at a theoretical level, as has previously occurred in Liberman (1993) and Brooks (1999), we focus on work that has proven directly relevant to empirical contributions examining the relationship between development, trade, and conflict.

Rosecrance's idealized depiction of states choosing to interact in the trading or military-political worlds (1986) highlights the importance of development in the possibilities available to contemporary states. Development affects four key variables that are crucial to a state's choice in this framework: it increases the gains from trade, it increases both the economic and political costs of war, and it decreases the benefits of conquest relative to trade. Overall, Rosecrance suggests that as states develop economically, they are much more likely to opt for the trading world rather than the military-political world. Drawing upon Rosecrance's logic, Hegre (2000) tests prevailing claims in the literature concerning the relationship between interdependence, development, and conflict. Hegre finds that trade and development both significantly reduce the occurrence of fatal militarized interstate disputes (MIDs). In addition, an interaction term also demonstrates that the pacifying effect of trade increases with the level of economic development. This empirical support for Rosecrance's suggestion that development would lead to a peaceful world of trading states has also been explored from other perspectives relying on different underlying mechanisms.[4]

Gartzke (2007) attempts to take this work one step further in his development of an argument for a "capitalist peace" as an alternative to the democratic peace. He argues that economic development, financial markets, and monetary policy coordination are much more likely to achieve that goal. Similarly to Rosecrance (1986) and Hegre (2000), Gartzke suggests that development has altered state preferences away from conquest and toward trade, since modern production processes "de-emphasize land, minerals, and rooted labor in favor of intellectual and financial capital" (172). Thus Gartzke also implicitly posits a conditional relationship between development and trade.[5]

We think that the aforementioned empirical studies have demonstrated an important boundary condition on the relationship between trade and conflict, heeding calls for greater nuance in the literature (for example, Mansfield and Pollins, 2001). While building on the importance of development in conditioning the effect of trade on conflict, we also suggest the need to reconsider the prevailing approach that treats all trade as equivalent in its impact on conflict. We are certainly not the first to make this claim, as scholars have previously debated the potential theoretical effects of strategic versus nonstrategic goods on conflict (for example, Schelling, 1958; Gowa, 1994; Morrow, 1997).

Yet, as Dorussen (2006, 88–89) demonstrates, very few have actually disaggregated trade flows for empirical analysis. Park, Abolfathi, and Ward (1976) and Polachek (1980) focus on the effects of trade in oil, Gasiorowski and

Polachek (1982) differentiate between agriculture and manufactured goods in U.S.-Warsaw Pact trade, Polachek and McDonald (1992) differentiate manufactures and raw materials in analyzing the sources of conflict, and Reuveny and Kang (1998) and Reuveny and Li (2004) analyze nine categories of commodity goods, though at a high level of aggregation. Dorussen himself distinguishes between manufactured and non-manufactured goods, which he then decomposes into ten subcategories. He finds that trade in manufactured goods significantly reduces conflict, while nonmanufactured goods do not; even as aggregate measures of trade retain their overall pacifying effect. We believe these efforts to disaggregate trade are a move in the right direction, though we suggest that the key distinction is between intra-industry and inter-industry trade. In fact, Dorussen's finding that manufactured goods reduce conflict could follow from the effect of intra-industry trade.

Intra-Industry Trade, Liberalization, Development, and Peace

We contend that intra-industry trade is pacifying while liberalization alone may have countervailing effects on the stability of peace. We do not dispute the aforementioned causal mechanisms proposed by scholars advocating a pacifying impact of liberalization, or even their operation in the contemporary world; however, we suggest that there are additional consequences of liberalization that could introduce aggravating influences along with pacifying ones, ultimately leading to an ambiguous connection between liberalized trade and conflict in the aggregate.

Peterson and Thies (2012a) demonstrate that intra-industry trade—but not inter-industry trade—facilitates peace between trade partners because it provides mutual trade gains but does not evoke dependence on, and therefore vulnerability to, trade partners.[6] For example, in the United States, automobiles from Japan, Germany, South Korea, and elsewhere compete openly with domestic brands. These states enjoy gains from globalized automotive markets, but do not rely on their trade partners for automobiles. If trade were to terminate, states could easily adjust by increasing domestic production. Importantly, even if importers and exporters face different costs for terminating trade (for example, Dorussen 2006; see also Crescenzi 2003; Peterson 2014), incentives for coercion nonetheless diminish as intra-industry trade increases, because both trade partners are importers and exporters of the same commodities.[7]

Given that intra-industry trade should promote political affinity among trade partners, it could therefore promote liberalization as well. This relationship follows from the logic that firms engaging in intra-industry trade are less likely to fear foreign competitors and therefore less likely to lobby for protectionism (for example, Balassa 1966; Aquino 1978; but see Gilligan 1997; Kono 2009). Yet the causal link from liberalization to trade composition is less clear. In many cases, liberalization might promote inter-industry trade. For example, when relative factor abundance differs between potential trade partners, they are more likely to specialize in the absence of trade barriers (Krugman 1981). Economists typically view this specialization in favorable terms, as trade gains result in aggregate welfare improvements for both states. Yet, increasingly, liberalization occurs between developed and developing states (no longer in a colonial relationship as in earlier periods), which could result in trade relationships in which poorer countries rely on exports of primary commodities, which typically offer lower value-added, while developed states export more profitable manufactured goods.[8] The problematic nature of these dependent relationships has long been described in the literature from a variety of theoretical perspectives (for example, Gallagher and Robinson 1953; Caporaso 1978; Dos Santos 1970; Pollins 1985). Even among mutually developed states, liberalization (particularly if it follows for political reasons [for example, Gowa 1994, Gowa and Mansfield 1993]), while fostering trade generally, may actually promote relatively more inter-industry trade because this alliance-induced liberalization could be indicative of lower willingness to protect strategically vital domestic protection against foreign competitors.[9]

When liberalization occurs in these cases, inter-industry trade will increase as a proportion of total dyadic trade.[10] Peterson and Thies (2012a) show that inter-industry trade should have an ambiguous impact on conflict because specialization introduces the potential for strategic vulnerability. The classic example is the case in which one country relies on fuel imports for its manufacturing sector. An oil embargo would be devastating to this state, which state leaders will be quick to recognize. Polachek (1980) demonstrates that oil exporters are more hostile as exports increase, a phenomenon that Dorussen (2006) claims follows from the lack of high opportunity costs for those exporters. This asymmetry, and the potential for coercion resulting from it, is precisely what Hirschman (1945) refers to as the crux of the dependence literature. As others have pointed out, dependence on trade tends not to prevent conflict because one side's decreased incentive to demand change in the status quo is balanced by the other's increased incentive therein (for example, Morrow 1999).

By instilling similar interests among trade partners without promoting dependence and vulnerability, intra-industry trade precludes conflicts of interest from ever originating, with trade gains as added incentives to provide value to a given relationship. Liberalization could facilitate intra-industry trade (and therefore increase the stability of peace); however, this outcome is likely only if states' factor endowments are similar. Since liberalization can lead to either increased specialization or higher intra-industry trade depending on market structure of liberalizing states, we contend that it could have an ambiguous impact on conflict between trade partners in the aggregate.

Given this argument, how does one explain existing work suggesting a uniformly pacifying effect of liberalization? We suggest that previous findings in this regard could follow from the influence of intra-industry trade, which was likely responsible for lower resistance to liberalization. In addition, limitations in previous studies may be responsible for results showing a pacifying influence of liberalization. Extant work makes the most of limited liberalization data; however, these data are available primarily for more developed countries. Given Krugman's work (1979; 1981) demonstrating that mutually developed states tend to have similar factor endowments, and therefore are more likely to engage in intra-industry trade, empirical work supporting a pacifying impact of liberalization may be capturing an effect limited to mutually developed states, in which liberalization is more likely to increase intra-industry specialization. However, given that a considerable volume of trade flows between developed and less-developed states, liberalization arguably increases the potential for exploitation if trade is structured such that less developed countries are dependent on developed states.

It is important to stress that liberalization serving to increase inter-industry trade in accordance with comparative advantage is not likely to *increase* the likelihood of conflict. Liberal trade policy does suggest weakness among import competitors, who might otherwise prefer the use of force to protect their monopoly rents (see, for example, McDonald 2004).[11] However, although the liberalization process reflects the weakness of protectionist interests who favor closure, it is possible that the consequences of liberalization (possible inequality, reliance on exports of primary commodities) would lead to a wide-scale, public backlash against cooperation with trade partners. Furthermore, the state-level consequence of vulnerability due to inter-industry trade—if only for the fact that it can provoke conflicts of interest more easily than can intra-industry trade—is also important to consider. These countervailing influences introduce more ambiguity regarding the impact of liberalization on conflict propensity. Accordingly, our first hypothesis notes that trade will be pacifying regardless of trade and liberalization levels.

Hypothesis 5.1: A higher proportion of intra-industry trade between states is associated with a lesser likelihood of the onset of a militarized dispute, irrespective of the extent of trade or liberalization.

The Role of Development

It is impossible to disentangle completely intra-industry trade from development. Studies have shown that bilateral intra-industry trade is more likely as both states have higher GDP and when GDP per capita is similar (for example, Bergstrand 1990). It tends to be richer states in which consumers develop varied tastes (and are not preoccupied merely with survival). Further, similarly large-sized economies suggests convergence in relative factor endowment, typically toward capital abundance. Krugman's model cites these consequences of increased wealth as necessary for the growth of intra-industry trade. However, we contend that although development (that is, relatively high GDP per capita) may be necessary, it is not sufficient to facilitate intra-industry trade—hence the rather modest correlation of 0.26 between our intra-industry trade proportion variable and (the natural log of) the lower dyadic GDP per capita in our sample. Russia is an illustrative example of a relatively developed state, the exports of which consist mainly of primary commodities (fuels, timber, metals, and so on), while its main imports are manufactured goods.

Prior work suggests that development and trade together reduce the likelihood of dyadic conflict (Rosecrance 1986; Hegre 2000). However, we contend that development and *overall* trade interaction have ambiguous influence on conflict, both separately and interactively. This ambiguity stems from synthesizing arguments regarding the costs of conquest relative to trade with Keohane and Nye's argument regarding vulnerabilities inherent in trade (1977). First, given that inter-industry trade may have as a consequence strategic dependence and vulnerability as well as trade gains, we expect these cross-cutting influences to lead to an uncertain impact of overall trade on conflict when we control for intra-industry trade.[12]

Similarly, Rosecrance's contention (1986) that development secures the ability to gain without resorting to conquest while simultaneously increasing the costs of conflict must be balanced against Liberman's similarly reasonable argument (1993) that development raises the benefits as well as the costs of (attempted) conquest. Liberman provides the classic example: Hitler was able to employ the subjugated, developed economies in Europe for his military aims, suggesting that the added costs of invading developed states seem to be outweighed, at least under certain circumstances, by the benefits thereof. Taken together, these arguments suggest crosscutting influences of development, some pacifying and some aggravating. We contend that these forces will cancel out in the aggregate, leading to an unclear impact of development.[13] However, the exclusion in existing studies of intra-industry trade, a pacifying force, may cause omitted variable bias in which development appears pacifying. We argue that development is pacifying only when intra-industry trade accompanies it. These expectations lead to a second hypothesis:

Hypothesis 5.2: Mutual development is not associated with the likelihood of the onset of a militarized dispute when intra-industry trade is low; however, this association becomes increasingly negative and significant as intra-industry trade is held at higher values.

Research Design

We test our hypotheses with data spanning 1962 to 2001—the upper limit of this timespan being determined by our data on militarized interstate disputes. Our unit of analysis is the nondirected dyad year. Our dependent variable is *fatal MID onset*, a binary variable equal to 1 only in years in which one dyad member initiates an MID against its dyadic partner with the consequence that there is at least one battle death, coded using data from the Correlates of War Militarized Interstate Dispute data 3.1 (Ghosn, Palmer, and Bremer 2004). While MIDs incorporate a spectrum of militarized conflict including threats, displays, and uses of force, fatal MIDs exclude the less severe threats and displays. Furthermore, many uses of force are likewise excluded from our dependent variable because many uses of force are arguably minor events (for example, the seizure of fishing vessels by armed forces that are later released with no further hostility).

To illustrate the occurrence of fatal MIDs in our data, the left-hand graph of Figure 5.1 presents the frequency of fatal MIDs over time, from 1962 to 2001. We also graph the mean level of bilateral intra-industry trade as a proportion of all

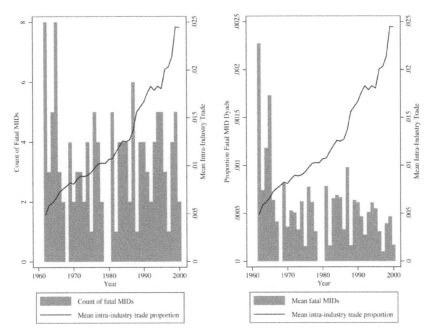

Figure 5.1   Count of fatal MIDs (left) and proportion of fatal MID dyads (right) over time, along with mean dyadic proportion of intra-industry trade, 1962–2000.

bilateral trade, to provide some initial illustration of the relationship between trade composition and militarized conflict. The figure shows that the frequency of fatal MIDs has declined somewhat over time, concurrent with an increase in the average level of intra-industry trade. However, there remains a relatively uneven pattern to the instance of fatal MIDs. The right-hand graph of Figure 5.1 examines the mean level of dyadic fatal MIDs and intra-industry trade over time. In other words, this figure shows the proportion of all dyads engaging in a fatal MID each year, useful given that the number of states in the system has increased over time due to the process of decolonialization. This figure more clearly shows a decline in the likelihood of fatal MID onset over time as intra-industry trade increases. However, these figures present aggregated data for the international system each year, insufficient to test our dyadic hypotheses. Accordingly, we turn to explanation of our primary statistical models.

Given that our primary dependent variable is binary, we specify probit models to test our hypotheses.[14] We lag most explanatory variables by one year to mitigate the potential for simultaneity bias.[15] To account for duration dependence, we include variables for *peace years, peace years squared,* and *peace years cubed* (Carter and Signorino 2010). To account for non-independence by country pair, we cluster standard errors on the dyad.[16] Finally, we exclude all dyad years in which conflict is ongoing from the previous year.

Similar to Chapters 3 and 4, our primary independent variable is the intra-industry trade index developed in Chapter 2. Again, this variable varies from 0, representing no intra-industry trade in a dyad year, to 1, representing a dyad year in which all bilateral trade flows within industries. Primary explanatory variables also include an indicator of trade levels, development, and, in alternate models, liberalization among dyadic states.[17] To capture dyadic trade levels, we use a measure of total trade flows (state A's imports from state B and A's exports to state B), taken from the UN Comtrade data from World Integrated Trade Solution (WITS),[18] divided by the less wealthy state's GDP, taken from the Penn World Table 8.0 (Feenstra, Inklaar, and Timmer 2013). We capture joint development by taking the lower of the states' GDP per capita in 2005 U.S. dollars, from the Penn World Table. As discussed in Chapter 4, liberalization measures are considerably more difficult to obtain. Accordingly, we use the estimated liberalization data from Chapter 4 again in models of fatal MID onset. Specifically, we estimate modified, yearly gravity models, specifying importer fixed effects and then utilizing the estimates of unit-specific error to create a state-year measure of trade restrictiveness (Hiscox and Kastner 2002). For each dyad-year observation in our fatal MID onset models, we include the lower of the two states' restrictiveness estimates. Accordingly, we have a measure of the lower liberalization—or highest restrictiveness—in the dyad.

Our remaining explanatory variables look similar to those used in previous chapters. In general, variables are included to account for political affinity, as well as opportunity for conflict, which could correlate both with trade composition and with the occurrence of militarized conflict. First, we include the lower of the two states' Polity combined scores using data from the Polity IV project (Marshall and Jaggers 2010), given that more democratic states tend to be more developed and engage in more trade. We include a measure of the log of (1 plus) relative military capabilities, specifically the ratio of the higher to the lower Composite Index of National Capabilities (CINC) score (Singer, Bremer, and Stuckey, 1972). We also include the higher CINC score in order to capture opportunity for conflict. Similarly, we include a measure of logged distance in miles between borders (plus 1), given that more proximate states could trade more and have more opportunity for conflict. Finally, we include a dichotomous indicator of alliance using the Correlates of War Formal Interstate Alliance Dataset version 4.0 (Gibler 2009).

Analysis

We find strong support for our hypotheses. Specifically, we find that a greater proportion of intra-industry trade is pacifying regardless of the extent of dyadic trade, and regardless of the extent of liberalization. We also find some evidence that development is aggravating—or at least is not pacifying—in the absence of intra-industry trade, but becomes pacifying as intra-industry trade increases as a proportion of total dyadic trade.

As in Chapters 3 and 4, we present tables of model coefficients and standard errors in the appendix to this chapter,[19] presenting here a series of figures that summarize our findings. Figure 5.2 summarizes the marginal effects of our explanatory variables, specifically illustrating how a one-unit increase in each explanatory variable is associated with the probability of fatal MID onset.[20] To determine the marginal effect of each variable, we hold all other explanatory variables at their median value. Accordingly, the point estimate for each variable's marginal effect can be considered the influence of that variable on MID propensity in an otherwise average dyad. The figure also presents 95 percent confidence intervals, summarizing our uncertainty regarding these relationships. According to Figure 5.2, intra-industry trade has a negative and significant association with fatal MID onset.[21] The magnitude of intra-industry trade appears larger than every other variable save higher CINC score in the dyad, which captures the opportunity of the dyad to engage in militarized conflict. However, magnitudes should be considered with respect to the range of the variables in question. Notably, the lower liberalization level in the dyad is associated with a reduced probability of fatal MID onset, although its marginal effect appears smaller than that of intra-industry trade.[22]

To illustrate the influence of intra-industry trade substantively, we present the left-hand graph in Figure 5.3, which plots the probability of fatal MID onset as intra-industry trade increases from the value of 0 to 2 standard deviations above its mean value, equal to approximately 15 percent of dyadic trade; we also hold all other variables at their medians. The figure shows that the probability of fatal MID onset among the dyadic states falls from approximately

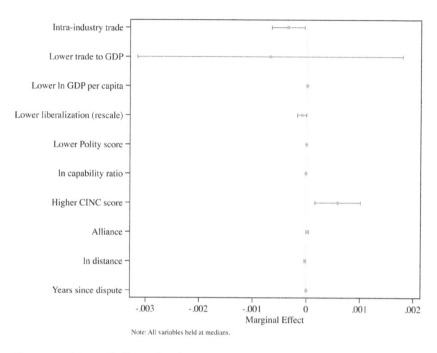

Figure 5.2   Marginal effects of explanatory variables on dyadic fatal MID onset, with all variables held at their medians, including 95 percent confidence bounds. From Model 5.7.

0.00003 to 6×10^{-6}, becoming statistically insignificant at the 0.05 level when intra-industry trade increases to 9 percent of dyadic trade. While all probabilities are quite small, it is important to remember that these estimates are associated with a median dyad, the members of which are separated by over four thousand miles and have experienced seventeen years of peace. The right-hand graph of Figure 5.3 replicates the left-hand graph, holding ln distance at 0, years since last fatal MID at 0, and capability ratio at 0, thereby capturing the effect of intra-industry trade on "dangerous dyads" most likely to experience conflict (Bremer 1992).[23] The figure shows a similar pattern: the probability of fatal MID onset decreases as intra-industry trade increases. When no dyadic trade flows within industries, the probability of fatal MID onset is equal to 0.05 (p < 0.02). When intra-industry trade is equal to 15 percent of dyadic trade, the probability of fatal MID onset falls to 0.02, but this probability is not statistically significant (p < 0.06). We remain confident (at the 0.05 level) that the probability of fatal MID onset is positive until intra-industry

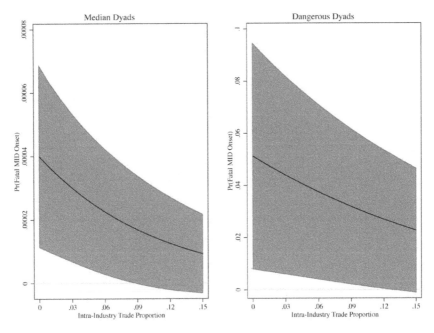

Figure 5.3   The probability of fatal MID onset by intra-industry trade level, for median dyads and "dangerous dyads," with 95 percent confidence intervals. From Model 5.7.

trade composes 13.5 percent of dyadic trade. Notably, confidence bounds are wider in the right-hand plot, which we suspect is a consequence of the general pattern that uncertainty associated with conflict tends to rise along with the overall probability of conflict.

To compare the influence of intra-industry trade to that of liberalization, we specified a statistical model in which these variables are interacted (Model 5.11, presented in Table 5.3). The interaction term is not significant in this model, suggesting that the influence of intra-industry trade and liberalization are not mutually conditioning. Although interaction terms are limited in explanatory power when used in nonlinear models, subsequent tests confirm that the influence of intra-industry trade and liberalization do not depend greatly on the value at which we hold the other variable. Accordingly, we omit a detailed discussion of conditional marginal effects. Instead, we present a simpler discussion, explaining how an increase in each of the two variables from its mean to its mean plus one standard deviation is associated with reduction in fatal MID onset. For both variables, we consider this change holding the other variable at the mean and mean plus one standard deviation (that is, at the same two values). We find that this one-standard-deviation increase in intra-industry trade is associated approximately with a 40 percent decrease in the probability of fatal MID onset, averaged over the two values of lower liberalization. Conversely, the same mean-to-mean-plus-one standard deviation change in lower liberalization is associated with a 33 percent decrease in the probability of fatal MID onset, averaged over the two values of intra-industry trade. Accordingly, we confirm that both intra-industry trade and liberalization can foster peace; however, the influence of intra-industry trade is somewhat greater. These results reaffirm the importance of domestic politics, given that both intra-industry trade and liberalization imply the absence (or political weakness) of domestic groups that seek to enact trade barriers.

Finally, we examine the conditional relationship between intra-industry trade and dyadic development (measured as the log of the lower GDP per capita, rescaled such that the minimum value is coded as 0). We specify models including an interaction of these two variables, the results of which suggest that both variables become increasingly pacifying at higher levels of the other variable.[24] In fact, neither variable has a statistically significant association with fatal MID onset when the other variable is at its minimum. With respect to intra-industry trade, a null effect in the presence of minimum development makes sense because intra-industry trade is unlikely to exist within a mutually undeveloped, poor dyad. However, the fact that development is not associated with peace in the absence of intra-industry trade suggests that the ability to prosper from commerce is insufficient to preclude conflict, supporting Hypothesis 5.2. We present a figure to illustrate the association of each constituent variable over meaningful ranges of the other variable. First, we present the left-hand graph of Figure 5.4, which examines the marginal effect of *intra-industry trade* over a standard deviation range, centered around the mean, of *lower GDP per capita*. The figure shows that intra-industry trade does not have a statistically significant association with fatal MID onset when lower GDP per capita is held at one-half standard deviations below its mean (equal to 1,618 U.S. dollars when transformed back from its logged value). However, the marginal effect of intra-industry trade becomes negative and significant as lower GDP per capita increases (specifically, at values above 1,976 U.S. dollars). These empirical results support our theoretical expectation that development could be necessary, but is not sufficient, for a dyadic peace.

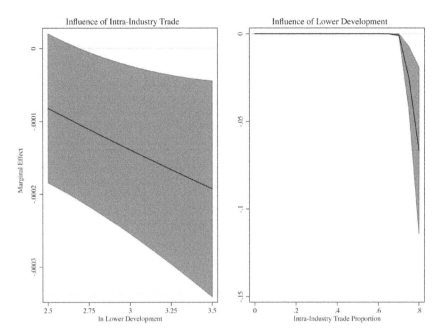

Figure 5.4   The marginal effect of intra-industry trade over lower development, and the marginal effect of lower development over intra-industry trade, with 95 percent confidence intervals. From Model 5.11.

The right-hand graph of Figure 5.4 illustrates the marginal effect of lower GDP per capita at different levels of intra-industry trade. The figure shows that lower development is not statistically associated with fatal MID onset over most of the range of intra-industry trade. Specifically, its marginal effect becomes negative and significant when intra-industry trade composes 70 percent of total dyadic trade. Notably, the mean level of intra-industry trade among states in our analysis is 2.5 percent; 70 percent is approximately 10 standard deviations above this mean value. Given this, we find evidence that development only facilitates peace when states engage primarily in two-way trade of similar commodities. This result further confirms our theoretical expectations that intra-industry trade is a—perhaps the—primary pacifying force within dyads. Overall trade volumes and development have no clear association. Peace also seems to follow as the less liberalized dyadic state lowers its trade barrier, yet the substantive impact of liberalization is less than that for intra-industry trade.

Finally, it's worth noting that our variable for lower Polity score is not significant in any of our models. This result stands in stark contrast to a wide body of evidence supporting the democratic peace hypothesis. There are a few possible explanations of this finding. First, it could be that previous findings in support of the democratic peace are spurious, following instead from the fact that jointly democratic dyads happen to be those most likely to engage in high proportions of intra-industry trade. Indeed, this interpretation would support recent findings that peace follows from capitalism rather than democracy (for example, Gartzke 2007). However, it is also possible that missing data for our intra-industry trade variable are responsible for the nonsignificance of democracy. Yet given that missing observations for this variable are most likely among less developed states, this explanation of the nonsignificance of democracy still could support the capitalist peace hypothesis, given the associated argument that more developed states will experience less conflict.

Conclusion

We find empirical support for our hypotheses linking intra-industry trade to peace within dyads. Higher levels of intra-industry trade are associated with lower levels of dyadic militarized conflict. Overall trade interaction typically has no effect on the likelihood of dyadic conflict when we control for intra-industry trade. Liberalization appears relatively less pacifying than intra-industry trade and, importantly, is not necessary for intra-industry trade to have a pacifying impact. Finally, development has no effect on the likelihood of dyadic conflict in the absence of intra-industry trade. Our study is the first to demonstrate these important boundary conditions on the commercial peace.

Adherents to the liberal perspective that trade promotes peace view the rapid increases in global trade in the post–World War II era with optimism. Yet the case of World War I, which occurred despite record levels of global trade and investment, serves as a reminder that interdependence by itself may do little to prevent massive conflicts from erupting. In this chapter, we point to a key factor distinguishing the contemporary period from that preceding World War I. Our results suggest that there is a distinct element of the current trend toward globalization that raises the prospects for peace; due to the unprecedented increases in intra-industry trade, the contemporary trade regime is more conducive to peace than was the more asymmetric, arguably exploitative trading environment that flourished in the late nineteenth century. Nonetheless, our results suggest that there are crosscutting effects and, potentially, militarized consequences to the continuing prevalence of inter-industry trade.

Our results have important implications for trade patterns and policy worldwide, suggesting that research would benefit from continuing to explore the relationship between the commodity makeup of bilateral trade and militarized conflict. Although ongoing scholarship examines (and typically commends) rapidly expanding trade ties worldwide, little attention is paid to the commodity composition thereof. The potential for states to become dependent on trade partners or alternatively to cooperate in large, interstate markets for similar, potentially branded goods suggests that expanding trade may only pacify interstate relationships in specific circumstances.

Appendix to Chapter 5

The preceding analysis discusses the results of eleven models, which we present in detail here in two tables. Table 5.1 replicates the results of our previous work (Peterson and Thies 2012a), using updated data as discussed in Chapter 2. Table 5.2 again replicates these results, but also adds the variable for lower liberalization in the dyad, and adds a model interacting lower liberalization with intra-industry trade.

Table 5.1 presents models 5.1 through 5.5. Model 5.1 includes our primary explanatory variable, *intra-industry trade proportion*, as well as a series of control variables. Model 5.2 adds variables for trade as a proportion of the poorer state's GDP and the lower of the two states' GDP per capita. Model 5.3 interacts *lower trade to GDP* with *lower (logged) GDP per capita*, while Model 5.4 interacts intra-industry trade with lower trade to GDP. Finally, Model 5.5 interacts intra-industry trade with lower GDP per capita. The results of Table 5.1 are essentially identical to those in Peterson and Thies (2012a). The coefficient of intra-industry trade is significant in four of the five models. The exception is Model 5.5, in which the coefficient for intra-industry trade is not statistically significant, suggesting that intra-industry trade is not associated with reduced conflict propensity at the minimum level of lower GDP per capita (which is rescaled to equal 0). However, as we show in the chapter text, intra-industry trade becomes associated with reduced conflict propensity when lower GDP per capita is held at approximately one-quarter of a standard devia-

Table 5.1 Probit coefficients and robust standard errors for models examining the association between intra-industry trade and fatal MID onset, excluding liberalization, 1962–2000.

	Model 5.1	Model 5.2	Model 5.3	Model 5.4	Model 5.5
Intra-industry trade	−2.215**	−2.253**	−2.058***	−2.663**	2.600
	(0.800)	(0.761)	(0.788)	(0.884)	(1.569)
Lower trade to GDP		−7.345	36.283**	−13.816	−8.862
		(9.290)	(13.334)	(12.460)	(9.509)
Lower ln GDPpc		0.058	0.082	0.061	0.081
		(0.046)	(0.045)	(0.046)	(0.044)
Lower trade to GDP X lower ln GDPpc			−15.156*		
			(7.509)		
Intra–industry trade index X lower trade/GDP				39.129	
				(27.906)	
Intra–industry trade index X lower ln GDPpc					−1.415*
					(0.598)
Lower Polity score	−0.003	−0.004	−0.004	−0.004	−0.004
	(0.009)	(0.009)	(0.009)	(0.009)	(0.009)
Ln capability ratio	−0.072	−0.078*	−0.078*	−0.079*	−0.076
	(0.040)	(0.039)	(0.039)	(0.039)	(0.039)
Higher capability score	4.363***	4.546***	4.657***	4.577***	4.530***
	(1.255)	(1.230)	(1.215)	(1.223)	(1.224)
Alliance	0.078	0.097	0.089	0.104	0.089
	(0.098)	(0.099)	(0.099)	(0.098)	(0.100)
ln Distance	−0.174***	−0.179***	−0.181***	−0.180***	−0.180***
	(0.012)	(0.012)	(0.012)	(0.013)	(0.012)
Years since fatal MID	−0.053	−0.051	−0.051	−0.050	−0.052
	(0.033)	(0.033)	(0.033)	(0.033)	(0.033)
Years since fatal MID ^{2}	0.001	0.001	0.001	0.001	0.001
	(0.002)	(0.002)	(0.002)	(0.002)	(0.002)
Years since fatal MID ^{3}	−0.000	−0.000	−0.000	−0.000	−0.000
	(0.000)	(0.000)	(0.000)	(0.000)	(0.000)
Constant	−1.882***	−2.033***	−2.094***	−2.031***	−2.099***
	(0.180)	(0.233)	(0.231)	(0.233)	(0.232)

continued

Table 5.1   Probit coefficients and robust standard errors for models examining the association between intra-industry trade and fatal MID onset, excluding liberalization, 1962–2000. (*continued*)

	Model 5.1	*Model 5.2*	*Model 5.3*	*Model 5.4*	*Model 5.5*
Observations	217,243	215,298	215,298	215,298	215,298
χ^2	456.7***	467.9***	472.5***	473.4***	475.7***
Log likelihood	−635.8	−625.5	−622.0	−624.8	−622.3

Notes: Robust standard errors adjusted for clustering on the dyad in parentheses.

*** $p < 0.001$, ** $p < 0.01$, * $p < 0.05$; two–tailed tests.

DV = fatal MID onset.

tion below its mean. Notably, the interaction term for *intra-industry trade X lower trade to GDP* is not significant in Model 5.4, suggesting that the impact of intra-industry trade does not depend on the overall extent of dyadic trade. In other words, irrespective of absolute trade volumes, it is the intra-industry composition thereof that provides a pacifying impact.

Table 5.2 presents Models 5.6 through 5.10, which replicate Models 5.1 through 5.5 with one key difference: we add a variable for *lower liberalization* to each model (using the method from Hiscox and Kastner 2002 to calculate each dyadic state's liberalization). We also add Model 5.11, in which we interact intra-industry trade and lower liberalization. The results of Models 5.6 through 5.10 are nearly identical to those from Models 5.1 through 5.5. In addition, the variable for lower liberalization is negative and significant in each model. In Model 5.11, the variables for intra-industry trade and lower liberalization are both negative and significant, while the interaction term is not significant at the 0.05 level. As discussed in the chapter text, the impact of both these constituent terms appears relatively constant regardless of the value at which the other variable is held.

Table 5.2 Probit coefficients and robust standard errors for models examining the association between intra-industry trade and fatal MID onset, including liberalization, 1962–2000.

	Model 5.6	Model 5.7	Model 5.8	Model 5.9	Model 5.10	Model 5.11
Intra-industry trade	−2.396**	−2.457**	−2.245**	−2.859**	2.767	−2.133**
	(0.840)	(0.765)	(0.788)	(0.908)	(1.632)	(0.915)
Lower liberalization	−61.237*	−62.971*	−64.926**	−62.124*	−66.582**	−68.101**
	(26.255)	(25.652)	(24.777)	(25.759)	(25.439)	(27.381)
Lower trade to GDP		−4.802	44.518**	−10.842	−6.076	−4.987
		(8.927)	(14.076)	(12.268)	(9.280)	(8.419)
Lower ln GDPpc		0.067	0.092	0.069	0.091*	0.067
		(0.049)	(0.047)	(0.049)	(0.047)	(0.049)
Low trade/GDP X low ln GDPpc			−16.561*			
			(7.828)			
IIT index X low trade/GDP				36.545		
				(27.914)		
IIT index X low ln GDPpc					−1.513*	
					(0.622)	
IIT X lower liberalization						219.999
						(401.733)
Lower Polity score	−0.003	−0.005	−0.004	−0.004	−0.004	−0.005
	(0.009)	(0.009)	(0.009)	(0.009)	(0.009)	(0.009)
Ln capability ratio	−0.076	−0.076*	−0.077*	−0.077*	−0.074*	−0.077**
	(0.039)	(0.038)	(0.038)	(0.038)	(0.038)	(0.038)
Higher capability score	4.326***	4.118***	4.211***	4.155***	4.085***	4.160***
	(1.211)	(1.214)	(1.203)	(1.207)	(1.209)	(1.209)
Alliance	0.117	0.109	0.101	0.116	0.103	0.112
	(0.098)	(0.099)	(0.100)	(0.099)	(0.101)	(0.100)
ln distance	−0.175***	−0.180***	−0.183***	−0.181***	−0.181***	−0.180***
	(0.012)	(0.012)	(0.012)	(0.012)	(0.012)	(0.012)
Years since fatal MID	−0.046	−0.047	−0.047	−0.046	−0.047	−0.048
	(0.034)	(0.033)	(0.033)	(0.033)	(0.033)	(0.033)
Years since fatal MID ^{2}	0.001	0.001	0.001	0.001	0.001	0.001
	(0.002)	(0.002)	(0.002)	(0.002)	(0.002)	(0.002)
Years since fatal MID ^{3}	0.000	0.000	0.000	0.000	0.000	0.000
	(0.000)	(0.000)	(0.000)	(0.000)	(0.000)	(0.000)

continued

Table 5.2 Probit coefficients and robust standard errors for models examining the association between intra-industry trade and fatal MID onset, including liberalization, 1962–2000. (*continued*)

	Model 5.6	Model 5.7	Model 5.8	Model 5.9	Model 5.10	Model 5.11
Constant	−1.945***	−2.120***	−2.189***	−2.117***	−2.196***	−2.131***
	(0.185)	(0.246)	(0.244)	(0.246)	(0.245)	(0.247)
Observations	213,730	213,730	213,730	213,730	213,730	213,730
χ^2	468.6***	488.5***	499.7***	497.4***	495.3***	491.9***
Log likelihood	−622.2	−620.1	−616.3	−619.5	−616.5	−619.9

Notes: Robust standard errors adjusted for clustering on the dyad in parentheses.
*** $p < 0.001$, ** $p < 0.01$, * $p < 0.05$; two–tailed tests.
DV = fatal MID onset.

Chapter 6

The Political Economy of International Affinity: How the Composition of Trade Influences Preference Similarity and Alliance

A S discussed in the preceding chapter, a large literature examines the question of whether trade flows between states can prevent war and secure enduring friendship. Similarly, numerous studies explore the ways in which international conflict or expectations thereof could preclude trade. Yet these studies focus almost exclusively on the *extent* of trade flows, typically ignoring how the *composition* of trade between states may condition the structure of their political relationships. In this chapter, we argue that the composition of trade affects the degree to which states develop complementary or divergent preferences, thereby influencing states' choice of alliance partners. Specifically, we contend that intra-industry trade, which consists of trade in similar, often branded goods, encourages the emergence of similar preferences among trade partners, which will manifest in their interactions with each other. On the other hand, inter-industry trade, the classic form of trade wherein dissimilar products are traded in accordance with the theory of comparative advantage, may occasionally sow the seeds of discord due to the security externalities inherent in such exchange. Ultimately, inter-industry trade could have a crosscutting influence on preference similarity.

We draw inspiration from Rogowski (1987), who focuses on the effect that trade may have on shaping democratic institutions within the state. Our interest is in how different forms of trade may shape political relationships between states. If trade can generate changes within domestic political structures through the reshaping of societal preferences, and if those preferences are also related to decisions about restriction or expansion of trade, then we believe it stands to reason that decisions about the characterization of states' larger political relationships with each other are also at stake. Preference similarity, and even formal alliances, may be born of many expedient factors, but underlying societal views about other states must also figure into this decision. Those views are shaped by the cultural information conveyed by different forms of trade. Trading relationships should therefore be an important structural consideration for policymakers when forging larger political relationships between states. Those decisions could then influence future trade between states, as an allied relationship casts a very different light on intersocietal relations than a rival relationship.

We test our expectations about the relationships between intra- and inter-industry trade and political relationships using error correction models and simultaneous equations models, finding evidence that when dyadic trade follows more from intra-industry specialization, states have more similar foreign policy preferences. We also find that intra-industry trade is associated with a higher likelihood that states will form and maintain alliances, while, simultaneously, alliance formation and presence do not have a clear effect on trade composition.

This chapter proceeds with a discussion of the literature linking trade to political relationships, including its primary focus on the extent of trade and relative lack of attention to the composition of trade. We then present our theoretical expectations, which synthesize expectations from the literatures on the security externalities of trade and the Kantian Peace with those from recent studies demonstrating that peace through trade is conditional on the commodity composition of trade. Next, we present our research design and discuss the results of our empirical analysis. We conclude with a discussion of the implications of our results for scholars and policymakers.

Trade and International Relationships

Most of the existing literature has focused on the effect of alliances and political similarity on trade, with no explicit consideration of the effect that the composition of trade might have on alliances or political similarity. Much of the initial wave of research on alliances and trade was born out of scholarship on the Cold War and hegemonic stability theory (Gowa 1994; Mansfield 1994). Gowa identifies the primary motivation for concern about trade in the context of international competition (see also Hirschman, 1945; Baldwin 1980; Keohane and Nye 1977; Mastanduno 1998):

The security externalities of trade arise from its inevitable jointness in production: the source of gains from trade is the increased efficiency with which domestic resources can be employed, and this increase in efficiency itself frees economic resources for military uses.... Thus, trade increases the potential military power of any country that engages in it. (1989, 1246)

States considering trade agreements may therefore be likely to use their military alliances as the basis for such agreement, since this is the best way to manage the security externalities of trade. Gowa (1989, 1249) notes that, even given an existing alliance, a member could exit and join another alliance. Given this risk of exit, any attempt to capture the security externalities of trade with an alliance in order to benefit members and exclude rivals may fail. Even so, Gowa argues that free trade agreements are more likely to occur within alliances than outside of alliances, and more likely to occur in a bipolar than a multipolar system. These arguments are replicated by Gowa and Mansfield (1993), who provide statistical analyses that demonstrate that alliances significantly increase trade, in particular during periods of bipolarity.

Mansfield and Bronson (1997) elaborate on the argument that freer trade is more likely among allies than adversaries by highlighting the incentives to both governments and firms. A government that trades with an adversary will increase the national income of that trading partner, thus undermining its own security. Governments that have the ability to influence their terms of trade should therefore discriminate in favor of allies in setting economic policy. Firms also have an incentive to act in accordance with government policy, since trade barriers imposed or left in place on adversaries should raise the local price for an imported good, thus reducing demand for it. Domestic-import-competing firms are thus rendered more competitive as a result of government discrimination against rivals. Firms that invest to support trade between countries are more likely to do so when political conditions mitigate against the risk of expropriation or an unanticipated increase in trade barriers. A political alliance between two states thus reduces the risk to firms that engage in production, distribution, and sale of traded goods. Mansfield and Bronson's statistical analysis confirms that alliances increase bilateral trade, and alliances accompanied by a preferential trade agreement (PTA) increase trade even more. Alliances and PTAs therefore reduce opportunism by foreign governments. Further, major powers embedded in alliances also generate increased trade as a result of the ability to capture security externalities within the allied relationship.

Morrow, Siverson, and Tabares (1998) cast some doubt on the findings from the work by Gowa and Mansfield, since they argue that the three prevailing arguments about the effect of international politics on trade flows must be empirically tested simultaneously. First, they argue that trade flows should be higher between states with similar, rather than dissimilar, interests (see also Pollins 1989). Second, they argue that trade flows should be higher between democracies than between nondemocracies (see also Dixon and Moon 1993). Finally, they consider the Gowa and Mansfield arguments that trade flows should be higher between allies. The statistical analyses support the idea that similarity of political relations and democratic dyads increase trade flows. Alliances increase trade under multipolarity, but decrease it under bipolarity (or in many cases have no significant effect in the models). However, as the authors themselves note, the measure of similarity used in the analyses, tau_b, is itself a correlation of alliance portfolios. Thus the findings do not necessarily contradict the general notion that alliances increase trade flows, and the polarity findings should also be taken with a grain of salt.

Long (2003) suggests that some of the confused results about the relationship between alliance and trade may result from failure to distinguish between defense and nondefense pacts. He attempts to improve operationalization of alliance such that it conforms more closely to theoretical expectations regarding security externalities. The expectation is that true defense pacts that involve a commitment of military assistance in the event of an attack provide a much firmer grounding for firms engaged in trade. The risk of opportunism is greatly reduced in this type of alliance, as opposed to nondefense pacts that do not involve extensive intergovernmental commitments. The statistical analysis demonstrates that trade is higher among alliances that are true defense pacts, while trade between nondefense pact allies is indistinguishable from that between non-allies. Further, the relationship between defense pact allies and trade is not contingent on polarity, as has been debated in the aforementioned contributions to the literature. This chapter nicely demonstrates a mechanism implicit in the type of alliance that resolves the problem posed by Gowa (1989) that even in alliances, one could still face the problems associated with exit costs for firms engaged in trade.

Long and Leeds (2006) provide yet another mechanism that explains why trade should be higher between allies. They focus on issue linkage between military alliances and economic agreements. Issue linkage can increase both the type and range of benefits to be distributed within a relationship as well as reduce incentives for opportunism. Issue linkage therefore helps governments overcome bargaining and enforcement dilemmas to enable cooperation. The explicit occurrence of issue linkage between military alliances and economic agreements is found within thirty-nine of the treaties (18 percent of the total) in the Alliance Treaty Obligations and Provisions dataset. The statistical results show that when alliances are linked to economic agreements, trade is significantly higher than found in non-allied state dyads in the periods 1885–1938 and 1920–1938. Nonlinked alliances do not exert an effect on trade that is distinguishable from non-allies in any period. Joint democracy is always significantly related to higher trade, while foreign policy interest similarity using Signorino and Ritter's S score (1999) is never significant in the models.

In general, we have fairly reliable evidence that alliances in general increase trade flows among member states, and that our confidence in these findings is improved when we look at subsets of alliances that have built-in commitment devices such as defense pacts or explicit linkages to economic agreements. Most of the literature assumes that alliances are an independent variable that affects trade as a dependent variable. Political dissimilarity—including rivalry—could also be associated with reduced trade between states due to the negative security externalities. The literature on rivalry more generally would also lead us to expect diminished trade between such states. Diehl and Goertz (2000, 4) conceptualize enduring rivalry as "a relationship between two states in which both use, with some regularity, military threats and force as well as one in which both sides formulate foreign policy in military terms." Thompson (2001, 560) argues that strategic rivalries occur when states view each other "as (a) competitors, (b) the source of actual or latent threats that pose some possibility of becoming militarized, and (c) enemies." These conceptualizations of rivalry are explicit in their understanding of the relationship as one of hostility that would probably lead to an expectation of reduced trade between states.

Long (2008) provides one of the few empirical pieces that includes explicit consideration of rivalry, which is conceived as a measure of the "shadow of conflict." The argument is that firms engaged in trade are risk averse and look for indications that armed conflict may disrupt their normal trading relationship (Li and Sacko 2002). If such indications look likely, as in the case of a rivalry, then trade should be lower. Long includes Thompson's measure of strategic rivalry, which is negatively associated with overall trade, as are his other measures of external conflict. Allies that are members of a defense pact are positively associated with overall trade, as are PTA membership and joint democracy. Similarity measured by Signorino and Ritter's S score (1999) is again not associated with trade.

Kastner (2007) highlights the fact that there are cases of rivalry when states do actually trade with each other, such as China and Taiwan, West Germany and rival Eastern European states during the Cold War, and even North and South Korea. Kastner suggests that domestic politics can help us get a better grasp on cases in which rivals trade in the shadow of conflict. In particular, when internationalist economic interests are strong within the states, then trade can flourish despite an overall hostile political relationship. If anything, the increase in trade may help build constituencies within society that have no vested interest in the political rivalry but that may work for peace and stability. This is a variant of the traditional liberal argument that commerce can produce peace through changing societal preferences, which are ultimately reflected in intergovernmental relations. Using an index of expected versus actual trade as a measure of trade barriers and as a proxy for international economic interests within a state, Kastner finds evidence that such barriers reduce bilateral trade. The case study of China and Taiwan shows that government reliance on internationalist economic interests helped to expand trade despite high levels of political hostility. Thus far, on balance, we expect that alliances should tend to promote trade while rivalries should tend to reduce trade. We also know that there are aspects of these relationships that are conditional, such as the kind of alliance or linkage between an alliance and an economic agreement or the importance of societal preferences in favor of trade within a rivalry.

Yet all of the aforementioned literature assumes trade in its undifferentiated form—there are no expected differences due to the composition of trade. The literature on trade interdependence and militarized conflict has moved toward differentiating trade in analyses (for example, Polachek and McDonald 1992; Reuveny and Kang 1998; Dorussen 2006). We believe these efforts to disaggregate trade are the right direction, though the key distinction for the purposes of this book is between intra-industry and inter-industry trade (see Peterson and Thies 2012a, 2012b).

Gowa and Mansfield's work (2004) represents the only paper in the literature on alliances and trade that began to investigate the distinction between intra-industry and inter-industry trade, supporting our belief that this is an important avenue of investigation. Gowa and Mansfield note that increasingly in the post–World War II era trade between developed states has taken on a different form from that in the preceding century. Trade between developed states, in particular, is primarily intra-industry in nature, meaning that it is trade of similar, often branded goods. Trade between developing and developed states still frequently takes the form of inter-industry trade, which is the classic form of trade in undifferentiated commodities based on specialization according to comparative advantage. New trade theory developed by Krugman (1980) and others was developed precisely to account for intra-industry trade.

While standard trade theory assumes constant returns to scale (unit costs do not change with output), and therefore market entry is free and cross-national differences in factor endowments drive trade, new trade theory makes different assumptions. Rising incomes in society generate demands for product diversity, while production processes exhibit increasing returns to scale (unit costs drop as output increases) and market entry requires substantial sunk costs; thus countries may engage in trade despite relatively similar factor endowments. Since increasing returns to scale (IRS) often occur because of substantial fixed costs, firms interested in engaging in intra-industry trade bear additional risks. As Gowa and Mansfield (2004, 780) note, "*Ex ante*, a firm has a wide array of alternative investment and production opportunities available to it. *Ex post*, however, the firm locks itself into a bilateral monopoly whenever its investment is to some degree 'specific to an export destination.'" The sunk costs associated with intra-industry trade make exporting firms especially vulnerable with regard to *ex post* attempts to renegotiate, thus weakening their incentive to export. While firms themselves may create mechanisms to deter opportunism on the part of other states, alliances between governments are argued to be especially desirable in this regard. Alliances reduce the risks associated with sunk costs in export production, since the income of both the exporting and importing state depends on the relationship. Government and firms have an interest in maintaining stability and peace under conditions of intra-industry trade.

Gowa and Mansfield (2004) thus argue that alliances will promote trade overall, but that due to this time inconsistency problem they will foster intra-industry trade to an even greater extent than inter-industry trade. They find statistical evidence to support these claims, though we take issue with the case selection and data. First, they limit their analyses to just major powers. While major power alliances are certainly important, they do not exhaust the range of alliance options. Second, they are not actually able to obtain data on intra-industry trade. Instead, they confine their analyses to major powers in the post–World War II era, simply assuming that the majority of their trade will be intra-industry in nature. While this is probably fairly accurate (see, for example, Milner 1999; Alt and others 1996), we now have better sources of data that will allow us to test directly claims about the relationship between allied relationships and intra-industry trade in a pool of all states. We also compare the expectations associated with the time inconsistency problem addressed by Gowa and Mansfield to the first mover advantage serving as an incentive for states to pursue trade with scale economies. Finally, we suspect that previous calls by Morrow, Siverson, and Tabares (1998) and Kastner (2007) to explore simultaneity are important, since trade may condition political relationships just as much as political relationships may condition trade.

Theory

We believe that Gowa and Mansfield (2004) have moved in the right direction to consider the composition of trade; however, we believe their logic distinguishing between intra- and inter-industry trade may be incomplete. Consideration of the simultaneous effects of trade on political relationships, plus the composition of trade, leads us to the following theory. Intra-industry trade is typically enabled by the existence of common factor endowments,[1] increasing returns to scale, and mutual development, which facilitates higher disposable incomes and preference for variety among consumers.[2] Intra-industry trade does not invoke security concerns because, by definition, domestic sources of imported commodities exit. If trade were terminated, states would lose only sources of variety. Simultaneously, trade is a source of cultural information, thus trade in similar, often branded products should promote intercultural understanding and a sense of common interests between states, in accordance with the expectations of the Kantian Peace (for example, Oneal and Russett 1997). For example, in the Untied States, imports of automobiles from Germany—including brands such as Volkswagen, Mercedes, and BMW—competing with domestic brands likely promotes interest and affinity among consumers for Germans in general, while these trade ties simultaneously provide economic ties that "encourage accommodation" over conflict (Oneal and Russett 1997, 269). The same pacifying effects would not necessarily accompany the import of oil from a state such as Saudi Arabia, given that (1) the oil does little to promote interest in or understanding of Saudi Arabian culture, and (2) concerns for strategic dependence might offset the pacifying effect associated with trade gains. Although oil from the Middle East may represent an extreme case, it illustrates a phenomenon accompanying inter-industry trade in general: the one-way flow of commodities (and particularly primary commodities) may not bestow positive cultural effects, and could potentially evoke concerns for strategic dependence. Accordingly, an increased proportion of intra-industry trade in the overall trading mix therefore should encourage the emergence of similar interests and preferences among trade partners over time as consumers and political leaders absorb the cultural information and economic gains provided by trade. In short, given that intra-industry trade promotes mutual economic gains from scale and common understanding but not vulnerability, it has a high likelihood of facilitating political similarity in general, as well as alliance formation specifically, among trading partners.

As pointed out in Chapter 1, the link between domestic politics and political outcomes is crucial, and yet depends on the relative complementarity of domestic interests between states. While the preceding discussion focuses on public opinion and state leaders' assessments of security interests, the link between intra-industry trade and alliance formation could be strongest following from its impact on domestic interests—particularly firms—in each trade partner. A higher proportion of intra-industry trade suggests the presence of mutual interests favoring maintenance (and expansion) of favorable trade relationships in order to maximize profit. Accordingly, a higher proportion of intra-industry trade could suggest conditions in which firms will lobby their respective governments for more similar policy, and for stronger ties up to and including the formation of alliances.

However, political affinity and alliance themselves do not necessarily promote intra-industry trade, because the lessened risk of vulnerability stemming from common interests may actually foster inter-industry trade.[3] For example, the United States imports a number of primary commodities—most notably oil—from Canada, a state with which it has many similar interests.[4] U.S. trade barriers against Canada historically have been low, and largely have been eliminated through mutual membership in free trade agreements beginning in 1989. Conversely, states may intervene to prevent imports of strategic commodities from—thereby preventing dependence on—trade partners with whom conflicts of interest tend to arise. For example, the United States recently (as of March 2012) announced the imposition of a tariff on solar panels originating from China, claiming that Chinese firms receive government subsidies that give them unfair advantage in the solar panel market (Joyce, 2012). This move aims to prevent U.S. solar panel manufacturers from being driven out of business by more competitive Chinese firms. Although the tariff results in a higher solar panel price for U.S. consumers in the short run, the lack of a response by the U.S. government could have resulted in the elimination of the U.S. solar industry, an outcome that would have left the United States dependent on, and therefore vulnerable to, China amidst growing energy needs and dwindling fossil fuels.

Although Gowa and Mansfield (2004) find that trade following primarily from increasing returns to scale is enabled by alliance and harmed by conflict, we contend that their findings could be due to reversed causation. While their logic that alliances can facilitate IRS trade that would otherwise face time inconsistency problems is sound, there are other factors that could offset this effect. For example, for two states having similar factor endowments and consumer preferences favoring the emergence of intra-industry trade, there is an incentive to facilitate such trade (primarily by removing trade barriers) because the productivity gains that would accompany participation in a larger market would render the states more productive relative to third parties. As discussed in Chapter 3, there is a first-mover advantage associated with such behavior: the first states to promote increased intra-industry trade will become relatively more productive than third parties. Accordingly, all states face incentives to find trade partners with whom to liberalize and promote trade. While the existence of an alliance might suggest a good trade partner, it is just as likely that the potential for expanded trade leads to the pursuit of a closer political relationship. Therefore, it is unclear that the correlation between political similarity and intra-industry trade implies causation from the former to the latter. Contrary to Gowa and Mansfield, the overall influence of alliances (and political affinity more generally) on intra-industry trade could be ambiguous when accounting for reverse causation. Two hypotheses follow from these observations:

Hypothesis 6.1: A higher proportion of intra-industry trade between states is associated with more similar foreign policy preferences.

Hypothesis 6.2: A higher proportion of intra-industry trade is associated with a higher probability of alliance formation and prevalence.

Research Design

To test our hypotheses connecting the composition of trade to political affinity, we use data spanning from 1962 to 2010. Our unit of analysis is the dyad year. We examine three dependent variables to capture political affinity. The first is *UN voting similarity*, a measure of how frequently dyadic states vote together in the UN General Assembly. This variable was developed by Gartzke (1998) and updated by Voeten, Strezhnev, and Bailey (2009). It is a continuous indicator that varies between–1 (perfect disagreement on General Assembly votes) and 1 (perfect agreement on General Assembly votes). We use the three-category variant of this affinity index.[5] Importantly, voting similarity is an imperfect measure of political affinity. The primary limitation of this measure is that it captures final agreement on an issue without specifying whether states' original interests were in harmony or whether one state coerced the other side into agreement. Indeed, states could be unaware of agreement on many issues that are considered trivial. Nonetheless, UN voting similarity serves as a rough proxy of revealed preference similarity within a dyad, which we expect to be conditioned by the composition of trade.

We also examine two additional dependent variables that address Hypothesis 6.2. First, we code *alliance prevalence*, a dichotomous variable equal to 1 in every year in which a dyad maintains a formal alliance (including the formation year). Second, we code *alliance formation*, a dichotomous variable equal to 1 in the year an alliance enters into force. Both of these variables are taken from the COW Formal Interstate Alliance Dataset (Gibler 2009). Looking at alliance formation and presence, we find that there are 500 dyad years in which an alliance is formed, relative to 35,137 total dyad years in which alliances are present.

Given the concern for bias due to reciprocal causation in models testing the impact of intra-industry trade on political affinity, we specify models in order to isolate whether intra-industry trade drives each of our affinity indicators amid potential for endogeneity. First, we use an error correction model (ECM) to address the relationship between intra-industry trade and UN voting similarity (see, for example, De Boef and Keele 2008).[6] The ECM allows us to examine how a shock to intra-industry trade influences change in UN voting in both the short and the long term. Accordingly, the dependent variable, UN voting similarity, is specified as a change from year $t-1$ to year t. In accordance with the error correction framework, we also include a lagged dependent variable (that is, UN voting similarly in year $t-1$).[7]

Given prior evidence that alliances enable intra-industry trade (Gowa and Mansfield 2004), we use simultaneous equations models to isolate the impact of intra-industry trade on alliance prevalence and formation from the reverse relationship. Specifically, we use the two-stage probit least squares model developed by Keshk (2003) to model simultaneous causation between one continuous and one dichotomous variable. The ECMs include fixed effects by dyad to account for unmodeled heterogeneity at the dyad level.[8] We specify alternative ECMs that in addition include year fixed effects to account for time-specific factors influencing agreement in the UN, for example, shocks to the international system such as the occurrence of a natural disaster or major war. In all ECMs we use robust standard errors to account for heteroskedasticity.[9] In our two-stage probit models examining alliance formation, we exclude all dyad years after the formation of an alliance given that subsequent formation of a second alliance is highly unlikely (although not absent in our data).

Primary Explanatory Variables

As in Chapters 3 through 5, our primary explanatory variable is the intra-industry trade index developed in Chapter 2, capturing the proportion of dyadic trade that flows within industries. In the ECMs, we include both the *change in intra-industry trade* (from year $t-1$ to year t) as well as the *lagged* indicator of intra-industry trade (that is, in year $t-1$). The change indicator captures the immediate impact of intra-industry trade on change in UN voting similarity. The lagged indicator, when divided by the lagged dependent variable, provides an estimate of the long-run multiplier—the total change in UN voting similarity given change in trade composition.

In alternative models, we include an interaction between intra-industry trade and a measure of trade level in order to address whether the influence of trade composition on political affinity depends on the extent of dyadic trade. Specifically, we include a measure of trade divided by the less wealthy state's GDP, as used in Chapters 3 through 5. Given the error correction framework, we include two indicators of *trade to GDP*: a *change* variable and a *lagged* variable. To specify the conditional relationship between trade composition and trade level, we include multiplicative interaction terms for *change in intra-industry trade X change in trade to GDP* as well as for *lagged intra-industry trade X lagged trade to GDP.*

Other Explanatory Variables

In our error correction models, we include additional explanatory variables to account for factors that could correlate with both trade composition and UN voting similarity. All explanatory variables are included in two forms: a change from year $t–1$ to year t, and a lagged indicator for year $t–1$. First, we account for regime type with a measure of the lower Polity combined score in the dyad, as well as a measure of the absolute difference in Polity combined scores across the dyad, using data from the Polity IV project (Marshall and Jaggers 2010). These variables together account for the fact that more democratic dyads trade more, whereas more divergent regime types could be associated with more frequent conflicts of interest. We also include variables for the lower (logged) GDP per capita in the dyad, as well as the difference between (logged) GDP per capita. We code these variables using data from the Penn World Table 8.0 (Feenstra, Inklaar, and Timmer 2013). Again, more developed states tend to trade more, all else equal. However, dyads with more divergent development levels could trade relatively more given that each state could have a distinct comparative advantage (for example, labor in the less developed state, and capitol in the more developed state). This economic complementarity would likely influence trade composition and could also influence conflicts of interest (although in ambiguous ways, as noted above and in Chapter 5).

In our two-stage probit least squares models, we include (some) different variables in each of the two equations. In the alliance prevalence or formation equations, we include variables for dyadic trade as a proportion of the less wealthy state's GDP—in other words, trade dependence. We include the lower Polity score and the lower (logged) GDP per capita, as well as the absolute difference between Polity scores. We calculate the log of the capability ratio, specifically the higher to the lower Composite Index of National Capabilities score within the dyad. In the alliance prevalence models, we include a lagged indicator for alliance prevalence, given the potential for time dependence. We include a dichotomous measure of contiguity to capture the increased prospects for interaction experienced by proximate states. In the alliance formation models, we include a dichotomous indicator of the Cold War, equal to 1 for years prior to 1989.

In the intra-industry trade equations, we include lower dependence, the lower Polity score, lower (logged) GDP per capita, and contiguity, as in the alliance equation. Unlike the alliance equation, we include a variable for the difference between states' GDP per capita, to capture the fact that different development levels likely correspond to comparative advantage rather than the presence of scale economies. Finally, we include a lagged indicator of intra-industry trade given potential for autocorrelation following from unmodeled factors that influence the composition of trade over time.

Analysis

UN Voting Similarity

We find strong support for our hypotheses in our error correction models examining UN voting similarity as well as in simultaneous models examining potential reciprocal causation between intra-industry trade and alliances. As in Chapters 3 through 5, we present the coefficients and standard errors of our statistical models in the appendix to this chapter, presenting figures and substantive interpretations of results here. We begin with a discussion of marginal effects, presented in Figure 6.1 (taken from Model 6.2, an error correction model that includes dyad and year fixed effects). The figure shows that the marginal effects for both *change in intra-industry trade* and *lagged intra-industry trade* are positive and significant. Conversely, the marginal effect for *lower trade to GDP* is not statistically significant at the 0.05 level.[10] These initial results suggest that the change in intra-industry trade has a positive impact on UN voting similarity immediately, and that it also leads to a long-run upward adjustment in voting similarity. However, short- and long-run impacts following from an error correction model must be interpreted using a combination of coefficients. The detailed discussion of the long-run multiplier is included in the appendix to Chapter 6. Here, we present estimates of the expected change in UN voting similarity over time following from an increase in the dyadic proportion of intra-industry trade from 0 to 1, using two separate examples.

From Model 6.1, a non-interactive specification, we find that, in the immediate aftermath of increasing intra-industry trade, UN voting similarity is expected to increase immediately by a very small amount (0.034, relative to a mean score of 0.61 and a standard deviation of 0.31).[11] However, after approximately one year, UN voting similarity increases by an additional 0.13, more than one-sixth of the mean value. The adjustment back to equilibrium contin-

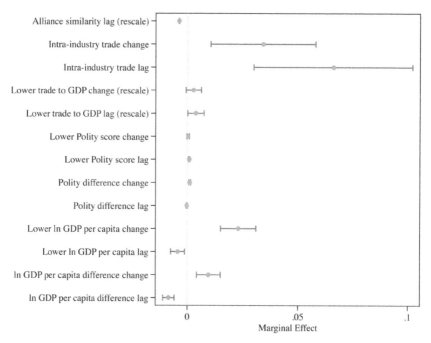

Figure 6.1   Marginal effects of explanatory variables on change in UN voting similarity, including 95 percent confidence bounds. From Model 6.1.

ues for several more years, with 50 percent of the total effect occurring after two years. After approximately six years, UN voting has increased by a total of approximately 0.25, nearly half of the mean value.

Similarly, using the results from Model 6.3, in which intra-industry trade is interacted with trade levels, we find that the increase in intra-industry trade proportion can have a much greater impact on UN voting if dyadic trade composes a larger share of each state's GDP (equal to 10 percent of the poorer state's total output). Under these conditions, an increase in intra-industry trade leads to an immediate 0.53 increase in the UN voting similarity score. After six years, UN voting similarity has increased by 0.75, more than two standard deviations in the UN voting similarity score (which is equal to 0.3).[12]

Alliance Prevalence and Onset

The results of simultaneous equations models suggest that intra-industry trade is associated with alliance prevalence, and with the onset of new alliances. The table of results is presented in the supplemental appendix to this chapter. However, the substantive results are substantial. We find that a 1 percent increase in intra-industry trade is associated with a 1 percent increase in the probability that the dyad maintains an alliance. The relationship between intra-industry trade and alliance formation is similar, with a 1 percent increase in intra-industry trade corresponding to a 1 percent increase in the probability that a new alliance is formed.

Given that we use simultaneous equations models, we also test for the possibility of reverse causation: that alliance leads to an increase in the proportion of trade following from intra-industry specialization. Previous research has found evidence that alliances foster an increase in intra-industry trade (Gowa and Mansfield 2004); our models confirm that the prevalence of alliance is associated with a higher proportion of intra-industry trade. However, our model examining the formation of alliances suggests that a new alliance is associated with a lower proportion of intra-industry trade. The idea that a new alliance might lead to a subsequent decrease in intra-industry trade as a proportion of dyadic trade could follow because new allies reduce trade barriers in industries wherein exposure to trade could render them vulnerable to trade partners; new allies might reduce protectionism that prohibits dependence following from inter-industry specialization. Overall, the results of our simultaneous equations models suggest support for our hypothesis that the direction of causation goes from intra-industry trade to alliance. The effect of alliance on trade composition is less clear, with contradictory findings given our two measures of alliance.

We can illustrate our findings more intuitively by examining the dyadic relationships between some of the central and eastern European states and major North Atlantic Treaty Organization (NATO) states prior to and after joining the multilateral alliance. Slovenia and Slovakia joined NATO in 2004, and Albania and Croatia joined in 2009. Their intra-industry trade with the United States, the United Kingdom, Germany, and France reveals a strikingly similar pattern: increases in the proportion of their intra-industry trade relative to total trade preceded their accession to NATO. Slovenia and Slovakia went from no intra-industry trade with the United States at the end of the Cold War to between 20 and 30 percent prior to joining NATO in 2004. Slovenia's intra-industry portion was even higher with its European neighbors, at nearly 40 percent with the United Kingdom, 50 percent with France, and 45 percent with Germany prior to joining NATO. Croatia at one point was over 30 percent in intra-industry trade with the United States, 15 percent with the United Kingdom, 15 percent with France, and 30 percent with Germany prior to joining in 2009.

Slovakia demonstrates the somewhat counterintuitive pattern in a few of its dyadic relationships with the NATO great powers, in which intra-industry trade increased to over 30 percent with the United Kingdom prior to joining, then dropped steadily over time to rest at around 13 percent in 2010. Its proportion of intra-industry trade also dropped with France after joining the alliance, from a high of nearly 40 percent to just under 30 percent in 2010. Yet, vis-à-vis Germany, its proportion was 45 percent at joining and went on to increase to well over 50 percent by 2010. Just why we see this variability even in one country's dyadic relationships is worthy of future research.

Albania presents another interesting case for analysis. Albania's proportions of intra-industry trade are much lower than those of Slovenia, Slovakia, or Croatia, but still demonstrated an increase to nearly 10 percent (from zero) with the United States and the United Kingdom, and nearly 20 percent with France prior to joining NATO in 2009. Albania's proportion of intra-industry trade with Germany was, however, relatively flat, hovering in the 2 to 3 percent range the entire time. Albania's case may offer some guidance to the current state of affairs regarding Ukraine and the NATO alliance. Ukraine's proportion of intra-industry trade is relatively low with the major NATO countries—the maximum proportion is around 15 percent with Germany in 2010, with most of the other dyads experiencing a proportion of somewhere between 5 and 10 percent over time. The societal interests that develop along with intra-industry trade may simply not be strong enough to overcome uncertainty among the NATO allies that comes with the relatively hostile security environment faced by Ukraine. Albania now is a relatively pacified and peaceful security environment, so increases in intra-industry trade even at a low level may have been enough for societal and governmental interests to work on behalf of NATO membership in 2009. The relatively low proportions present across time in independent Ukraine may simply represent a failure of the development of overlapping societal and governmental interests to press for NATO membership in the face of a threatening Russia (and one that ultimately intervenes in Ukraine after our data end).

Conclusion

In this chapter, we presented strong evidence that the composition of trade influences the degree to which states develop similar interests with trade partners. Preference similarity and even formal alliances are obviously a product of many factors, but, fundamentally, underlying societal views about other states must also figure into this decision. We argued theoretically that those views are shaped by the cultural information conveyed by different forms of trade. Over time trading relationships then become an important structural consideration for policymakers when developing political relationships between states, whether these are informal in terms of political similarity or formal alliances.

Empirically, the challenge in this chapter was to sort out the potentially endogenous relationship between the composition of trade and preference similarity and alliance decisions. The existing literature has often come to competing conclusions about the direction of the causal effect, but we believe our statistical modeling approaches have helped to overcome the methodological shortcomings in this literature that cloud our ability to observe the real underlying relationship. We are also able to sort out short- and long-term effects of intra-industry trade on preference similarity and alliances, which is also new to this literature. The evidence suggests we were correct on both counts. First, intra-industry trade is substantially associated with both the onset of new alliances and their prevalence. We also find evidence that the causal arrow also runs in the other direction, with the prevalence of alliances being associated with higher levels of intra-industry trade, though new alliance onsets actually reduce such trade (something observed in the Slovakian case discussed earlier). Second, intra-industry trade has a small, positive effect on preference similarity in the short run, though its longer-run effects are more dramatically positive. Higher overall levels of trade increase the short- and long-run effects of intra-industry trade even more.

Our findings have important implications for the literature connecting economic ties to political relationships—and particularly for studies tying trade to conflict. It is not just the extent of trade relationships that matters for states' propensity to cooperate, but also the composition of that trade. In this case, we have demonstrated that the proportion of dyadic intra-industry trade is central to the type of political relationship that emerges between states. A further finding from our work is that the political consequences of changing trade composition take time to manifest. Therefore, yearly variation in trade levels or composition may not be as useful of an indicator of conflict propensity as scholars typically hold it to be. This fact may be in part responsible for the considerable variation in findings by scholars examining a link between trade and conflict.

Appendix to Chapter 6

This appendix presents the results of our error correction models and simultaneous equations models. First, Table 6.1 presents coefficients and robust standard errors for Models 6.1 through 6.4, error-correction models assessing the short- and long-run association between intra-industry trade and UN voting similarity. Models 6.1 and 6.2 are additive specification, while Models 6.3 and 6.4 include an interaction of intra-industry trade and lower trade to GDP. Models 6.1 and 6.3 include dyad fixed effects, while Models 6.2 and 6.4 also include year fixed effects. As noted in the chapter text, the coefficients for change in intra-industry trade and lagged intra-industry trade are positive and significant in all four models. Models 6.1 and 6.2 are non-interactive specifications, in which the impact of intra-industry trade does not depend on the level at which we hold other variables. In the interactive models (6.3 and 6.4), these coefficients suggest that intra-industry trade has short- and long-run effects on UN voting similarity under the specific condition that lower trade to GDP is equal to o. We calculate the long-run multiplier and its standard error, as well as median and mean lag lengths in accordance with a strategy presented by De Boef and Keele (2008), specifically using a Bewley transformation of the ECM to estimate these values directly.[13] Our long-run multiplier for intra-industry trade is positive and significant in all four models. However, the long-run multiplier for the interaction term is significant only in Model 6.3, which excludes year fixed effects. In the interactive model, we calculated the short- and long-run effect of intra-industry trade following from the interaction holding lower trade to GDP at 10 percent (.1 in our data). The immediate impact of intra-industry trade is a linear combination of the coefficient for the change in intra-industry change and the change interaction term, specifically: $\beta_{\Delta \text{ Intra-industry trade proportion}} + .1^* \beta_{\Delta \text{ IIT X} \Delta \text{ Lower trade to GDP}}$. The long-run effect is similarly calculated as a linear combination of the long-run multipliers: $\beta_{\text{LRM Intra-industry trade proportion}} + .1^* \beta_{\text{LRM IIT X Lower trade to GDP}}$.

Next, we turn to the results of our two-stage least squares probit models, presented in Table 6.2. In Model 6.5, we find that both alliance and intra-industry trade have positive and significant coefficients, suggesting a mutu-

Table 6.1 Error correction model coefficients and robust standard errors for models assessing the short- and long-term effect of change in intra-industry trade on change in UN voting similarity.

	Model 6.1	Model 6.2	Model 6.3	Model 6.4
UN voting similarity $_{t-1}$	−0.388***	−0.374***	−0.388***	−0.374***
	(0.005)	(0.006)	(0.005)	(0.006)
Δ Intra-industry trade proportion	0.034**	0.026*	0.033**	0.025*
	(0.012)	(0.012)	(0.012)	(0.012)
Intra-industry trade proportion $_{t-1}$	0.066***	0.063***	0.064***	0.061***
	(0.018)	(0.018)	(0.019)	(0.018)
Δ Lower trade to GDP	0.271	0.176	0.224	0.130
	(0.177)	(0.143)	(0.171)	(0.136)
Lower trade to GDP $_{t-1}$	0.374*	0.304	0.312	0.242
	(0.187)	(0.170)	(0.174)	(0.157)
Δ IIT X Δ lower trade/GDP			2.913*	5.120*
			(1.407)	(2.323)
IIT $_{t-1}$ X lower trade/GDP $_{t-1}$			0.581	0.577
			(0.810)	(0.801)
Δ Lower Polity score	0.000	−0.000	0.000	−0.000
	(0.000)	(0.000)	(0.000)	(0.000)
Lower Polity score $_{t-1}$	0.001***	0.001***	0.001***	0.001***
	(0.000)	(0.000)	(0.000)	(0.000)
Δ Polity difference	0.001***	0.001***	0.001***	0.001***
	(0.000)	(0.000)	(0.000)	(0.000)
Polity difference $_{t-1}$	−0.000*	−0.000*	−0.000*	−0.000*
	(0.000)	(0.000)	(0.000)	(0.000)
Δ Lower ln GDPpc	0.023***	0.011**	0.023***	0.011**
	(0.004)	(0.004)	(0.004)	(0.004)
Lower ln GDPpc $_{t-1}$	−0.004**	−0.008***	−0.004**	−0.008***
	(0.002)	(0.002)	(0.002)	(0.002)
Δ GDPpc difference	0.010***	−0.005	0.010***	−0.005
	(0.003)	(0.002)	(0.003)	(0.002)
GDPpc difference $_{t-1}$	−0.008***	−0.016***	−0.009***	−0.016***
	(0.001)	(0.001)	(0.001)	(0.001)
Constant	0.265***	0.355***	0.265***	0.355***
	(0.006)	(0.008)	(0.006)	(0.008)

continued

Table 6.1   Error correction model coefficients and robust standard errors for models assessing the short- and long-term effect of change in intra-industry trade on change in UN voting similarity. (*continued*)

	Model 6.1	Model 6.2	Model 6.3	Model 6.4
Long-run multiplier: Intra-industry trade proportion	0.170***	0.168***	0.163***	0.164***
	(0.018)	(0.018)	(0.019)	(0.018)
Long-run multiplier: IIT X lower trade to GDP			1.699*	1.071
			(0.857)	(0.805)
Observations	298,420	298,420	298,420	298,420
Number of dyads	14,561	14,561	14,561	14,561
Dyad fixed effects	Yes	Yes	Yes	Yes
Year fixed effects	No	Yes	No	Yes
R^2	0.205	0.325	0.205	0.325
F test	575.9***	486.7***	500.0***	471.5***

Notes: Robust standard errors in parentheses.
*** $p < 0.001$, ** $p < 0.01$, * $p < 0.05$; two–tailed tests.
DV = Δ UN voting similarity.

ally reinforcing relationship. Conversely, in Model 6.6, alliance formation has a negative and significant coefficient, while the coefficient for intra-industry trade remains positive and significant. Again, these results suggest that, although alliances and intra-industry trade might be mutually reinforcing once alliances are formed, intra-industry trade has a robust alliance-promoting impact.

Table 6.2 Two-stage least squares probit models assessing simultaneous causation between intra-industry trade and alliance.

	Model 6.5		Model 6.6	
	IIT Proportion	*Alliance Presence*	*IIT Proportion*	*Alliance Formation*
Alliance prevalence	0.000***			
	(0.000)			
Alliance formation			−0.002***	
			(0.000)	
Intra-industry trade proportion		1.186***		1.257***
		(0.189)		(0.226)
Alliance prevalence $_{t-1}$		5.282***		
		(0.029)		
Intra-industry trade $_{t-1}$	0.893***		0.887***	
	(0.001)		(0.001)	
Cold War				0.084*
				(0.033)
Lower trade to GDP	0.693***	−3.679	0.651***	−10.274*
	(0.014)	(2.843)	(0.018)	(4.279)
Lower Polity score	0.000***	−0.004	0.000***	−0.006*
	(0.000)	(0.002)	(0.000)	(0.003)
Lower ln GDP pc	0.002***	0.015	0.001***	−0.018
	(0.000)	(0.013)	(0.000)	(0.015)
Contiguity	0.005***	0.559***	0.009***	0.808***
	(0.000)	(0.044)	(0.000)	(0.043)
ln GDP pc difference	0.001***		0.000**	
	(0.000)		(0.000)	
Polity difference		−0.025***		−0.030***
		(0.003)		(0.003)
ln Capability ratio		0.022***		0.009
		(0.006)		(0.007)
Constant	−0.003***	−2.954***	−0.009***	−2.862***
	(0.000)	(0.046)	(0.001)	(0.055)
Observations	294,303	294,303	266,574	266,574
R^2	0.830		0.802	
χ^2		176845***		540.5***

Notes: Standard errors in parentheses.
*** $p < 0.001$, ** $p < 0.01$, * $p < 0.05$; two–tailed tests.

Part IV

Conclusion

Chapter 7

Conclusion

OUR main objective in writing this book has been to convince scholars of the global political economy that they are laboring under outdated theoretical arguments about trade that have been unthinkingly smuggled into our explanations of political outcomes. The Ricardian approach to trade theory based on specialization and comparative advantage is the norm, despite the fact that the composition of global trade has changed dramatically over the course of the past half-century. Thus, as scholars of global political economy, they are using nineteenth century theorizing for twenty-first century outcomes. Stated that bluntly, it either seems quite natural to those with realist inclinations rooted in *realpolitik,* or those with classical liberal leanings, yet it undoubtedly strikes a chord with those whose interests were piqued with the complex interdependence literature of the late 1970s, the neoliberal institutionalists of the 1980s and 1990s, and the varied developments in the interdependence and conflict and institutional design literatures of the 2000s and beyond. Theories and empirical approaches to the effect of trade on a variety of cooperative and conflictual political outcomes are due for a renovation. We hope that the work in this book will be taken in the spirit of offering the chance for renewal in any number of literatures in which trade is an important element.

Theoretically, we have attempted to make the case that a higher proportion of intra-industry trade will change the decision-making calculus of groups within society as well as governments. We suggested that the characteristics of this type of trade, such as increasing returns due to economies of scale and the consumer demand for variety, increase the leverage of forces pushing for trade liberalization. In particular, we suggested that this is especially true of preferential liberalization under PTAs, though we are more agnostic about multilateral liberalization. Governments that choose to pursue PTAs for a variety of reasons, including potential lobbying from pro-liberalizing groups, should meet less resistance in economies characterized by higher proportions of intra-industry trade. On the security side of the global political economy, we argued that dyads characterized by higher proportions of intra-industry trade should be less vulnerable to disruptions in trade; thus a traditional source of vulnerability associated with inter-industry trade is greatly ameliorated. Such dyads should therefore engage in fewer militarized disputes and be more likely to have higher degrees of political affinity.

Empirically, we outlined a way of conceptualizing and operationalizing intra-industry trade that we think is useful for most of the topics that scholars of the global political economy might investigate. This required tackling three issues: the level of product-level aggregation, horizontal and vertical intra-industry trade, and the appropriate level of analysis. We suggested that each of these decisions carries implications for empirical analyses. Our primary concern was that we develop a measure that would capture consumer substitutability of commodities; thus we defined an industry as a group of trade goods that could generally be considered substitutes by consumers (that is, individuals or firms). The level of aggregation chosen would thus need to ensure that we were picking up on primarily horizontal rather than vertical intra-industry trade. We suggested that the SITC 4-digit level was sufficient for these purposes. Our concern was that, in many, although not all, cases, vertical intra-industry trade looks much like inter-industry trade on the basis of comparative advantage due to differing factor endowments between economies. Capturing the horizontal part of intra-industry trade allows a focus on trade between economies with relatively similar factor endowments, thus reducing the likelihood of lobbying for protection and security vulnerabilities. Finally, we suggested that the dyadic, rather than the state level of analysis is appropriate for most analyses. This allows us to identify complementary interests in a pair of states that may push for liberalization or maintain relatively peaceful interstate relations. These choices allowed us to develop a dataset covering 190 states from 1962 through 2010 using the Grubel and Lloyd measure of intra-industry trade.

The aforementioned theoretical and empirical innovations were then developed further in the subsequent four empirical chapters. The first two chapters were devoted to understanding the implications of intra-industry trade for cooperation in international institutional outcomes. Chapter 3, on

PTA formation, revisits the classical argument that higher intra-industry trade reduces barriers to liberalization, which has been challenged in recent years. We argued that intra-industry trade is associated with preferential liberalization, even as its effects on multilateral liberalization may be unclear. This is in part because PTA formation is a competitive process; thus firms face incentives to join a PTA in order to gain a productivity advantage or to avoid falling behind firms in other states that join PTAs. Firms will enjoy the economies of scale presented by the enlarged market, and are unlikely to be driven out of business since trade partners are not specializing according to comparative advantage. The presence of third-party PTAs is critical to ensuring PTA formation, since even relatively uncompetitive firms within a bilateral PTA will gain from the enlarged market.

Our two hypotheses from this chapter were

Hypothesis 3.1: A higher proportion of intra-industry trade between states is associated with a higher likelihood of PTA formation.

Hypothesis 3.2: The magnitude of the association between intra-industry trade and PTA formation is weakest when there are no third-party PTAs in force, becoming larger as the number of third-party PTAs in force increases.

Both hypotheses receive support in the analysis. Intra-industry trade has a strong substantive effect on the formation of PTAs. Further, it has an even stronger impact on agreements with deeper levels of integration. The conditional effect of third-party PTAs on the relationship between intra-industry trade and PTA formation is also confirmed, though its substantive effect is more modest. Given our sense that even the threat of third-party PTA formation is enough to drive PTA formation, it may not be surprising that the actual number of third-party PTAs has only a modest conditional impact.

The effects of intra-industry trade on dispute initiations under the WTO's DSP were examined in Chapter 4. Unlike in other chapters in this book, trade itself is the subject of conflict. Thus we argue that the composition of trade on dispute initiation will matter most when trade flows are high. When trade flows are low, we do not expect much in the way of dispute initiation in a dyad. Given that intra-industry trade consists of similar, often branded products, we expect that it is occurring in a relatively high-velocity business environment. We expect, similarly to the rest of the literature, that firms in these environments are more likely to pursue bilateral talks between governments or make use of WTO committees or PTA fora, rather than engage in the more long-term, costly WTO DSP. Our two hypotheses from this chapter were

Hypothesis 4.1: A higher proportion of intra-industry trade between states is associated with a lesser likelihood of WTO dispute onset. The magnitude of the association between intra-industry trade and WTO dispute onset is weakest when dyadic trade flows are small, becoming larger as dyadic trade flows increase.

Hypothesis 4.2: A higher level of dyadic trade is associated with a higher probability of WTO dispute onset in the absence of intra-industry trade. The magnitude of this relationship diminishes as intra-industry trade increases as a proportion of total trade.

Our analysis was restricted to the years 1995–2009, since the WTO DSP began to operate in 1995. Our hypotheses received support from the data analysis. We find that higher trade levels leads to an increased probability that a trade dispute is filed between two states. This effect is especially pronounced when the proportion of trade in a dyad is inter-industry. As the proportion of intra-industry trade increases, the probability of filing a trade dispute is reduced. Further, when the proportion of intra-industry trade exceeds 50 percent, an increase in trade is actually associated with a decline in the number of disputes filed.

Our next two substantive chapters dealt with aspects of conflict in relationships found in the global political economy. Chapter 5 examined how intra-industry trade affects the onset of militarized disputes between countries. We argued that intra-industry trade is pacifying, while liberalization may have countervailing effects on the stability of peace between countries. Intra-industry trade provides mutual gains to trading partners but does not produce dependence or vulnerability between them. If trade were to terminate, then firms within states could easily adjust by increasing domestic production to replace foreign products. As a result, the incentives for coercion decrease as intra-industry trade increases. Liberalization might induce intra- or inter-industry trade, producing crosscutting effects on militarization of disputes. Finally, development is often entangled with intra-industry trade, but we suggested that development alone could have either positive or negative effects on conflict; only in combination with intra-industry trade is it pacifying. Our two hypotheses from this chapter were

Hypothesis 5.1: A higher proportion of intra-industry trade between states is associated with a lesser likelihood of the onset of a militarized dispute, irrespective of the extent of trade or liberalization.

Hypothesis 5.2: Mutual development is not associated with the likelihood of the onset of a militarized dispute when intra-industry trade is low; however, this association becomes increasingly negative and significant as intra-industry trade is held at higher values.

Both hypotheses are supported by the data analysis. A higher proportion of intra-industry trade reduces the likelihood of militarized disputes, regardless of the extent of trade and liberalization. There is some evidence that development is not pacifying on its own (or is even aggravating), though in combination with intra-industry trade it becomes pacifying.

Finally, Chapter 6 examined the relationship between intra-industry trade and preference similarity as well as decisions to ally. Once again, we argued that the lack of security concerns that accompany intra-industry trade, combined with the cultural information and economic gains such trade provides, should lead to similar preferences between states. It should also mean that such states are more likely to ally. Importantly, we argued that political affinity and alliances themselves do not necessarily promote intra-industry trade, suggesting that the alliance literature may indeed suffer from reverse causation. Our hypotheses from this chapter were

Hypothesis 6.1: A higher proportion of intra-industry trade between states is associated with more similar foreign policy preferences.

Hypothesis 6.2: A higher proportion of intra-industry trade is associated with a higher probability of alliance formation and prevalence.

Our hypotheses receive confirmation in the analysis. Both the proportion of and increase in intra-industry trade are associated with high political affinity as measured by UN voting preferences. A higher proportion of intra-industry trade was also associated with alliance prevalence, and with the onset of new alliances. In examining the possibility of reverse causation, we also found that the prevalence of alliances produced a higher proportion of intra-industry trade, though the onset of an alliance is associated with a lower proportion of intra-industry trade. These mixed results lead us to suggest that the main effect is from intra-industry trade to alliance.

Overall, we think our theoretical rationale underpinning the effect of intra-industry trade on both institutionalized cooperation and militarized conflict held up well. The specific hypotheses we derived from our theoretical framework also received support in the empirical analyses. In all cases, we dealt with possible confounding factors, as well as endogeneity questions that were pertinent. We are therefore confident that intra-industry trade is shaping the global political economy in ways that we were heretofore unaware of in the absence of this combination of theorizing and empirical analyses. We wish to conclude this book with a discussion of the role that intra-industry trade could be playing in a few key relationships in the global political economy, followed by some suggestions for how intra-industry trade may be an important yet unexamined factor in a variety of other literatures.

Applications to Key Relationships

Social scientists can be skittish about predictions or forecasts of future behavior. While we cannot predict with precision when a conflict will occur between two states, or when they might choose to ally, whether they will form a PTA or file a trade dispute with the WTO, we can examine a few key relationships in the global political economy to shed some light on general tendencies in these areas.

The United States and China in the Global Political Economy

The future of the relationship between the United States and China is one of the most important for scholars to study, given the likely rise of China as an economic and military power rivaling the United States. Our theory can be applied to understand some pressures toward U.S.-China cooperation or conflict in the future. The trend we see is generally positive: while the United States and China engaged in no intra-industry trade before 1987, the proportion of U.S.-China two-way trade of similar commodities increased to approximately 17 percent of total trade by 2000. Interestingly, China's ascension to the World Trade Organization correlates with a brief decline in intra-industry trade, although its share of total trade appears to have recovered to approximately 16.8 percent by 2010. The solid line in Figure 7.1 highlights this trend. Given our analyses in Chapters 3 through 6, at the current proportion of intra-industry trade, we predict that the United States and China are relatively likely to cooperate, with a greater than average probability of forming a PTA

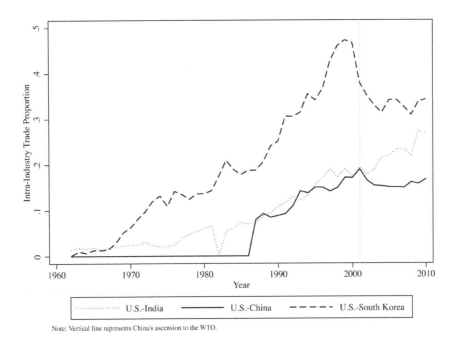

Figure 7.1   Intra-industry proportion over time for the U.S.-China, U.S.-South Korea, and U.S.-India dyads.

(all else equal) and a low probability of initiating militarized conflict. Interestingly, however, contemporary U.S.-China levels of intra-industry trade are low enough that an increase in trade flows overall is still predicted to lead to an increase in the frequency of WTO disputes—a model prediction that is supported in our data.

From the perspective of the United States, the economic relationship with China is perhaps most enlightening when viewed with respect to U.S. relationships with comparable states. Accordingly, we also graph the proportion of U.S.-India and U.S.-South Korea intra-industry trade over time. India and South Korea were chosen given the sizes of their economies (generally large for continental East and South Asia) and their geographical proximity to China. However, some other factors suggest that these states are similar to China. Like China during the Cold War, India maintained a somewhat rocky relationship with the United States, particularly after the assassination of President Kennedy, as it appeared to align itself with the Soviet Union. U.S. relations with India and China alike warmed toward the end of and after the Cold War.

Nonetheless, the United States and India maintained a greater proportion of intra-industry trade than did the United States and China in almost every time point between 1962 and 2010. The dotted line in Figure 7.1 illustrates this pattern. Most notably, the years since 2001 (when China joined the WTO) have seen an increase in the gap between India's and China's intra-industry trade proportion with the United States. In 2010, nearly 30 percent of U.S.-India trade is composed of two-way trade of similar commodities. This trend suggests that there will be relatively more pressure by interests in India and the United States to pursue cooperation. If U.S.-India trade continues to evolve toward increasing intra-industry specialization, we could see the formation of a preferential trade agreement or alliance—possibly one that excludes China.

South Korea is relatively similar to China in terms of geography, while historically it has assimilated some Chinese culture during periods in which China was dominant in East Asia. The post–World War II period led to considerable political and economic divergence between China and South Korea, although recent years arguably have seen more economic convergence as Chinese economic policy has moved toward a market orientation. Interestingly, while the United States and South Korea have experienced a greater proportion of intra-industry trade than have the United States and China at all time points, the relative disparity appears to have declined over time. This convergence is largely explained by the fact that U.S.-South Korean intra-industry trade hit a maximum of nearly 50 percent in 1998, after which it has fallen to approximately 35 percent. The dashed line in Figure 7.1 illustrates this trend. Given considerable difference in U.S. political orientations with each of these two states (formal alliance with South Korea versus an icy, yet thawing over time, relationship with China), differences in trade composition could be at least in part a consequence rather than a cause of political affinity. Nonetheless, relatively high proportions of intra-industry trade suggest considerable pressure toward cooperation between the United States and South Korea. Although outside the scope of our data, which end in 2010, a free trade area between the United States and South Korea entered into force in 2012—an event our models would predict. The formal alliance between these states also remains in effect. Given South Korea's higher level of intra-industry trade with the United States relative to China's, we would expect fewer WTO disputes for a given level of trade between these states. Notably, between 2002 and 2010, our data show that South Korea has filed four complaints against the United

States, while China has filed six. The United States has filed no complaints against South Korea during this time period, while filing eleven complaints against China.

Given our emphasis that intra-industry trade creates complementary incentives for cooperation to gain an advantage against third parties, we can potentially gain insight into possible economic and political blocs that could form in the future by examining with whom the United States and China engage in the most intra-industry trade. Indeed, if there were considerable overlap in intra-industry trade partners, we might expect these indirect ties also to facilitate cooperation (see, for example, Dorussen and Ward 2010). Taking data from 2010, we find that there are forty-one states with which the United States maintains higher intra-industry trade than it does with China (with a mean proportion of 35 percent). Conversely, China has twenty-one trade partners with which it maintains intra-industry trade greater than that with the United States (with a mean proportion of 26 percent). Nineteen of these twenty-one states also maintain greater intra-industry trade with the United States, leaving China only two states with which it uniquely maintains higher intra-industry trade (Ireland and Zimbabwe). These findings suggest that the United States has more opportunity to form cooperative agreements, potentially to the extent that it could seek to isolate or gain an economic advantage over China. Overall, trends between the United States and China suggest increasing opportunity for cooperation. Yet the United States maintains an advantage in terms of trade partners with high levels of intra-industry trade.

Brazil's Rise and the Latin American Regional Political Economy

The emergence of Brazil as a regional leader and potential contender for great-power status has begun to occupy a fair amount of scholarly attention (for example, Malamud, 2011; Wehner, forthcoming). As one of the BRICs (Brazil, Russia, India, China, and sometimes South Africa), Brazil's emergence is seen as emblematic of the rise of regional powers to global power status. However, the relationship between economic power and military power has always troubled theorists of great-power rise and decline. Much as with the aforementioned U.S.-China example, we can consider how Brazil's rise as an economic and military power has shaped and been shaped by the South American region. Argentina and Brazil have long been considered historic rivals for leadership in the Southern Cone. Their rivalry reached an apex in the 1980s as both countries secretly engaged in nuclear weapons development programs; however, in 1991, both countries formally renounced their nuclear rivalry by signing the Quadripartite Agreement that established the Brazilian-Argentine Agency for Accounting and Control of Nuclear Materials and opened both countries to International Atomic Energy Agency inspections. Chile was also a historic rival to Argentina, with many militarized confrontations (perhaps the most of any South American rivalry) spanning large parts of the late nineteenth and mid-twentieth centuries, only coming to a close after the Malvinas-Falkland Islands war with the United Kingdom and democratization in Argentina (Thies, 2001). Chile is now seen as a state that plays a role of a regional supporter to Brazil (Wehner, forthcoming). Our theory can be applied to understand some pressures toward Argentine-Brazilian cooperation or conflict in the future.

The trend we see is generally quite positive. During the height of the rivalry in the 1970s and 1980s, only 10 to 20 percent of Argentine-Brazilian trade was intra-industry. Intra-industry trade began to expand between the two toward the end of the 1980s, and by the formal end of the nuclear rivalry was at 30 percent of total trade between the two countries. Since the two countries have been members of a military alliance, the Inter-American Treaty of Reciprocal Assistance, or "Rio Pact," since 1947, we cannot directly assess the relationship between intra-industry trade and alliance decisions. However, it does appear that the growth of intra-industry trade preceded the end of the rivalry between the two states in 1991. The trend in the growing proportion of intra-industry trade between Argentina and Brazil was also solidified with the signing of the 1985 Argentina-Brazil Integration and Economics Cooperation Program. This agreement laid the groundwork for the official formation of Mercosur in 1991. Our analysis of intra-industry trade and PTAs is certainly suggestive for this originally bilateral agreement between Argentina and Brazil, which has expanded to take on new members and associate members and deepen cooperation over time. Intra-industry trade between the two has expanded, with minor setbacks, such as that generated by the Argentine "great depression" of 1998–2002, to the point at which nearly half of all trade is intra-industry. It is notable that Argentina and Brazil have only had three official WTO disputes—two of which occurred during the height of Argentina's great depression and currency crisis in 2000 and 2001 when there was a temporary decline in the overall upward trend of intra-industry trade. Our expectations for Argentina and Brazil suggest that the high proportion of intra-industry trade between the two is likely to continue to encourage cooperation in both the security and economic realms, which will likely contribute to a peaceful rise of Brazil as a regional hegemon and potential global power.

The increase in cooperation stemming from the growth of intra-industry trade between Argentina and Brazil also stands in stark contrast to the relationships that Argentina and Brazil have with Chile. The economic relationship between Brazil and Chile is dominated by inter-industry trade, which has steadily composed 90 percent or more of total trade. The overall amount of trade between the two countries is relatively small compared to their major trading partners, though it has grown recently. It is perhaps unsurprising from our perspective that Chile has never become more than an associate member of Mercosur, instead rebranding itself as an "Asia-Pacific" country to join APEC in 1994. Chile's goal in joining APEC was to serve as an entry-point for Asian goods into the South American market (Wehner and Thies, 2014). Similarly, Chile is also a member of the Pacific Alliance, forged between Mexico, Chile, Colombia, and Peru for export-oriented trading states. Many of Chile's early PTAs were negotiated outside of Latin America. Brazil and Chile have never engaged in a formal WTO dispute, likely due to the small amount of trade that occurs between the two countries. Both are already members of the Rio Pact military alliance as well, yet the formation of several other regional alliances has produced some element of competition between the two. Chile has taken an active role in UNASUR (Union of South American Nations), formed in 2008 to handle issues of regional security, as a way of containing what it sees as a Brazilian-dominated institution. The exclusion of Brazil from the Pacific Alliance is also seen as a way of Chilean "soft-balancing" that has created some distance between the two countries (Wehner, forthcoming). Overall, the relative lack of intra-industry trade has meant the general lack of institutionalized economic cooperation between Chile and Brazil, and perhaps introduced an element of competitive institution building. Similarly, the lack of intra-industry trade has not completely stymied cooperation on the security front, yet Chile does seem to try to check Brazilian influence through participation in multilateral alliances.

The relationship between Chile and Argentina provides another view of this triangular relationship in the Southern Cone. The proportion of intra-industry trade between the two countries historically has been small (less than 10 percent), as has the overall amount of trade between the two countries. Intra-industry trade began to pick up in the early 1980s prior to the end of the historic rivalry between the two (who are also both members of the Rio Pact). Intra-industry trade's proportion jumped in 1991 to nearly 20 percent, but again suffered from Argentina's great depression, plummeting to about 5 percent by 2001. As we know, the low level of intra-industry trade likely prevented Chile from becoming more than an associate member of Mercosur, and its PTA emphasis would be focused more on countries bordering the Pacific Ocean. Argentina and Chile have had seven formal WTO disputes starting in 2000, as the proportion of intra-industry trade between the two was nearing 5 percent. Intra-industry trade has grown since then, but it was still around 10 percent by 2010. The very low proportion of intra-industry trade in the 1960–1985 era is associated with the historic rivalry and many militarized interstate disputes between the two countries. The return to historic lows in the proportion of intra-industry trade is somewhat worrying given the hypothesized effects we believe it has on cooperation and conflict, but we also recognize that many factors are at work in this and other interstate dyads.

Our South American triangle of relationships is suggestive of the future of cooperation and conflict in the cone. First, we expect that the Argentina-Brazilian relationship should continue to be one of cooperation on both the economic and security fronts. Intra-industry trade constitutes nearly half of all trade between the two countries today. Given our arguments and evidence that such trade is pacifying militarily and institution-promoting in the economic realm, we view the Argentine-Brazilian relationship as central to the way in which Brazil's rise as a regional leader is managed in the region. We of course recognize lingering historical animosity that leads Argentina to see itself as a "soft-balancer" to Brazil's regional leadership, as well as its sense of a "competitive partnership" with Brazil (Wehner, forthcoming). Yet we suggest that the societal forces underlying the growth in intra-industry trade will likely overcome such animosity over time. Second, Chile's general support of Brazil as a regional leader and lack of economic or security conflict are likely a result of Chile's purposeful orientation toward the Pacific and trading partners outside of the region. Despite very low levels of intra-industry trade in the Brazil-Chile dyad, this relationship is unlikely to become overly competitive economically or conflictual militarily. Third, the Argentine-Chilean relationship will never serve as a true counterweight to Brazil's rise despite desires and attempts to soft-balance by both states. The basis for cooperation that we see emerging from societal forces attached to intra-industry trade simply is not present in this relationship. Overall, we suggest that Brazil's rise and regional leadership should be accomplished in a relatively peaceful fashion.

Directions for Future Research

Given the novelty of our arguments about trade composition and international political outcomes, there are really many directions for future research. In the conflict literature, we have already examined how trade composition affects political affinity, alliance, and militarized disputes. Yet we could probe in more detail the effect of intra-industry trade on war. If McDonald and Sweeney (2007) are correct, then specialization according to comparative advantage during the nineteenth century made the desire for and possibility of carrying out great-power war possible. Could the seeming decline of great-power war (Mueller 1989) in part be traceable to the shift from inter-industry to intra-industry trade between the most powerful states in the system? This argument poses a strong alternative hypothesis to the notion that institution building within the European Union helped to forge a lasting peace between France and Germany. It is also an alternative hypothesis to the notion that the heavy hand played by the United States as a hegemon or the establishment of NATO were ways to bind the military forces of Western Europe together to preserve peace. One might also read postwar history as the U.S. hegemon instilling its liberal values through the Bretton Woods system, which provided opportunities for intra-industry trade to expand via the GATT and the WTO. While the institutions themselves are often credited with providing cooperation in the absence of a hegemon or after hegemonic decline (Keohane 1984), it could very well be that the solidification of that cooperation came as trade expanded and shifted in composition among the more powerful members of the system. The effect of the Cold War and bipolarity on peace within the West may also have diminished over time as intra-industry trade increased.

Alongside changes in great-power war propensity, and polarity or polarization in the international system in the postwar era, we also saw waves of democratization (Huntington 1991). The scholarly focus shifted to the role of democracy in pacifying dyadic relationships. The democratic peace, as it came to be known, later evolved into the notion of a Kantian peace supported by joint democracy, trade interdependence, and membership in intergovernmental organizations. The trade interdependence piece of this argument still relies on a notion of trade as specialization according to comparative advantage. This is somewhat odd given the Keohane and Nye (1977) arguments about vulnerability and sensitivity to changes in trade. While some early studies found evidence that trade openness and other measures such as asymmetry were not associated with pacific relations (Barbieri 1996), most of the literature on trade interdependence has concluded that trade helps to produce peace. Our own work has suggested that the peaceful parts of trade are the intra-industry portions. While this argument and empirical finding is relatively new, it should become a more standard feature of analyses when conflict short of war (for example, MIDs) is the dependent variable.

Building on the early work of Karl Deutsch (1957) and the identification of pluralistic security communities, a body of work on regional variation in conflict and peace has developed in the aftermath of the Cold War. Buzan and Waever (2003) identify regional security complexes that are based on their geographic boundaries, polarity, and patterns of amity and enmity among members. A regional security complex may be categorized as a conflict formation, security regime, or security community in large part on the basis of the patterns of amity and enmity. Kacowicz (1998) similarly talks about zones of peace ranging from a zone of conflict to a zone of negative peace to a zone of positive or stable peace. Trade interdependence is seen as a positive force generating patterns of amity in these and other approaches (for example, Miller, 2005; Ripsman, 2005). Yet the findings are somewhat mixed in this regard. Thies (2008; 2010) finds that dyadic interdependence increases the likelihood of rivalry in Latin America and West Africa, the two regions analyzed by Kacowicz. In these regional cases, was the composition of trade largely inter-industry? Might trade composition be a useful way to help identify the variation in zone of peace or conflict that a region occupies, with more pacific regions being dominated by intra-industry trade?

Further, what is the relationship between trade composition and democracy? Rogowski's seminal contributions (1989) might be usefully reanalyzed considering the distinction between intra- and inter-industry trade. While historically most states analyzed in his *Commerce and Coalitions* opened up to trade under conditions of inter-industry trade, thus generating the factor- or class-based divisions within society that Rogowski expected, this may no longer be the case. It might be useful to examine how new states, perhaps those of post–Cold War Central and Eastern Europe or the Balkan states, adjusted to trading relationships with Europe. To the extent that the opening to trade was of the intra-industry variety, what kinds of coalitions formed within those new countries? Rogowski (1987) also suggested that trade could itself condition the kinds of democratic political institutions we observe within countries. Rogowski argues that democratic states can achieve autonomy through strong parties, especially through proportional representation electoral systems. States can achieve insulation from interest group pressure through the use of large electoral systems. Finally, stability is best achieved through proportional representation, large districts, and a parliamentary system (rather than a presidential system). Can we see differences in the institutional composition of new democratic states that are exposed to primarily intra- versus inter-industry trade? Do the purported functions of existing institutional arrangements continue to work in older states that initially opened up to inter-industry trade but are now faced with primarily intra-industry trade?

While most of the literature continues to think of both the demand for and supply of trade in terms of inter-industry trade and the potential cleavages it creates within society, this book has suggested that such traditional divisions may not be relevant when intra-industry trade becomes more prevalent. For example, import competitors may not always be opposed to trade liberalization, especially since they can benefit from economies of scale and consumer tastes for variety in foreign markets. In terms of demand, we should also examine how trade composition intersects with geographic concentration and other factors that promote organization to demand protectionism. Given that intra-industry trade often comprises branded goods, the focus on trade composition should also shift the literature's attention to consumers and groups within society that organize for liberalized trade (see, for example, Rogowski and Kayser, 2002). In addition, a focus on intra-industry trade may force us to reconsider the supply of protectionism as well.

The literature on the design of international institutions, especially those of an economic nature, might consider how trade composition affects some of the key dependent variables they identify. Koremenos, Lipson, and Snidal (2001) consider membership, scope, centralization, control, and flexibility in institutional design. Are there differences in the design of an institution that might be focused on members with a high proportion of intra-industry trade versus one that is focused on inter-industry trade or a mix of the two?

Might states engaging in a higher proportion of intra-industry trade take more advantage of escape clauses (a form of adaptive flexibility) rather than pursue the DSP of the WTO (for example, Pelc, 2009). The design of PTAs might be a particularly fruitful area within which to investigate the effect of intra-industry trade on institutional design, especially given our findings that such trade increases the likelihood of PTA formation.

North-South relations and economic dependency are cast in a new light when the composition of trade is considered. North-South relations in general are conditioned by inter-industry trade in which raw materials are exchanged for finished goods, particularly high-value-added goods, and services. North-North relations are now increasingly dominated by intra-industry trade. Those states that moved out of the periphery and into the semi-periphery have done so largely by producing the types of goods produced in the core economies. State-led economic growth strategies that funneled resources into creating infant industries worked well in the rapidly developing Asian states, the so-called "Asian tigers," at least prior to their blame by some for the Asian financial crisis, even as import-substitution industries seemed to fail in Latin America. The composition of trade is thus tied up with economic dependency and development, as well as models of economic growth tied to trade. Revisiting these issues in light of the distributional consequences of intra- versus inter-industry trade at the global level might shed some light on the long-standing North-South divide.

Finally, how does trade composition condition the rise of emerging powers? Much has been made of the rise of the BRICs (Brazil, Russia, India, and China). Do emerging powers that engage in higher proportions of intra-industry trade with the hegemon, or with the subset of major status quo powers, experience a more peaceful rise? Do those who engage in more inter-industry trade, such as Russia, experience more conflict-laden rises? Could an emerging power that still engages in primarily inter-industry trade rise to great-power status in today's global economy? And does the decline of a hegemon owe in part to the catching up of the rest of the world due to their production and trade of similar goods? If the literature on systemic war is correct, then hegemonic rise and decline is inexorable (Thompson 1988), so it may make sense to foster intra-industry trade within rising powers so as to make this transition as pacific as possible.

These are just some of the areas in which refocusing our understanding of international trade may cause some theoretical and empirical changes. Most of the literatures in international relations, to the extent that they consider trade an important variable, consider inter-industry trade to be dominant. This is a default position, since by and large, international relations theory has adopted unthinkingly the Ricardian notion of specialization according to comparative advantage. All of our thinking about trade's effects on a variety of cooperative and conflictual outcomes thus draws on that underlying theoretical perspective. We hope that the theoretical and empirical contributions in this book will prompt scholars to consider carefully both the composition of trade and their theoretical assumptions about how trade may or may not produce various effects on political outcomes. It may be the case that for some types of political phenomenon the composition of trade will not matter. Yet if our initial inquiries in this volume are on target, then the composition of trade does matter to many of the central issues in the study of international conflict and international political economy. We look forward to seeing future work that takes these ideas into consideration to develop the next generation of theoretical models of and empirical applications to the global political economy.

Notes

Chapter 1

1. Similarly, in the eighteenth century, economic philosophers such as David Hume (1752) and Adam Smith (1776) began to challenge the logic of mercantilism, contradicting the conventional wisdom that restrictions on trade are a means for states to achieve power.

2. Future scholars at times have implied that Sir Norman Angell argued that the occurrence of war itself was the great illusion, whereas his intention was only to stress that all sides to the war would lose more than they could conceivably gain. Indeed, his argument mirrors later, seminal work by James Fearon (1995), who developed the "rational explanations of war," starting with the puzzle that war occurs despite the fact that its costs imply that there always exists an *ex ante* bargain that both sides would prefer.

3. This chapter incorporates material previously published in Peterson and Thies (2015).

4. In this case, each state holds an absolute as well as comparative advantage. However, the same logic would hold if, for example, England were more efficient producing both textiles and wine. It would still hold a comparative advantage in textiles if its relative efficiency with respect to Portugal were greater for textiles than for wine.

5. This section is reproduced with permission from Thies and Porche (2007, 172–175).

6. Notably, opportunity costs are costs associated with the loss of *future* trade. Existing trade does not necessarily imply that there will be future trade, nor is contemporary trade necessary for states to trade in the future; however, scholars typically use it as a proxy of opportunity costs via the fact that trade flows tend to be sticky over time for various reasons.

Chapter 2

1. This chapter contains previously published material (from Peterson and Thies 2012a; 2015). However, this material has been updated and expanded for this volume.

2. Its classification as vertical is probable because price differentials would likely exceed the 15 or 25 percent threshold used to distinguish vertical from horizontal intraindustry trade.

3. However, the fact that production is internationalized could imply the existence of intra-firm trade across states. This form of trade could also have implications for international politics, although we leave examination of these effects to future researchers.

4. In addition to those data hosted by the UN, Feenstra and others (2005) have made available SITC 4-digit-level data.

5. Again, we except trade following from what appears to be vertical intra-industry specialization, but which actually follows from production sharing, from our conceptualization and operationalization of intra-industry trade.

6. We use the SITC revision 1 classification scheme. Although there have been subsequent revisions (the current version is revision 4), the later revisions are not available as far back as 1962.

7. COMTRADE records exports as "free on board" (FOB), excluding these extra costs. As such, using state i's imports from state j along with i's exports to j could lead to bias given that export values would be inflated as much as 20 percent. A better practice is to use *either* the imports *or* the exports of each dyadic state, but not to mix the two.

8. We do not observe all states in 2010 because some states leave the international system: for example, East Germany and South Vietnam. Although we do not have data on every state in the system in any given year, missing data typically occur for very small states (in terms of economy and population), which have much less impact on international politics.

9. The numbers we discuss examine only intra-region dyadic trade. However, we replicated these numbers to include inter-region dyadic trade, finding similar results. Importantly, the inclusion of inter-region dyadic trade leads to the duplication of some intra-industry trade values. For example, the dyadic proportion of intra-industry trade in the U.S.-Japan dyad is included in the aggregate values for both the North American region and the Asian region.

10. Notably, joint European Union dyads have much higher intra-industry trade than does the average dyad (mean equals 0.27). This issue led us to examine all results from later chapters excluding EU dyads from the analysis. All results are consistent with this change. Notably, EU dyads do not have much influence on overall results because they represent only 1 percent of all dyads.

11. We adjusted the value by subtracting the minimum (4.89), thereby coding the lowest value of lower development as equal to 0.

12. Given that we subtract the minimum logged value of lower development, we must add this value back before calculating the dollar value. Accordingly, this value is calculated as e to the power of $3 + 4.89$.

13. According to our data, intra-industry trade, by value, has increased from approximately 12 percent of all trade in 1962 to approximately 37 percent in 2010. Notably, these estimates of intra-industry trade as a proportion of total trade value are considerably lower than those from Milner's study (1999). We suspect that this difference follows from our use of the SITC 4-digit level trade data. Using these more refined data, our measures could exclude much of the vertical intra-industry trade, which likely composes a large portion of total intra-industry trade given the increasing prevalence of regional trade between states with differing incomes. The difference could also follow from the globalization of production, which could lead a less disaggregated measure of intra-industry

trade to include trade that we find occurs in related but distinct commodities. We contend that our measure of intra-industry trade arguably is superior when one's goal is to understand how the composition of trade affects a state's propensity for conflict and cooperation following from complementarity of domestic producer groups, consumer demands, and avoidance of vulnerability. However, a comparison of our SITC 4-digit measure to an alternate SITC 3-digit measure shows a relatively high correlation.

Chapter 3

1. Other preferential trade agreements exist outside of the WTO.

2. Veto players are defined according to their prevailing use in the literature as party or institutional actors whose assent is needed to alter existing policy (Tsebelis 1995; 2002).

3. The propensity to view domestic preferences regarding PTAs similarly to those for multilateral liberalization may contribute to the tendency to assume away variation of these factors. Specifically, when a state considers reducing trade barriers to all other states (as occurs in multilateral liberalization), it follows that there is a reasonably high likelihood that foreign products will compete with domestic firms. However, given that PTAs tend to involve as few as two states, there is far less certainty that any given domestic industry will be harmed by selective trade barrier reduction.

4. Prior work by economists suggests that PTA formation leads to increases in intra-industry trade (Egger, Egger, and Greenaway 2008). We discuss the consequential concern for endogeneity in the research design further on. Ultimately, we find both that intra-industry trade facilitates PTA formation and vice versa.

5. This effect is also beneficial at the state level, as PTAs in this case would result in enhanced terms of trade with non-members.

6. Levy's conception of factor endowments (1997) mirrors our discussion of similar productivity (assuming that relative abundance of capital and labor determine productivity in most trade goods). Levy contends that if two states have identical factor endowments, there would be zero costs associated with forming a bilateral PTA. Yet on the multilateral level, similar or identical factor endowments are impossible.

7. Importantly, in both of these cases, there is an implicit assumption that, within a dyad, a higher level of intra-industry trade in a given industry suggests relatively similar levels of productivity. Due to the fact that intra-industry trade results from product differentiation, some degree of differential productivity is possible. However, if there is a considerable difference in productivity, then a price differential will result, and intra-industry trade will be less likely to exist at all, given that consumers in the more productive state will be less likely to import a much more expensive foreign brand. A salient example is automotive trade between the United States and Japan. Because Japanese car companies were more productive for many years, the United States imports millions of Japanese cars while Japan imports just a few thousand cars from the United States.

8. Specifically, Grossman and Helpman's conditions apply to the creation of a PTA in which essentially all trade is liberalized. In the absence of the criteria presented ear-

lier, Grossman and Helpman's model suggests that PTA formation could also occur if it would benefit the average voter and if organized interests fail to coordinate an organized resistance; however, the authors contend that PTA formation due to these latter criteria is much less likely. The authors also demonstrate that agreements are easier to reach when some industries are excluded from liberalization.

9. Interestingly, one of China's goals in this case may be to facilitate the development of its own "green" technology industry (that is, the manufacture of wind turbines and batteries) that utilizes rare-earth metals. Potentially, the development of such an industry could lead to more intra-industry trade in the green technology industry. Also, U.S. production of rare-earth metals appears to be ramping up, given Chinese restrictions; however, this market response tends to occur only in the long term, meaning that strategic vulnerabilities are most acute in the short term.

10. Although our primary models include both bilateral and multilateral (from the perspective of each dyad) agreements, we also examined these agreements separately, finding equivalent results, as discussed further on.

11. We use a one-year lag between explanatory and dependent variables in order to mitigate simultaneity bias, wherein joining a PTA could lead to increased intra-industry trade. As we show further on, we have reason to think that reversed causation is not a problem.

12. Non-reciprocal agreements typically fall under the generalized system of preferences, in which less developed states are afforded advantageous trade practices, often from former colonial masters. Mansfield, Milner, and Pevehouse (2007) refer to these non-reciprocal agreements as "hub and spoke" PTAs. They exclude PTAs in which terms are not reciprocal.

13. Many of these low-level PTAs establish MFN status consistent with membership in the World Trade Organization, but on a bilateral or otherwise member-restricted basis.

14. Specifically, the language in GATT article XXIV, paragraph 8, states that for customs unions, trade barriers on third parties "shall not on the whole be higher or more restrictive" (emphasis added) than those for members. This flexible language reflects the fact that joiners to existing CUs may need to raise barriers to match those of existing members. For free trade areas, the language omits this ambiguous condition, requiring that external barriers "shall not be higher or more restrictive" than those within the FTA. However, rules of origin may be applied to similar ends in FTAs.

15. Kono (2007) points out that not all PTAs of the same class are equally successful in liberalizing. The experience of the European Economic Community has certainly been more successful than, for example, the African Economic Community (AEC) and the pillars thereof, which have successfully liberalized in some areas while losing momentum in others. Although distinguishing between PTAs, FTAs, CUs, and so on does not entirely capture the variance in subsequent liberation within each type of agreement, we contend that signings of a given agreement type nonetheless convey a

similar expectation of liberalization. Indeed, much of the difficulty experienced by the AEC stemmed from unanticipated conflicts in the region subsequent to signing.

16. 0 is the baseline, representing no agreement formation.

17. However, this could conceivably change if agreements become large enough that they encompass most states. At some point, the larger the proposed PTA, the more it converges towards multilateral liberalization.

18. Results are available by request from the authors.

19. PTA formation is a rare event (occurring in approximately 1 percent of dyad years). Accordingly, we estimated rare events logit models to test for the robustness of our primary results, in accordance with the suggestion of King and Zeng (2001). The results of these models were substantively equivalent, indeed nearly identical, to those presented. These models are available by request from the authors.

20. Specifically, we use the Conditional Mixed Process estimator in Stata 12 (Roodman 2011), specifying a Heckman selection process for a two-equation model in which the first equation dependent variable is dichotomous and the second equation dependent variable is ordinal. A typical Heckman model in Stata would treat the second equation dependent variable as continuous, possibly leading to biased results given that integration is an ordinal variable. However, results using a traditional Heckman model look reasonably similar to those presented in Tables 3.2 and 3.3.

21. We get a similar result if we include a year counter variable or a "system size" variable as used by Hegre, Oneal, and Russett (2010) in a study of the reciprocal relationship between trade and conflict. However, the substantive impact of these alternative variables is more modest than that of our third-party PTA dyad variable, which more directly measures the competition associated with PTA formation, in accordance with our theoretical argument.

22. Results are consistent when we look at the sum of veto player scores across both dyad members. These specifications are consistent with Mansfield, Milner, and Pevehouse (2007), who also present results using a weak link and dyadic total variant of their veto players measure.

23. Results look consistent if we use trade data from the Correlates of War (Barbieri, Keshk, and Pollins 2009), or from Gleditsch (2002). We prefer using WITS trade data because these are the data necessary to calculate our measure of bilateral intra-industry trade proportions.

24. While most of our independent variables are adapted from Mansfield, Milner, and Pevehouse (2007), we adjust their specifications to code explanatory variables at the dyad-year level of analysis. Mansfield, Milner, and Pevehouse code many of their variables at the country-year level, including variables for each state in the dyad. However, because dyads are ordered somewhat arbitrarily (by the lower then higher Correlates of War country code), we contend that it is more useful to code variables at the dyad-year level (for example, taking the higher of the two states' veto player scores, the lower of the two states' GDP, and so on). All of our results are consistent using country-year-level variables.

25. Results look similar if we instead include a measure of GDP, representing total wealth rather than development.

26. Results are robust to the substitution distance (calculated as the log of distance between state capitals plus one) in place of contiguity.

27. Previous studies find similar results in the U.S.-Mexico case. For example, Globerman (1992) finds that intra-industry trade between the United States and Mexico increased from 36 percent in 1980 to 51 percent in 1988. Globerman attributes this increase in intra-industry trade to Mexico joining GATT, the result of this multilateral liberalization being an influx of foreign capital to the maquiladoras.

28. These models suggest a mutually reinforcing pattern of causation in which intra-industry trade facilitates PTA formation and PTAs facilitate intra-industry trade.

29. That is, the figure presents the rate at which the probability of PTA formation would change given a one-point increase in each explanatory variable. The estimates for each variable are taken holding all explanatory variables at their median value.

30. However, the scales of our explanatory variables are not all equal. Accordingly, we must interpret substantive effects using relevant values of each explanatory variable. We discuss this issue in detail further on.

31. In this case, we calculate probability change rather than rely on marginal effects. Accordingly, to the extent that the marginal effect of intra-industry trade is not constant, we obtain a better estimate of its substantive impact than we would if we relied on marginal effects alone.

32. In both of these figures, the curve illustrating the change in probability of PTA formation as intra-industry trade increases is convex, its slope becoming ever steeper at higher ranges of intra-industry trade. This result suggests that the marginal effect of intra-industry trade increases at an increasing rate as the value of intra-industry trade increases. This finding complements that of Figure 3.2, in which the marginal effect of intra-industry trade is approximately 0.1; the marginal effect in Figure 3.2 is an estimate from a scenario in which intra-industry trade is held at a low value (in fact, near 0).

33. Specifically, Model 3.4 examines the formation of agreements that are at least customs unions, also including more integrative agreements (applying primarily to the European Union).

34. Indeed, patterns of intra-industry trade increasing from very low values (close to 0) to values higher than 0.6 are relatively common among developed states in Europe and North America. Although it is rare to see intra-industry trade values approach 1, there is meaningful variation along two-thirds of the scale.

35. Again, the marginal effect (essentially) represents the change in probability of PTA formation as intra-industry trade increases from its minimum (0) to its maximum (1).

36. In alternative models, we included an additional variable for multilateral liberalization (used in subsequent chapters in this book), given the possibility that more globalized dyads would find less need to engage in preferential liberalization. Results for intra-industry trade remain robust in these models, however. Furthermore, the coef-

ficient for the lower of the dyadic state's liberalization is not significant. These results support the argument that even those states having low overall trade barriers nonetheless see potential to gain from preferential liberalization—or perhaps face compulsion to pursue PTAs to counter the advantage other states receive from previously formed third-party agreements.

37. We also considered the potentially conditional relationship between those factors affecting opportunity to form PTAs and those affecting the willingness of domestic actors to support PTAs. At the multilateral level, Kono (2009) demonstrates that if electoral institutions reward narrow interests, then intra-industry trade leads to higher protectionism. However, we contend that, due to the third-party consequences of preferential liberalization, a higher degree of bilateral intra-industry trade prompts firms and industries to lobby for PTA formation, even as they may organize to resist broader liberalization. Given that more intra-industry trade with a given trade partner suggests less domestic pressure to maintain trade barriers against that specific trade partner, a higher number of veto players should not diminish the facilitating effect of intra-industry trade. Although the opportunity to derail a PTA exists, veto players, channeling domestic interests, will be less willing to use their veto power.

38. Specifically, in the interactive specifications, the coefficients for the component terms represent the influence of each component when the other component is held at zero (that is, the intra-industry trade coefficient represents its influence when there are no veto players, and the veto players coefficient represents its effect when there is no intra-industry trade). An examination of marginal effects using the margins command in Stata confirms that the effects of both intra-industry trade and higher veto players remains significant regardless of the level at which we hold the other variable (see, for example, Braumoeller 2004; Brambor, Clark, and Golder 2006; Kam and Franzese 2007).

Chapter 4

1. The source material for this section is from the WTO website. Please see http://www.wto.org/english/tratop_e/dispu_e/dispu_e.htm for more information.

2. For the figure, we code the presence of a dyadic dispute between a state and all EU members if the state in question is involved in a dispute with the EU. However, the general pattern we find is robust to alternative codings, either excluding EU disputes, or counting only one bilateral dispute for each dispute in which the EU is a party.

3. See Conti (2010) for an analysis of experience gained during the dispute settlement process.

4. Furthermore, the use of non-directed dyads reduces (although it does not necessarily eliminate) problems of dependence between dyads (Erikson, Pinto, and Rader 2014).

5. One could make the argument that higher GDP per capita is a consequence of trade. However, we suspect that the influence of dyadic trade on higher GDP per capita is indirect. Furthermore, GDP per capita typically is viewed as a determinant of trade (often in terms of relative capital endowment) rather than vice versa.

6. One alternative is to use a Heckman model in which the outcome variable is assumed to be continuous. Given that our outcome variable is a highly skewed count in which over 99 percent of observations (110,616 out of 110,815) are coded as 0, we do not trust the results that such a model would return.

7. We re-ran these models including UN voting similarity in the outcome equation, finding no association between it and WTO dispute onset.

8. The only feasible alternative to these two approaches is to count the EU as a single actor. However, most of our explanatory variables do not aggregate easily to the single market. Arguably, the best option is to code average levels of trade, distance, and so on; doing so returns equivalent results, which are available by request.

9. Results look similar if we include a square and cube term for this counter variable. However, cubic polynomials were developed for binary dependent variables (Carter and Signorino 2010); therefore, we include only the counter variable in the models presented in this chapter.

10. Intra-industry trade levels this high are very rare, consisting primarily of dyads including one EU state (especially the United Kingdom, Ireland, and Belgium) with a small number of other states (especially Israel, Singapore, and the Philippines).

11. As noted earlier, all dyads in which both states are EU members are excluded from the analysis, given that the EU is a single customs territory.

12. And, in Models 4.3 through 4.6, this coefficient represents the association between intra-industry trade and the frequency of WTO disputes when the other constituent terms are also equal to zero. Accordingly, we must take care to consider meaningful marginal effects of this interacted variable.

Chapter 5

1. Note: some sections of this chapter are adapted from Peterson and Thies (2012a). However, new sections have been introduced, and the analysis has been updated and expanded.

2. In fact, the ability of trade to constrain conflict is debated by proponents of its informational effect. Morrow (1999) argues that dependence on trade is simply subsumed in bargaining, with an ambiguous impact on constraint. For example, one state's trade dependence may be a deterrent for that state, yet it is simultaneously an incentive for its trade partner to demand change to the status quo (see also Wagner 1988).

3. Notably, Mansfield and Pevehouse (2000) examine the influence of *preferential* liberalization on conflict.

4. For example, Mousseau (2000) similarly suggests that development plays a strong role in pacifying relationships among states. In fact, he suggests that the well-known democratic peace is largely a developed democratic peace. Yet, Mousseau, Hegre, and Oneal (2003, 299) find that the pacifying effects of democracy and development only occur when both are present, while trade interdependence has "a robust pacifying impact independent of a dyad's level of democracy or development."

5. Schneider and Gleditsch's special issue of *International Interactions* (2010) finds substantial empirical support for the capitalist peace along with debate over the inde-

pendent effects of democracy. The role of trade openness is not highlighted to a great extent in any of the contributing papers, nor is the notion of a conditional relationship between development and trade.

6. We refer primarily to horizontal intra-industry trade: in other words, the trade of essentially the same commodity. As we discuss in Chapter 2, we distinguish this type of trade from vertical intra-industry trade, unless two-way trade occurs of commodities at the SITC 4-digit level. Our aim is to remove vertical intra-industry trade that follows from the globalization of production.

7. Dorussen's finding that trade in manufactured goods is relatively more pacifying (2006) may stem from this impact of intra-industry trade (which tends to consist of manufactures). Yet isolating intra-industry trade can uncover conditions in which, for example, trade in agriculture is pacifying—as long as it is bidirectional.

8. More recently, manufacturing value-added has declined in relative terms (simultaneously with an increase in manufacturing by less-developed states). Currently, intellectual property exports offer the highest return, with developed states dominating exports in these commodities and services.

9. We address the issue of how trade composition affects political affinity and vice versa in Chapter 6.

10. Previous research suggests that preferential liberalization leads to higher levels of intra-industry trade on average (for example, Egger, Egger, and Greenaway 2008). However, there is variation in this relationship, and even when it does occur, it could be that states choose to enter into preferential trade agreements (PTAs) when they are confident they will obtain returns from scale (for example, Chase 2003). Furthermore, PTAs could actually lead to higher external protectionism (Bhagwati 1991), such that states do not liberalize overall when they enter into a preferential trade agreement.

11. However, there are other reasons to suspect that liberal trade policy does not always serve as a constraint on state behavior. For example, although advocates of the capitalist peace contend that lower tariff revenue suggests less income that governments can use to make war (for example, McDonald 2007), modern states tend to collect more revenue from direct taxation of citizens rather than from taxation of imports. Indeed, none other than Adam Smith was doubtful that taxation due to war would burden enough people to provoke political action, arguing that, for citizens reading about war in the news, the "amusement compensates the small difference between the taxes which they pay on account of the war, and those which they had been accustomed to pay in time of peace" (Smith 1776, 552). Adam Smith's pessimism aside, the potential for rallies-around-the-flag (for example, Mueller 1970; 1973), as well as potential sources of funding beyond taxes (including borrowing, which can be enabled by a strong, liberalized economy), suggests that lack of tariffs for revenue is not sufficient to preclude conflict.

12. This argument suggests the question, when is specialization aggravating or pacifying? Perhaps specialization is pacifying when states do not face incentives to use a trade partner's dependence as leverage in coercion attempts. Although this question is beyond the scope of this book, it presents a potentially very lucrative avenue for future research.

13. Ultimately, we think that the occasionally coercive aspects of vulnerability introduce variation into an otherwise pacifying impact of trade gains. As mentioned earlier, future research can benefit from examining conditions in which specialization leads to coercion.

14. Our conflict variable captures a rare event. Accordingly, we tested for the robustness of our results using rare events logit models (King and Zeng 2001). All findings are consistent, which is not surprising given that rare events logit is intended primarily to prevent false negatives (a.k.a. type II error)—findings of no association when one actually exists, or, more generally, to an underestimation of the probability of a rare event.

15. Keshk, Pollins, and Reuveny (2004) point out that lags do not eliminate concerns for endogeneity, as conflict—or expectations thereof—may lead to reductions in trade rather than vice versa. In robustness check models available by request from the authors we utilize simultaneous equations models to test for the reciprocal relationship between trade and conflict (Keshk 2003). All results are robust in these models. In fact, we find no evidence of a reverse relationship between conflict and intra-industry trade.

16. In addition, all results are consistent using dyad fixed effects or country fixed effects; however, the former requires the removal of some control variables. Furthermore, all dyads (countries) that never experience fatal MID onset are dropped from the analysis when we use dyad (country) fixed effects. Accordingly, interpretation of those results changes: for example, a negative and significant coefficient for intra-industry trade would suggest that a higher proportion of intra-industry trade is associated with a lower probability of fatal MID onset among dyads (states) that experienced at least one such instance between 1962 and 2001.

17. We estimate models excluding liberalization in order to more directly replicate Peterson and Thies (2012a). However, we devote most of the discussion of our analysis to the models that include a measure of lower liberalization.

18. As in Chapters 3 and 4, we find robust results if we use Correlates of War (COW) trade data (Barbieri, Keshk, and Pollins 2009) or Gleditsch's trade data (2002). Our use of UN trade data follows from a desire for consistency, given that these data are used to construct the measure of intra-industry trade.

19. We present two tables. In both, we present models that include, along with control variables, (1) only *intra-industry trade*, (2) intra-industry trade along with *lower development* (that is, lower GDP per capita) and *lower dependence* (that is, lower trade to GDP), (3) interactive models examining *lower development X lower dependence*, (4) interactive models examining *intra-industry trade X lower dependence*, and (5) interactive models examining *intra-industry trade X lower development*. Table 5.2 includes a variable for *lower liberalization* in all models, and also adds a model interacting lower liberalization and intra-industry trade.

20. This one-unit interpretation is technically only correct for dichotomous explanatory variables, although in most cases the marginal effects presented for continuous explanatory variables are close approximations for their one-unit change effect.

21. These marginal effects are taken from Model 5.7, presented in Table 5.2. Because the marginal effect for each variable is taken holding all other variables at their medians, the marginal effects are all quite small as they represent dyad years in which states have experienced seventeen years of peace and are separated by over four thousand miles.

22. To make this marginal effect appear on the same scale, we multiplied the raw variable by 100. However, the change in probability associated with a min-to-max change in lower liberalization still is lower than the equivalent change in intra-industry trade.

23. We also hold maximum capabilities at 0.05 (5 percent of the total global capabilities) in order to examine a dyad with more opportunity for conflict.

24. Specifically, Model 5.5 in Table 5.1 (excluding a variable for lower liberalization), and Model 5.10 in Table 5.2 (including a variable for lower liberalization) include the interaction between intra-industry trade and lower GDP per capita.

Chapter 6

1. Although perhaps not strictly necessary, capital abundance has been the norm among states engaging primarily in intra-industry trade.

2. One might expect these conditions for intra-industry trade to have direct effects on dyadic political similarity. However, for these conditions to exist in the absence of intra-industry trade suggests that states are competitors, producing similar goods for export to third parties. In this case, similar factor endowments and joint development in particular could actually be aggravating if states view each other as economic rivals.

3. Also, the emergence of preferential liberalization among allies could be in part responsible for the lack of an influence of political similarity on intra-industry trade. Preferential trade agreements (PTAs) typically require the reduction of trade barriers in "substantively all the trade" between members (GATT article XXIV) such that states cannot restrict imports of strategic commodities from PTA partners holding a comparative advantage in producing these goods.

4. According to Signorino and Ritter's weighted, global S score, the United States consistently has a more similar foreign policy with Canada than with (1) Mexico, the other state with which it shares a border, and (2) the United Kingdom, with which it shares common language and heritage.

5. The three-category variant of the measure incorporates abstentions along with "yes" and "no" votes on UN General Assembly resolutions. All results are consistent when we use the two-category version of the affinity index.

6. This is a one-equation ECM, appropriate when our variables are not co-integrated (see De Boef and Keele 2008). De Boef and Keele point out that all stationary variables have an equilibrium relationship. Tests for unit roots in our panel data suggest that they are stationary. Specifically, using Stata 12, we specified Fisher-type tests, which can account for multiple panels. For both UN voting and intra-industry trade, we reject the null hypothesis that all panels have unit roots ($p < 0.0001$).

7. We specify a one-year lag length for practical reasons, given that most of our data—including the measure of our dependent variables—are unavailable at more frequent intervals. Otherwise, we would have considered one-quarter and two-quarter lag lengths, given that trade data are often available to state leaders on a quarterly basis.

8. The use of fixed effects with a lagged DV could potentially cause violation of the assumption of zero conditional mean. However, we find that all primary results are consistent when we omit fixed effects.

9. Given the use of dyad fixed effects, robust standard errors are equivalent to standard errors clustered on the dyad.

10. We rescaled the coefficient for trade to GDP as well as the lagged dependent variable because the raw marginal effects were very large (yet not statistically significant in the case of trade to GDP), obscuring the marginal effect of other variables.

11. Yet these changes associated with increasing intra-industry trade are quite large relative to the mean yearly change: 0.002. The standard deviation of the mean yearly change is 0.14.

12. Again, the impact of intra-industry trade looks larger if compared to the mean and standard deviation of *change* in UN voting similarity. Specifically, the 0.75-point change in the score represents an increase of more than six standard deviations (equal to 0.14).

13. In the non-interactive models, we verified these values using the approximation method. Specifically, we calculated the long-run multiplier as equal to the ratio of the coefficient for *intra-industry trade t–1* to that of *UN voting similarity t–1*. The standard error of the long-run multiplier is approximated using the formula provided by De Boef and Keele (2008, 192).

Bibliography

Ai, Chunrong, and Edward C. Norton. 2003. Interaction terms in logit and probit models. *Economic Letters* 80:123–129.

Alt, James E., and Michael J. Gilligan. 1994. The political economy of trading states. *Journal of Political Philosophy* 2:165–192.

Alt, James E., Jeffry Frieden, Michael J. Gilligan, Dani Rodrik, and Ronald Rogowski. 1996. The political economy of international trade: Enduring puzzles and an agenda for inquiry. *Comparative Political Studies* 29:689–717.

Alter, Karen J. 2003. Resolving or exacerbating disputes? The WTO's new dispute resolution system. *International Affairs* 79 (4): 783–800.

Anderson, James E. 1979. A theoretical foundation for the gravity equation. *The American Economic Review* 69 (1): 106–116.

Angell, Sir Norman. 1913. *The great illusion: A study of the relation of military power to national advantage.* London: Heinemann.

Aquino, Antonio. 1978. Intra-industry trade and inter-industry specialization as concurrent sources of international trade in manufactures. *Review of World Economics* 114 (2): 275–296.

Axelrod, Robert. 1984. *The evolution of cooperation.* New York: Basic Books.

Baccini, Leonardo. 2012. Democratization and trade policy: An empirical analysis of developing countries. *European Journal of International Relations* 18 (3): 454–478.

Bagwell, Kyle, and Robert W. Staiger. 2004. Multilateral trade negotiations, bilateral opportunism, and the rules of GATT/WTO. *Journal of International Economics* 63 (1).

Balassa, Bela. 1961. Towards a theory of economic integration. *Kyklos* 14 (1): 1–17.

Balassa, Bela. 1966. Tariff reductions and trade in manufactures among industrial countries. *American Economic Review* 56:466–473.

Balassa, Bela. 1986. The determinants of intra-industry specialization in United States trade. *Oxford Economic Papers* 38 (2): 220–233.

Baldwin, David A. 1980. Interdependence and power: A conceptual analysis. *International Organization* 34 (4): 471–506.

Baldwin, Richard. 1995. A domino theory of regionalism. In *Expanding European Regionalism: The EU's New Members*, ed. R. Baldwin, P. Haaparanta, and J. Kiander. New York: Cambridge University Press.

Barbieri, Katherine. 1996. Economic interdependence: A path to peace or a source of conflict? *Journal of Peace Research* 33 (1): 29–49.

Barbieri, Katherine, Omar M. G. Keshk, and Brian M. Pollins. 2009. Trading data: Evaluating our assumptions and coding rules. *Conflict Management and Peace Science* 26:471–491.

Becker, Gary. 1983. A theory of competition among pressure groups for political influence. *Quarterly Journal of Economics* 98.

Bennett, S., and A. Stam. 2000. EUGene: A conceptual manual. *International Interactions* 26 (2): 179–204.

Bergstrand, Jeffrey H. 1989. The generalized gravity equation, monopolistic competition, and the factor-proportions theory in international trade. *Economics and Statistics* 71 (1): 143–153.

Bergstrand, Jeffrey H. 1990. The Heckscher-Ohlin-Samuelson model, the Linder hypothesis, and the determinants of bilateral intra-industry trade. *The Economic Journal* 100:1216–1229.

Bhagwati, Jagdish N. 1991. *The world trading system at risk*. Princeton, NJ: Princeton University Press.

Bhagwati, Jagdish N. 2008. *Termites in the trading system: How preferential agreements undermine free trade*. New York: Oxford University Press.

Blanes, José V., and Carmela Martín. 2000. The nature and causes of intra-industry trade: Back to the comparative advantage explanation? The case of Spain. *Review of World Economics* 136:423–441.

Blonigen, Bruce A., and Chad P. Brown. 2003. Antidumping and retaliation threats. *Journal of International Economics* 60 (2): 249–273.

Brambor, Thomas, William Roberts Clark, and Matt Golder. 2006. Understanding interaction models: Improving empirical analysis. *Political Analysis* 14 (1): 63–82.

Braumoeller, Bear. 2004. Hypothesis testing and multiplicative interaction terms. *International Organization* 58:807–820.

Bremer, Stuart A. 1992. Dangerous dyads: Conditions affecting the likelihood of interstate war, 1816–1965. *Journal of Conflict Resolution* 36 (2): 309–341.

Brooks, Stephen G. 1999. The globalization of production and the changing benefits of conquest. *The Journal of Conflict Resolution* 43 (5): 646–670.

Brown, Chad P. 2004. Trade disputes and the implementation of protection under the GATT: An empirical assessment. *Journal of International Economics* 62 (2): 263–294.

Brown, Chad P. 2005. Participation in WTO dispute settlement: Complainants, interested parties, and free riders. *World Bank Economic Review* 19 (2): 287–310.

Busch, Marc L. 2000. Democracy, consultation, and the paneling of disputes under GATT. *Journal of Conflict Resolution* 44 (4): 425–446.

Busch, Marc L., and Eric Reinhardt. 1999. Industrial location and protection: The Political and economic geography of U.S. nontariff barriers. *American Journal of Political Science* 43:1028–1050.

Busch, Marc L., and Eric Reinhardt. 2000. Geography, international trade, and political mobilization in U.S. industries. *American Journal of Political Science* 44:703–719.

Busch, Marc L., and Eric Reinhardt. 2003. Developing countries and GATT/WTO dispute settlement. *Journal of World Trade* 37 (4).

Busch, Marc L., and Eric Reinhardt. 2006. Three's a crowd: Third parties and WTO dispute settlement. *World Politics* 58 (3): 446–477.

Buzan, Barry and Ole Waever. 2003. *Regions and powers: The structure of international security*. Cambridge, UK: Cambridge University Press.

Caporaso, James A. 1978. Dependence, dependency, and power in the global system: A structural and behavioral analysis. *International Organization* 32:13–43.

Carr, Edward Hallett. 1964. *The twenty years crisis, 1919–1939: An introduction to the study of international relations*, 2nd ed. New York: Harper.

Carter, David and Curtis Signorino. 2010. Back to the future: Modeling time dependence in binary data. *Political Analysis* 18:271–292.

Chase, Kerry A. 2003. Economic interests and regional trading arrangements: The case of NAFTA. *International Organization* 57:137–174.

Chase, Kerry A. 2005. *Trading blocs: States, firms, and regions in the world economy. Studies in international political economy*. Ann Arbor:University of Michigan Press.

Conti, Joseph A. 2010. Learning to dispute: Repeat participation, expertise, and reputation at the World Trade Organization. *Law & Social Inquiry* 35 (3): 625–662.

Copeland, Dale C. 1996. Economic interdependence and war: A theory of trade expectations. *International Security* 20:5–41.

Crescenzi, Mark J. C. 2003. Economic exit, interdependence, and conflict. *The Journal of Politics* 65 (3): 809–832.

Davis, Christina L., and Sarah Blodgett Bermeo. 2009. Who files? Developing country participation in GATT/WTO adjudication. *Journal of Politics* 71 (3): 1033–1049.

Davis, Christina L., and Yuki Shirato. 2007. Firms, governments, and WTO adjudication: Japan's selection of WTO disputes. *World Politics* 59 (2): 274–313.

De Boef, Suzanna, and Luke Keele. 2008. Taking time seriously. *American Journal of Political Science* 52 (1): 184–200.

Deutsch, Karl. 1957. *Political community and the north atlantic area: International organization in the light of historical experience*. Princeton, NJ: Princeton University Press.

Diehl, Paul F., and Gary Goertz. 2000. *War and peace in international rivalry*. Ann Arbor: University of Michigan Press.

Dixon, William, and Bruce Moon. 1993. Political similarity and american foreign trade patterns. *Political Research Quarterly* 46:5–25.

Doran, Charles F. 1991. *Systems in crisis: New imperatives of high politics at century's end*. New York: Cambridge University Press.

Dorussen, Han. 2006. Heterogeneous trade interests and conflict: What you trade matters. *Journal of Conflict Resolution* 50:87–107.

Dorussen, Han, and Hugh Ward. 2010. Trade networks and the Kantian peace. *Journal of Peace Research* 47:29–42.

Dos Santos, Theotonio. 1970. The structure of dependence. *American Economic Review* 60 (2): 231–236.

Egger, Hartmut, Peter Egger, and David Greenaway. 2008. The trade structure effects of endogenous regional trade agreements. *Journal of International Economics* 74:278–298.

Ehrlich, Sean D. 2007. Access to protection: Domestic institutions and trade policies in democracies. *International Organization* 61:571–606.

Eisenhardt, Kathleen M., and L. J. Bourgeois III. 1988. Politics of strategic decision making in high velocity environments: Toward a midrange theory. *Academy of Management Journal* 31 (4).

Elsig, Manfred and Cedric Dupont. 2012. European Union meets South Korea: Bureaucratic interests, exporter discrimination and the negotiations of trade agreements. *Journal of Common Market Studies.*

Ekaterina II. 1971. *Documents of Catherine the Great.* Cambridge: Cambridge University Press.

Erikson, Robert S., Pablo M. Pinto, and Kelly T. Rader. 2014. Dyadic analysis in international relations: A cautionary tale. *Political Analysis* 22 (4): 457–463.

Esserman, Susan, and Robert Howse. 2003. The WTO on trial. *Foreign Affairs* 82:288–298.

Falvey, R. E. 1981, Commercial policy, and intra-industry trade." *Journal of International Economics* 11 (4): 495–511.

Fearon, James D. 1995. Rationalist explanations for war. *International Organization* 49:379–414.

Feenstra, Robert. C., Robert Inklaar, and Marcel Timmer. 2013. PWT 8.0—a user guide. http://www.rug.nl/research/ggdc/data/penn-world-table. Data accessed January 15, 2014.

Feenstra, Robert C., Robert E. Lipseym, Haiyan Deng, Alyson C. Ma, and Hengyong Mo. 2005. World trade flows: 1962–2000." Working paper 11040. http://www.nber.org/papers/w11040.

Findlay, Ronald, and Kevin H. O'Rourke. 2007. *Power and plenty: Trade, war, and the new world economy in the second millennium.* Princeton: Princeton University Press.

Finger, J. M. 1975. Trade overlap and intra-industry trade. *Economic Inquiry* 13:581–589.

Fontagné, L., Freudenberg M. and N. Péridy. 1998. Intra-industry trade and the single market: Quality matters." Center for Economic Policy and Research (CEPR) discussion paper #1959.

Frieden, Jeffry. 1991. Invested interests: National economic policies in a world of global finance. *International Organization* 45:425–452.

Gallagher, John, and Ronald Robinson. 1953. The imperialism of free trade. *Economic History Review* 6 (1): 1–15.

Galtung, John. 1971. A structural theory of imperialism. *Journal of Peace Research* 8:81–117.

Gartzke, Erik. 1998. Kant we all just get along? Opportunity, willingness, and the origins of the democratic peace. *American Journal of Political Science* 42 (1): 1–27.

Gartzke, Erik. 2003. The classical liberals were just lucky: A few thoughts about interdependence and peace. In *Interdependence and international conflict: New perspectives on an enduring debate*, ed. Edward Mansfield and Brian Pollins. Ann Arbor: University of Michigan Press.

Gartzke, Erik. 2007. The capitalist peace. *American Journal of Political Science* 51 (1): 166–191.

Gartzke, Erik, and Quan Li. 2003. Measure for measure: Concept operationalization and the trade interdependence-conflict debate. *Journal of Peace Research* 40 (5): 553–571.

Gasiorowski, Mark, and Solomon Polachek. 1982. Conflict and interdependence: East-west trade and linkages in the era of detente. *The Journal of Conflict Resolution* 4:709–729.

Ghosn, Faten, Glenn Palmer, and Stuart Bremer. 2004. The MID3 data set, 1993–2001: Procedures, coding rules, and description. *Conflict Management and Peace Science* 21:133–154.

Gibler, Douglas. 2009. *International military alliances.* Thousand Oaks, CA: CQ Press.

Gilligan, Michael J. 1997. Lobbying as a private good with intra-industry trade. *International Studies Quarterly* 41 (3): 455–474.

Gilpin, Robert. 1981. *War and change in world politics.* New York: Cambridge University Press.

Gleditsch, Kristian Skrede. 2002. Expanded trade and GDP data. *The Journal of Conflict Resolution* 46:712–724.

Globerman, S. 1992. North American trade liberalization and intra-industry trade. *Review of World Economies* 128:487–497.

Gowa, Joanne. 1989. Bipolarity, multipolarity, and free trade. *American Political Science Review* 83 (4): 1245–1256.

Gowa, Joanne. 1994. *Allies, adversaries and international trade.* Princeton, NJ: Princeton University Press.

Gowa, Joanne, and Edward Mansfield. 1993. Power politics and international trade. *American Political Science Review* 87 (2): 408–420.

Gowa, Joanne, and Edward Mansfield. 2004. Alliances, imperfect markets, and major power trade. *International Organization* 58 (4): 775–805.

Greenaway, D., and C. Milner. 1986. *The economics of intra-industry trade.* Oxford, UK: Blackwell.

Grimwade, Nigel. 1989. *International trade: New patterns of trade, production, and investment.* London and New York: Routledge.

Grossman, Gene M., and Elhanan Helpman. 1995. The politics of free-trade agreements. *The American Economic Review* 85:667–690.

Grossman, Gene M., and Elhanan Helpman. 2002. *Interest groups and trade policy.* Princeton, NJ: Princeton University Press.

Grubel, H. G., and D. J. Lloyd. 1975. *Intra-industry trade: The theory and measurement of international trade in differentiated products.* London: Macmillan.

Guzman, Andrew, and Beth Simmons. 2002. To settle or empanel? An empirical analysis of litigation and settlement at the World Trade Organization. *Journal of Legal Studies* 31:205–235.

Hansen, Wendy, and Jeffrey Drope. 2004. Purchasing protection? The effect of political spending on U.S. trade policy. *Political Research Quarterly* 57(1).

Hegre, Havard. 2000. Development and democracy: What does it take to be a trading state? *Journal of Peace Research* 37 (1): 5–30.

Hegre, Havard, John R. Oneal, and Bruce Russett. 2010. Trade does promote peace: New simultaneous estimates of the reciprocal effects of trade and conflict. *Journal of Peace Research* 47 (6): 763–774.

Heinisz, Witold J. 2000. The institutional environment for economic growth. *Economics and Politics* 12:1–31.

Heinisz, Witold J., and Edward D. Mansfield. 2006. Votes and vetoes: The political determinants of commercial openness. *International Studies Quarterly* 50 (1): 189–212.

Hirschman, Albert O. [1945] 1980. National power and the structure of foreign trade. Berkeley: University of California Press.

Hiscox, Michael J. 2001. Class versus industry cleavages: Inter-industry mobility and the politics of trade. *International Organization* 55 (1): 1–46.

Hiscox, Michael J., and Scott L. Kastner. 2002. A general measure of trade policy orientations: Gravity-based estimates for 82 nations, 1960 to 1992. Unpublished manuscript.

Hollyer, James, and Peter Rosendorff. 2011. *Leadership survival, regime type, policy uncertainty and PTA accession.* Unpublished Manuscript.

Homans, Charles. 2010. Are rare earth elements actually rare? *Foreign Policy.* http://www.foreignpolicy.com/articles/2010/06/15/are_rare_earth_minerals_actually_rare. Accessed January 29, 2011.

Horn, Henrik, and Petros C. Mavroidis. 2008. Special issue. *World Trade Review* 7 (1): 1–7.

Horn, Henrik, Petros C. Mavroidis, and Håkan Nordström. 2005. Is the use of the WTO dispute settlement system biased? In *The WTO and international trade law/dispute settlement*, Petros C. Mavroidis and Alan Sykes, eds. Cheltenham, UK: Edward Elgar.

Hounshell, Blake. 2010. Is China making a rare earth power play? *Foreign Policy.* http://blog.foreignpolicy.com/posts/2010/09/23/is_china_making_a_rare_earth_power_play?hidecomments=yes. Accessed January 29, 2011.

Hume, David. 1752. *Political Discourses.* Edinburgh: Kincaid and Donaldson.

Huntington, Samuel L. 1991. *The third wave of democracy.* Norman, OK: University of Oklahoma Press.

Joyce, Christopher. January 12, 2012. Cheap Chinese panels solar power trade war. NPR.org. http://www.npr.org/2012/01/19/145403625/cheap-chinese-panels-spark-solar-power-trade-war.

Kacowicz, Arie M. 1998. *Zones of peace in the third world: South America and West Africa in comparative perspective.* Albany, NY: SUNY Press.

Kam, Cindy D., and Robert J. Franzese Jr. 2007. *Modeling and interpreting interactive hypotheses in regression analysis.* Ann Arbor: University of Michigan Press.

Kastner, Scott L. 2007. When do conflicting political relations affect international trade? *Journal of Conflict Resolution* 51 (4): 664–688.

Kegley, Charles W. 1993. The neoidealist moment in international studies? Realist myths and the new international realities. *International Studies Quarterly* 37:131–146.

Keohane, Robert O. 1984. *After hegemony.* New York: Columbia University Press.

Keohane, Robert O., and Joseph S. Nye. 1977. *Power and interdependence: World politics in transition.* Boston: Little, Brown.

Keshk, Omar M. G. 2003. CDSIMEQ: A program to implement two-stage probit least squares. *The Stata Journal* 3 (2): 1–11.

Keshk, Omar M. G., Brian M. Pollins, and Rafael Reuveny. 2004. Trade still follows the flag: The primacy of politics in a simultaneous model of interdependence and armed conflict. *Journal of Politics* 66 (4): 1155–1179.

Keshk, Omar M. G., Rafael Reuveny, and Brian M. Pollins. 2010. Trade and conflict: proximity, country size, and measures. *Conflict Management and Peace Science* 27:3–27.

Kim, M. 2008. Costly procedures: Divergent effects of legalization in the GATT/WTO dispute settlement procedures. *International Studies Quarterly* 52 (3): 657–686.

Kindleberger, Charles P. 1973. *The world in depression, 1929–1939*. Berkeley, CA: University of California Press.

King, Gary, and Langche Zeng. 2001. Explaining rare events in international relations. *International Organization* 55 (3): 693–715.

Kono Daniel Y. 2007. Who liberalizes? Explaining preferential trade liberalization. *International Interactions* 33:401–421.

Kono, Daniel Yuichi. 2009. Market structure, electoral institutions, and trade policy. *International Studies Quarterly* 53:885–906.

Koremenos, Barbara, Charles Lipson, and Duncan Snidal. 2001. The rational design of international institutions. *International Organization* 55 (4): 761–799.

Krasner, Stephen D. 1976. State power and the structure of international trade. *World Politics* 28 (3): 317–347.

Krugman, Paul R. 1979. Increasing returns, monopolistic competition, and international trade. *Journal of International Economics* 9:469–479.

Krugman, Paul. 1980. Scale economies, product differentiation, and the pattern of trade. *American Economic Review* 70(5): 950–959.

Krugman, Paul R. 1981. Intra-industry specialization and the gains from trade. *Journal of Political Economy* 89:959–973.

Lake, David A. 2009. *Hierarchy in international relations*. Ithaca, NY: Cornell University Press.

Levy, Philip I. 1997. A political-economic analysis of free-trade agreements. *The American Economic Review* 87 (4): 506–519.

Li, Quan, and David Sacko. 2002. The (ir)relevance of militarized interstate disputes for international trade. *International Studies Quarterly* 46 (1): 11–43.

Liberman, Peter. 1993. The spoils of conquest. *International Security* 18 (2): 125–153.

Long, Andrew G. 2003. Defense pacts and international trade. *Journal of Peace Research* 40(5): 537–552.

Long, Andrew G. 2008. Bilateral trade in the shadow of armed conflict. *International Studies Quarterly* 52 (1): 81–101.

Long, Andrew G., and Brett Ashley Leeds. 2006. Trading for security: Military alliances and economic agreements. *Journal of Peace Research* 43 (4): 433–451.

Lu, Lingyu, and Cameron G. Thies. 2010. Trade interdependence and the issues at stake in the onset of militarized conflict: Exploring a boundary condition of pacific interstate relations. *Conflict Management and Peace Science* 27 (4): 347–368.

Madeira, Mary Anne. 2013. The new politics of the new trade: The political economy of intra-industry trade. Doctoral dissertation. University of Washington.

Magee, Stephen P., William A. Brock, and Leslie Young, 1989. *Black hole tariffs and endogenous policy theory: Political economy in general equilibrium.* Cambridge: Cambridge University Press.

Maggi, Giovanni, and Andres Rodriquez-Clare. 2007. A political economy theory of trade agreements. *American Economic Review* 97 (4): 1374–1406.

Malamud, Andrés. 2011. A leader without followers? The growing divergence between the regional and the global performance of Brazilian foreign policy. *Latin American Politics and Society* 53 (3): 1–24.

Mansfield, Edward D. 1994. *Power, trade and war.* Princeton, NJ: Princeton University Press.

Mansfield, Edward D., and Rachel Bronson. 1997. Alliances, preferential trading arrangements, and international trade. *American Political Science Review* 91 (1): 94–107.

Mansfield, Edward D., Helen V. Milner, and Jon C. Pevehouse. 2007. Vetoing co-operation: The impact of veto players on preferential trading arrangements. *British Journal of Political Science* 37:403–432.

Mansfield, Edward D., Helen V. Milner, and Jon C. Pevehouse. 2008. Democracy, veto players and the depth of regional integration. *World Economy* 31 (1): 67–96.

Mansfield, Edward D., Helen V. Milner, and Peter Rosendorf. 2002. Why democracies cooperate more: Electoral control and international trade agreements. *International Organization* 56:477–514.

Mansfield, Edward D., and Jon C. Pevehouse. 2000. Trade blocs, trade flows, and international conflict. *International Organization* 54 (4): 775–808.

Mansfield, Edward D., and Brian M. Pollins. 2001. The study of interdependence and conflict: Recent advances, open questions, and directions for future research. *Journal of Conflict Resolution* 45 (6): 834–859.

Marshall, Monty G., and Keith Jaggers. 2010. Polity IV Project: Political regime characteristics and transitions, 1800–2009." http://www.systemicpeace.org/polity/polity4.htm.

Mastanduno, Michael. 1998. Economics and security in statecraft and scholarship. *International Organization* 52 (4): 825–854.

McDonald, Patrick J. 2004. Peace through trade or free trade? *Journal of Conflict Resolution* 48 (4): 547–572.

McDonald, Patrick J. 2007. The purse strings of peace. *American Journal of Political Science* 51 (3): 569–582.

McDonald, Patrick J. 2009. *The invisible hand of peace: Capitalism, the war machine, and international relations theory.* New York: Cambridge University Press.

McDonald, Patrick J., and Kevin Sweeney. 2007. The Achilles' heel of liberal IR theory? Globalization and conflict in the pre-World War I era. *World Politics* 59:370–403.

McGillivray, Fiona. 1997. Party discipline as a determinant of the endogenous formation of tariffs. *American Journal of Political Science* 41:584–607.

Melitz, Marc J. 2003. The impact of trade on intra-industry reallocations and aggregate industry productivity. *Econometrica* 71:1695–1725.

Melitz, Marc J., and Giancarlo I. Ottaviano. 2008. Market size, trade, and productivity. *Review of Economic Studies* 75:295–316.

Miller, Benjamin. 2005. When and how regions become peaceful: Potential theoretical pathways to peace. *International Studies Review* 7 (2): 229–267.

Milner, Helen V. 1999. The political economy of international trade. *Annual Review of Political Science* 2:91–114.

Milner, Helen. 2002. Reflections on the field of international political economy. In *Millennium Reflections on International Studies*, ed. Michael Brecher and Frank P. Harvey, 623–636. Ann Arbor: University of Michigan Press.

Moon, Don. 2006. Equality and inequality in the WTO dispute settlement system: Analysis of the GATT/WTO dispute data. *International Interactions* 32 (3): 201–228.

Morrow, James D. 1997. When do 'relative gains' impede trade?" *The Journal of Conflict Resolution* 41 (1): 12–37.

Morrow, James D. 1999. How could trade affect conflict? *Journal of Peace Research* 36 (4): 481–489.

Morrow, James D., Randolph M. Siverson, and Tressa E. Tabares. 1998. The political determinants of international trade: The major powers, 1907–90. *American Political Science Review* 92 (3): 649–661.

Most, Benjamin, and Harvey Starr. 1989. *Inquiry, logic, and international politics*. Columbia: University of South Carolina Press.

Mousseau, Michael. 2000. Market prosperity, democratic consolidation, and democratic peace. *The Journal of Conflict Resolution* 44 (4): 472–507.

Mousseau, Michael, Havard Hegre, and John R. Oneal. 2003. How the wealth of nations conditions the liberal peace. *European Journal of International Relations* 9(2): 277–314.

Mueller, John. 1970. Presidential popularity from Truman to Johnson. *American Political Science Review* 64 (1): 18–34.

Mueller, John. 1973. *War, presidents, and public opinion*. New York: John Wiley & Sons.

Mueller, John. 1989. *Retreat from doomsday: The Obsolescence of major war*. New York: Basic Books.

Nelson, Douglas. 1988. Endogenous tariff theory: A critical review. *American Journal of Political Science* 32: 796–837.

Nielson, Daniel L. 2003. Supplying trade reform: Political institutions and liberalization in middle-income presidential democracies. *American Journal of Political Science* 47:470–491.

Ohlin, Bertil. 1933. *Interregional and international trade*. Cambridge, MA: Harvard University Press.

Olson, Mancur. 1965. *The logic of collective action: Public goods and the theory of groups*. Cambridge, MA: Harvard University Press.

Oneal, John R., and Bruce M. Russett. 1997. The classical liberals were right: Democracy, interdependence, and conflict. *International Studies Quarterly* 41 (2): 267–293.

Oneal, John R., and Bruce M. Russett. 1999. Assessing the liberal peace with alternate specifications: Trade still reduces conflict. *Journal of Peace Research* 36 (4): 423–442.

Oneal, John R., Frances H. Oneal, Zeev Maoz, and Bruce Russett. 1996. The liberal peace: Interdependence, democracy, and international conflict, 1950–85. *Journal of Peace Research* 33 (1): 11–28.

Oye, Kenneth A. 1993. *Economic discrimination and political exchange: World political economy in the 1930s and 1980s.* Princeton, NJ: Princeton University Press.

Park, Tong, Farid Abolfathi, and Michael Ward. 1976. Resource nationalism in foreign policy behavior of oil exporting countries." *International Interactions* 2:247–263.

Pelc, Krzysztof. 2009. Seeking escape: The use of escape clauses in international trade agreements. *International Studies Quarterly* 53:349–368.

Peterson, Timothy M. 2014. Dyadic trade, exit costs, and conflict. *The Journal of Conflict Resolution* 58 (4): 564–591.

Peterson, Timothy M. 2015. Insiders versus outsiders: Preferential trade agreements, trade distortions, and militarized conflict. *The Journal of Conflict Resolution* 59 (4): 698–727.

Peterson, Timothy M., and Stephen L. Quackenbush. 2010. Not all peace years are created equal: Trade, imposed settlements, and military conflict. *International Interactions* 36 (4): 363–383.

Peterson, Timothy M., and Cameron G. Thies. 2012a. Beyond Ricardo: The link between intra-industry trade and peace." *British Journal of Political Science*, published online April 24, 2012. http://dx.doi.org/10.1017/S0007123412000099.

Peterson, Timothy M., and Cameron G. Thies. 2012b. Trade and the variety of international relationships: How intra- and inter-industry trade conditions alliances and rivalries. Paper presented at the American Political Science Association, New Orleans, August 30–September 2, 2012.

Peterson, Timothy, and Cameron G. Thies. 2015. Intra-industry trade and policy outcomes. In *Oxford handbook of the politics of international trade*, ed. Lisa Martin. New York: Oxford University Press.

Peterson, Timothy M., and Jerome Venteicher. 2013. The influence of trade dependence on asymmetric crisis perception. *Foreign Policy Analysis* 9 (2): 223–239.

Polachek, Solomon W. 1980. Conflict and trade. *Journal of Conflict Resolution* 24:55–78.

Polachek, Solomon W., and Judith McDonald. 1992. Strategic trade and the incentive for cooperation. In *Disarmament, economic conversion, and management of peace*, ed. Manas Chatterji and Linda Rennie Forcey, 273–284. New York: Praeger.

Polachek, Solomon W., and Jun Xiang. 2010. How opportunity costs decrease the probability of war in an incomplete information game. *International Organization* 64: 133–144.

Pollins, Brian M. 1985. Breaking trade dependency: A global simulation of third world proposals for alternative trade regimes. *International Studies Quarterly* 29 (3): 287–312.

Pollins, Brian M. 1989. Conflict, cooperation, and commerce: The effects of international political interactions on bilateral trade flows. *American Journal of Political Science* 33:737–761.

Reed, William. 2003. Information and economic interdependence. *Journal of Conflict Resolution* 47 (1): 54–71.

Reinhardt, Eric. 1999. Aggressive multilateralism: The determinants of GATT/WTO dispute initiation, 1948–1998. Presented at International Studies Association Meetings, Washington, DC.

Reuveny, Rafael, and Heejoon Kang. 1998. Bilateral trade and political conflict/cooperation: Do goods matter? *Journal of Peace Research* 35:581–602.

Reuveny, Rafael, and Quan Li. 2004. *Is all trade the same? Exploring the effect of disaggregated bilateral trade on militarized interstate disputes.* Paper presented at the Peace Science Society (International) Thirty-Eighth American Meeting, November 12–14, Houston, Texas.

Ricardo, D. [1817] 1981. *The principles of political economy and taxation.* Cambridge: Cambridge University Press.

Ripsman, Norrin M. 2005. Two stages of transition from a region of war to a region of peace: Realist transition and liberal endurance. *International Studies Quarterly* 49:669–693.

Rodrik, Dani. 1995. Political economy of trade policy. In *Handbook of international economics,* vol. 3., ed. Gene Grossman and Kenneth Rogoff. Amsterdam: Elsevier Science.

Rogowski, Ronald. 1987. Trade and the variety of democratic institutions. *International Organization* 41 (2): 203–223.

Rogowski, Ronald. 1989. *Commerce and coalitions.* Princeton, NJ: Princeton University Press.

Rogowski, Ronald, and Mark Andreas Kayser. 2002. Majoritarian electoral systems and consumer power: Price-level evidence from the OECD countries. *American Journal of Political Science* 46 (3): 526–539.

Roodman, David. 2011. Fitting fully observed recursive mixed process models with cmp. *The Stata Journal* 11(2): 159–206.

Rosecrance, Richard. 1986. *The rise of the trading state: Commerce and conquest in the modern world.* New York: Basic Books.

Russett, Bruce, and John Oneal. 2001. Triangulating peace: Democracy, interdependence and international organizations. New York: W. W. Norton.

Sattler, Thomas, and Thomas Bernauer. 2011. Gravitation or discrimination? Determinants of litigation in the World Trade Organization. *European Journal of Political Research* 50:143–167.

Schelling, Thomas C. 1958. *International economics.* Boston: Allyn and Bacon.

Schneider, Gerald, and Gleditsch, Nils Petter. 2010. The capitalist peace: The origins and prospects of a liberal idea." *International Interactions* 36 (2): 107–114.

Shaffer, Gregory. 2003. *Defending interests: Public-private partnerships in WTO litigation.* Washington, DC: Brookings Institution.

Signorino, Curtis S., and Jeffrey M. Ritter. 1999. Tau-b or not tau-b: Measuring the similarity of foreign policy positions. *International Studies Quarterly* 43:115–144.

Singer, David J., Stuart Bremer, and John Stuckey. 1972. Capability distribution, uncertainty, and major power war, 1820–1965. In *Peace, war, and numbers,* ed. Bruce M. Russett. Beverly Hills, CA: Sage.

Smith, Adam. 1776. *An inquiry into the nature and causes of the wealth of nations.* London: Methuen.

Smith, James McCall. 2003. WTO dispute settlement: The politics of procedure in appellate body rulings. *World Trade Review* 2(1).

Smith, James McCall. 2004. Inequality in international trade? Developing countries and institutional change in WTO dispute settlement. *Review of International Political Economy* 11 (3): 542–573.

Stolper, Wolfgang, and Paul Samuelson. 1941. Protection and real wages. *Review of Economic Studies* 9 (1): 58–73.

Tarullo, Daniel. 2004. Paved with good intentions: The dynamic effects of WTO review of anti-dumping action. *World Trade Review* 2(3).

Thies, Cameron G. 2001. Territorial nationalism in spatial rivalries: An institutionalist account of the Argentine-Chilean rivalry. *International Interactions* 27 (4): 399–431.

Thies, Cameron G. 2008. The construction of a Latin American interstate culture of rivalry. *International Interactions* 34 (3): 231–257.

Thies, Cameron G. 2010. Explaining zones of negative peace in interstate relations: West Africa's regional culture of interstate rivalry. *European Journal of International Relations* 16 (3): 391–415.

Thies, Cameron G. 2015. The declining exceptionalism of agriculture: Identifying the domestic politics and foreign policy of agricultural trade protectionism. *Review of International Political Economy.* 22 (2): 339–359.

Thies, Cameron G., and Schuyler Porche. 2007. Crawfish tails: A curious tale of foreign trade policy making. *Foreign Policy Analysis* 3:171–187.

Thompson, William R. 1988. *On global war: Historical-structural approaches to world politics.* Columbia: University of South Carolina Press.

Thompson, William R. 2001. Identifying rivals and rivalries in world politics. *International Studies Quarterly* 45:557–586.

Tsebelis, George. 1995. Decision making in political systems: Veto players in presidentialism, parliamentarism, multicameralism and multipartyism. *British Journal of Political Science* 25:289–325.

Tsebelis, George. 2002. *Veto players: How political institutions work.* Princeton, NJ: Princeton University Press.

Viner, Jacob. 1950. *The customs union issue.* New York: Carnegie Endowment for International Peace.

Voeten, Erik, Anton Strezhnev, and Michael Bailey. 2009. United nations general assembly voting data. Erik Voeten Dataverse, Georgetown University. http://hdl.handle.net/1902.1/12379. Accessed June 2015.

Wagner, R. Harrison. 1988. Economic interdependence, bargaining power, and political influence. *International Organization* 42: 461–483.

Waltz, Kenneth. 1970. The myth of national Interdependence. In *The International Corporation*, ed. Charles P. Kindleberger, 205–223. Cambridge, Mass.: MIT Press.

Wehner, Leslie E. Forthcoming. Role expectations as foreign policy: South American secondary powers' expectations of Brazil as a regional power. *Foreign Policy Analysis.* DOI: 10.1111/fpa.12048.

Wehner, Leslie E., and Cameron G. Thies. 2014. Role theory, narratives, and interpretation: The domestic contestation of roles. *International Studies Review* 16 (3):411–436.

Index

Note: Locators in italics indicate pages with figures or tables.